CONTENTS

REGIMENTAL

Steve Brown

To my small but mighty Mum. Fighter, Protector, Survivor.
Thanks for everything.

In memory of my friends who made the ultimate sacrifice
fighting the enemy and their demons:
Bryan Budd VC
Jon Hollingsworth CGC, QGM
Colin "Tom" Beckett
Nick Brown
Keith Butler
Eddie Collins
Lloyd Newell
Peter "Ronnie" O'Sullivan
Ian Plank
Shaun Sexton
Noah Stevenson

INTRODUCTION

I don't claim to be anyone special, and this account of my life is certainly not an attempt to prove that I am. I'm not a tough-guy, intellect, or big personality, I'm just an ordinary bloke who happens to have done a lot of extraordinary stuff with exceptional people. Besides, there's enough people out there claiming to be the world's foremost underwater knife-fighting, feng-shui super-soldier already. Over the years I've bought many books that I never finished reading because I couldn't tolerate the bullshit and bravado in the text, but that same waffle was no doubt lapped up by plenty of others with no comparable experiences of their own, who swallowed every word as if it were gospel. I've heard, read, and watched on TV as people recount their personal accounts of hardship, success, and apparent heroics, but I've learned to take most of them with a cynical pinch of salt. Rose-tinted glasses, hindsight, and time might cloud a person's memory, and poetic licence can always be a factor too, especially if the alluring potential of fame, notoriety, or financial gain are added to the mix. That said, I have also been extremely fortunate to work with some very special people, who have done amazing things that far surpass anything I'll ever achieve. Some have openly shared their stories, while others chose to remain anonymous. I have friends and family that have climbed Everest, crossed Antarctica, beat cancer, delivered babies, rescued hostages, and recovered from horrific injuries. Several of them have received distinguished honours and awards in recognition of their service or achievements, including the Victoria Cross, Military Cross, Queens Gallantry Medal, Conspicuous Gallantry Cross,

British Empire Medal, MBE, and OBE, sadly with some making the ultimate sacrifice in doing so. Friends of mine have survived child abuse, addiction, psychosis, paralysis, and tropical disease. They've suffered amputations and traumatic brain injuries, and they've watched their closest friends torn to pieces in front of them by both enemy and friendly fire. Being around people like that has humbled me time and time again and reaffirmed something an old friend used to say during hard times; "There's always somebody worse-off than you."

I've definitely had my fair share of adventures, and for some people my experiences might read like their own personal "bucket list" of things they'd like to do, or wish they'd had the opportunity to do. For others it might sound like an epic series of hellish nightmares that they're thankful I endured instead of them. Either way I hope my story, or at least parts of it, are relatable to everyone that reads it, and evokes an emotion, memory, or moment of quiet reflection that has a positive effect on them.

CHAPTER ONE
THE BOY

The great Greek philosopher Aristotle is credited with saying; "*Give me a child until he is seven and I will show you the man.*" This phrase suggests that the first seven years of our life determine how we'll turn out as adults, a theory that many people believe to be true.

I was seven years old the day I moved home for the first time. I remember sitting in the front cab of the removal lorry with my mum and brother as it pulled away from our house in Camelot Close, Andover. We didn't have a family car, we couldn't afford one, so we hitched a ride with the movers. My mum sat in the front with the removal men, and my brother and I sat in a small storage space behind their seat on top of some bags and coats. I waved goodbye to some of my friends and neighbours who stood outside to see us off, fighting back the tears that were welled-up in my eyes, boys didn't cry, especially not in front of their mates. Everyone and everything I knew was in that place, and I didn't want to leave. None of us did really, but we had to, for our own safety and security. As we pulled away I leant forwards nervously in my makeshift seat to scan the small car park and adjoining streets for an orange car. If we were followed, the whole move would be pointless, nothing would change.

That orange car was the main feature of the only recurring nightmare I've had in my entire life. I have violent dreams all the time and wake up my long-suffering wife regularly by shouting, punching the air, and even head-butting my pillow, but the only dream that I remember having many times, which has woken me up terrified, is the one with the orange car. In that dream I'm running down a shaded, single-track, country lane that has high earth embankments and tall deciduous trees on either side. The air is cold, but not cold enough to see my breath as I exhale, and the trees are almost bare of leaves like a typical late autumn morning. The road is a shallow decline which helps me run quickly as I flee from my pursuer, and although I'm terrified, I'm not panicking, seemingly confident that I've made my escape. But that confidence doesn't last long. At the bottom of the hill is a T-junction where another lane crosses from left to right at right angles, and as I approach it a car appears from the left, slowly drawing to a stop about fifty feet in front of me. The car is orange, with dark tinted windows that disguise the identity of the driver, but I know who it is, there's no doubt in my mind, there's only one car like that. I run a few more paces before I stop. Now I'm panicking, I'm petrified, and I stand still, staring at the driver's window as it slowly lowers, unable to move. The window goes down to reveal Terry, my mum's violent and abusive ex-boyfriend who sits behind the steering wheel facing forwards momentarily, before slowly turning his head to face me. Our eyes meet, and his blank gaze turns into a sinister grin. He's got me, and we both know it. At that point I'd always wake up, sweating and panting heavily. That man terrorised my mum, brother, and me when I was a young boy, even forcing us to leave our home and go into hiding in hostels and safehouses at one point. My clearest memory of that period is staying in a creepy old place that was infested with Crane Flies, or what we called "Daddy-Long-Legs'". I remember being in the communal shower room and sharing the cubicle with about ten of the little bastards. I was too proud to tell my mum I was scared of those annoying creatures, she had enough on her plate already.

I think everyone was afraid of Terry, probably due to

his unpredictability, because nobody from our family or community stepped in to help us. The worst thing he ever did was take our dog for a walk and return without her, claiming she'd mysteriously died, and he'd buried her in a field somewhere. That was our family pet that I'd had since I was a baby and adored, a beautiful little Sheltie called Lassie, who used to chase me around our house and gently bite the back of my clothing to bring me to a halt when she caught me. That's some sick, twisted stuff right there. I dread to think what he did to our dog, he was a psychopath.

Apart from Terry, my memories of Andover are almost all good, and we lived in a street where everyone knew each other. The boy and girl next-door were my best friends, an old man called Pat, who lived across the square acted as appointed medic, pulling out splinters and applying plasters to all the kids' minor injuries, and an old lady that lived around the corner called Kit handed out an endless supply of ice-pops anytime we knocked at her door and asked for one. On the route to school there was another old woman who lived in the flats known as "The Witch" by all the children from our estate. Seldom seen outside her home she would often sit in her living-room in the morning, looking out through the window as people filed past on their way to school. Most of us young kids would sprint across the frontage of her flat, daring to peek inside if we could pluck up the courage, and then report what we had seen to our friends when we met in the school playground. The conversation was always the same;

"What colour were the witches teeth?" we'd ask each other, and in turn the boys would describe what they'd seen.

"They were green!" One kid would shout in disgust.

"No, they were black when I saw her!" Another would claim.

"They've all fallen out!" Would be someone else's recollection.

"There was only one, and it was orange!"

"Red and yellow!"

Rarely would we see the same thing, but we were all equally convinced by our own version of events, as our imaginations ran wild. No wonder that poor old lady didn't like going outside when children shrieked at the mere sight of her and fled in fear. For all I know she wasn't even a witch! We'll never know.

In school I got into a lot of fights as a young boy and was the leader of my little gang. We used to practice trips and takedowns on one another before school started in preparation for the regular brawls we had with the other gang. To us it was all very real at the time, but obviously nobody really got hurt, we were only six or seven years old. There was one kid I was a bit scared of though. He was the same age as me, and he had a big brother, who was the same age as my brother. They went to a different school and lived at the other end of our estate where we didn't often venture. One day my brother and I were walking past their house while they played outside, and they saw us.

"Fucking wankers!" The younger one shouted angrily. We were very young, but we all had an exceptionally well-developed vocabulary of profanity.

I looked at my brother then replied with equal angst, yelling "Fuck off!" while sticking two fingers up at them.

Immediately the brothers began running towards us, which was when I realised my brother was also scared of the older one, because he starting running too, and suddenly I didn't feel quite so brave anymore. It wasn't far to our house, and we arrived at the front door quickly, only to find it locked, so we banged on it frantically. Unfortunately our pursuers reached the door a split second before my mum, who opened it just in time to see me punch the younger kid right on the nose in a pre-emptive strike before he could hit me. It was a cracking shot, and it busted his nose open, with blood running from both nostrils.

My mum grabbed me and my brother by the arms and dragged us inside yelling loudly "You naughty boys! What have you done?" But as soon as the door was closed she gave me a big pat on the back and smiled broadly. "Well done. Good for you Steve. I'm really proud of you." she said. They never bothered us again after that.

We left Andover in 1981 and never returned, starting our new life in the neighbouring county of Surrey. It was only fifty miles away, but it could have been a thousand for all I knew. Few people knew where we'd gone, we were starting over again like some kind of witness protection programme. Our new home in a place called Shottermill was another council house, but very different to our previous mid-terrace property. It was an old red-brick cottage divided into two homes and was on the side of a busy road. Inside the rooms were small but cosy, with uneven floors and walls and several open fireplaces. Adjacent to the house was a large plot of open waste ground that was owned by the council and led to the local waste disposal site. My brother and I spent hours there, climbing on the roofs of the offices and spying on the staff inside in a game we called "Roofs" and rummaging through the huge metal skips in another game we imaginatively called "Skips". Often we'd bring things home that other people had discarded as rubbish, we even managed to scavenge some items of furniture for the house, which was sparsely equipped. A lot of our stuff was donated by friends of the family or family members, including the black and white T.V and living room furniture. One day we invented another game, but we only ever played it once, we didn't give it a name, and we never told anyone about it. If I were to give it a name, it would probably be called something like "Car Inferno" because we torched a car that was parked in a nearby layby. After noticing the old, brown Austin Maxi for a second day we deduced that it had been abandoned, went home, collected some old newspapers and some matches, then returned. After a quick check to see nobody was coming, my brother scrunched up a load of the paper and held it still while I lit it with a match. Once nicely aflame he put the burning newspaper through the half-open passenger window, landing on the front seat. Excitedly we roughly screwed up the remaining paper and threw it inside, both surprised at how fast the fire developed, as the flames licked at the vehicle ceiling. At that point we realised the seriousness of what we'd done and scarpered back to our house. Returning to check the damage the following day we found a completely burned out car and swore to keep it a secret. We were poor, but we were happy, and our mum always made sure we had food in our stomachs and clothes on our backs. My mum was a very attractive and petite young woman, and this didn't go unnoticed by the council workers who drove past every day on their way to and from jobs. Two men in particular, whose names I still remember to this day were Frank and John, and they'd often pop in for a cup of tea and lend a hand with the more physical tasks, like chopping logs for the open fire with an axe or moving heavy objects around for us.

A year later we moved house once more, this time though it was to be closer to our school, rather than to get further away from a maniac. My brother and I had both moved to St. Bartholemew's Middle School on the other side of Haslemere, and it was a long walk from our old cottage, especially for my mum who was clocking up the miles going there and back twice every day. 6 Pepperham Road was in the middle of the High Lane council estate, close to the local shop, close to our new school, and surrounded on three sides by woodlands. I loved it there and spent as much time as possible exploring the woods, climbing trees, and building camps. At eight years old on a new estate and school I had to prove myself to the other boys and got into quite a few fights at first. I remember one boy having a go at me outside my own house, and I punched him so hard he tumbled down my front garden into a rose bush, I wasn't mucking about.

It was in Haslemere at about eight years of age that I was arrested for the first time in my life. Along with my brother and a couple of other kids, we'd decided to break into a World War Two air-raid shelter on the edge of town that had been bricked-up to deny access. There were a few of the old shelters dotted around the area that the kids played in, but this one was going to be our "secret bunker" that only we knew about. We grabbed a lump-hammer and crow-bar, walked to the site with our mates and went to work, bashing at the wall to make a hole in it. Before long my brother and I got bored and wandered off. There were four of us there, and only one person could swing the hammer at a time, so we decided to entertain ourselves by throwing sticks at cars that were driving past nearby. We were on some high ground in a small copse that handrailed a busy road, so the drivers couldn't see us as we threw the small branches down onto their roofs and bonnets, while we hid amongst the trees. However, they obviously knew we were there because some of them reported it to the police, and half an hour later a plain-clothed policeman came to investigate. He didn't find anyone throwing sticks, but he did catch me and my brother excitedly smashing a hole in the wall, by then almost big enough for us to crawl through. He grabbed us by the scruff of our necks and frog-marched us straight down to the police station in town, where he called my mum to come and collect us. It turned out not to be an air-raid shelter after all. It was in fact a very deep old well, that had been sealed off for the safety of the public, and if we'd climbed through that hole, we'd have probably plummeted to our deaths.

A few days later we were summoned back to the police station for a meeting with the station superintendent. His office was huge, but sparsely furnished, with old-fashioned mahogany cupboards, and a matching desk that he made us stand in front of while he sat behind it. I don't know if he was genuinely angry, or putting on an act, but he was very convincing, and I was terrified when he hinted that he could send us to Borstal, the infamous prison for boys. I was in tears and my brother was too as the big man shouted at us, but in the end he kicked us out of there with just a caution for vandalism, and a warning not to come back. Outside I asked my brother if he'd really been crying or putting it on.

"I was putting it on. I wasn't scared." he told me. "What about you?"

I was just as full of shit as he was. "I was pretending too." I lied.

It was also during my time in Haslemere, at eight years old, that I first decided I wanted to join the Parachute Regiment. A seven-part documentary on the BBC followed a platoon of young men through recruit training at Depot Para, and I was hooked from the very first episode. I'd sit with my mum and brother in front of our old black and white T.V and I'd be buzzing as soon as I heard the first beat of the theme tune. I can still hear it now, almost forty years later, it made such a huge impact on me. I think that show probably inspired an entire generation of future paratroopers, especially as it aired in the wake of the Falklands War of 1982. The recruits of 480 Platoon were beasted, harangued, and tormented relentlessly by the corporals, sergeants, and officers that made up their directing staff, but it looked exciting to me. They were firing weapons, running around assault courses, and jumping out of planes. What wasn't to like? Ten years later when I was in Depot myself, one of the recruits from the show was my platoon sergeant, and another one was my platoon sergeant in 3 PARA a few years after that too. It's a small world.

The local Spar shop and post office on the estate was a two minute walk from our house and owned by a man called Dave, who lived in the apartment above it with his mother and two children. Dave was a good bloke, he let my mum get shopping on an i.o.u when we were skint, and he paid my brother and I to work in his shop sometimes, stacking shelves and putting price tags on stuff. A few months after we moved there my mum and Dave started dating, and after a relatively short romance, they got married. Not long after the wedding we moved house again, this time to Aylesbury in Buckinghamshire where Dave had taken a new job in agricultural finance. I didn't want to leave Haslemere, I'd made good friends there, and I felt safe. I knew loads of kids on the estate and hung around with my brother and the older boys, who took me under their wing and helped me grow up quickly. I remember my mum asking me if I was alright with moving to Aylesbury one day. We were on the upstairs landing outside her bedroom, and she knelt down, put a hand on my shoulder and told me. "If you don't want to go, then we won't go." I really didn't want to leave but knew everything was already in place. She was married and the house was already bought. I was only nine years old, but well aware of the potential consequences of my response. "I don't mind moving Mum." I said.

Dave never really tried to assume the role of father figure to my brother and me. It was a strange set-up really, because he looked after and disciplined his children, and my mum did the same with us. We were two families that co-existed together rather than one coherent family unit. At first I was looking forward to having younger siblings, the idea of being a big brother was something I relished, but it didn't turn out like I hoped. We were all very different people, with incompatible personalities and very little in common.

Dave was a quiet, unassuming man who only had a few friends outside of work and kept to himself. If visitors ever came round the house you could tell he was uncomfortable, and he'd always make himself scarce by disappearing to his office to do some work. However, he was a man of many talents. We all knew he could play the guitar really well, because we'd seen him in action at barbeques and a couple of talent contests on holiday. He had a massive catalogue of tunes from the 60's that he could play and sing along to without the help of music sheets, but in retrospect I think he probably used the guitar as a kind of protective shield, so he didn't have to talk to people.

One year we were on holiday at Butlins Holiday Park in Skegness, getting ready to enjoy the evenings entertainment when there was an announcement. Earlier in the week Dave had been beaten into 4th place in a talent contest by a drunk old lady who sang "Whip-Crack-Away!" from the 1950's film "Calamity Jane", but he'd taken the defeat it in good spirits and humbly returned to watch the resident live band. However, when the announcer walked onto the stage he informed us that the drummer had not turned up, and the band would have to cancel the performance. It was a shame, because the rest of the band were obviously there, they'd been warming-up five minutes earlier. Without saying a word Dave got up and walked off, and we assumed he was going to get another drink or use the toilet, but a couple of minutes later the announcer returned to the stage.

"Ladies and gentlemen." he called out excitedly. "We have a volunteer from the audience to play the drums for us tonight, so I'm pleased to tell you that the show will go on! Please put your hands together for our new drummer.......... Dave."

With that there was a loud drum solo from behind the stage curtains, and as they slowly parted we saw our Dave sitting behind the drum kit, banging away like a rock 'n' roll star, finishing his intro with a dramatic clash of the cymbals. I was completely stunned and turned to my mum.

"I didn't know he could play the drums!" I shouted over the noise.

My mum also looked surprised. "Neither did I!" she laughed.

Dave played solidly for about half an hour, not missing a beat, and when he came back to the table he was rewarded with a round of applause from the audience and free pint of beer from the staff. He'd saved the day and was rightly looking quite pleased with himself.

On another holiday in Majorca we were getting a few essentials at a small supermarket, when a woman approached Dave and asked him a question in a foreign language. I looked at him to see how he'd react, expecting him to be awkward or flustered, he wasn't the best at talking to strangers in his own language, so I thought this would be amusing.

"Brot un milch sind im nachsten gang." he answered confidently, pointing across the shop, and the woman walked off, seemingly happy with the response. It turned out another of his hidden talents was speaking German, and the German tourist had randomly asked him where she could find some milk.

In 1983 we moved to a three-bedroom, semi-detached house in Aylesbury. My first friend there, and oldest friend to this day was a boy called Mayur. He was nine years old, the same age as me, and lived in the house opposite ours on Ingram Avenue, with his mum, dad, and younger brother. They were practising Hindus of Indian descent and great people, and our families got on really well with each other. When I started at the local school, Mayur and I were in the same year, but different classes, and it was there that I experienced racism for the first time in my life when another kid from his class said something derogatory about him. I punched that little shit straight in the head and he ran away crying. I realised early on in that school that I was made of tougher stuff than most of the other kids there, they seemed timid compared to my friends in previous towns, but like anywhere else they still wanted to have a go at the new boy. One kid smacked me over the head from behind with a football-boot bag and I turned around and punched him in the face. Another kid arranged to fight me before school one morning, so I set my alarm, got up early, and did some weight training and shadow boxing before heading in. My opponent wore a large gold bracelet and hit me in the mouth with it while swinging wildly, but I soon got him in a headlock and punched him in the head repeatedly until he pleaded with me to stop. I accidentally stabbed another kid in the face with a pencil when he got aggressive, and I used a taekwondo spinning-back-kick on another boy when he got angry because I'd pushed him into the girls toilets as a joke.

His mother came knocking at my house afterwards to tell my mum what I'd done and say that he was at home vomiting. I'd never heard that word before and had to ask what vomiting was.

"It means he's being sick." My mum explained. I was pretty pleased with that.

One day I attacked a kid in the year above mine after losing my temper, when he deliberately kicked my football to the other end of the playground. That fight sealed the deal, and nobody bothered me again. Beating up older kids was unheard of.

At a parent's evening a teacher from that school told my mum that I had a lot of charisma. It wasn't a compliment though, because apparently, I was using it in the wrong way to influence the other kids into being naughty. I'd never heard that word before either.

"What does charisma mean?" I asked her.

"It means, you're a natural leader." My mum informed me. She was paraphrasing of course, what it really meant was that I was a disruptive little shit, and I was leading the other kids astray and getting them in trouble.

By the time I was in my last year at Bedgrove Middle School I was "Top Dog", the toughest kid in the school, or so everyone said anyway, and I was happy to let them think that, because it meant I got left alone.

That reputation followed me to secondary school, so when I started at The Grange there were plenty of kids that wanted to see how I fared against the top dogs from the other schools now we'd all been put together. It wasn't long before I was fighting again, this time against the so-called hardest kid from another school that I'd been hanging around with. We had a fight over money at the top of a staircase on the way to maths class. I'd lent him a pound that he hadn't paid back, and he actually hit me first when I aggressively demanded repayment. It was only a short altercation, with him swinging wildly and me countering with a few straight punches to his face, and that one ended with him running away and me the victor, with word quickly spreading that I could look after myself.

I started off quite well at The Grange, knuckling down in class and doing my homework as soon as I got back from school, but it didn't last long. I think my main problem was the attitude of the teachers, who seemed to genuinely detest children. There were a few that I liked, but the vast majority were soulless, humourless, autocrats, who had long determined that children were the root cause of their miserable existence. The best one by a mile was a P.E teacher called Mr McCrystal, a down-to-earth, rugby playing, firm-but-fair, decent bloke. He'd been teaching there for many years and was well-established and respected by the other teachers and the kids alike. Nobody disrespected him, but at the same time he treated everyone else with respect too. As well as teaching P.E Mr McCrystal ran a hub known as "R5", which was a large room for kids who'd been kicked out of their class for one reason or another. It could be because they'd been naughty, or because they'd forgotten their P.E kit, either way you'd just go in there and crack on with some homework, or at least pretend to. As long as you were well behaved Mr McCrystal left you alone, and there were always the same familiar faces in there, including the naughty kids and the kids who hated doing P.E. As I slowly got ejected from more and more classes for bad behaviour I spent more and more time in R5, eventually finding myself in there for the majority of the week. One morning I was surprised to find myself banned from my form class where we assembled each day for registration. My form tutor was one of the other select teachers that I liked, a long haired man called Mr Bowles, who we all thought looked like Jesus, with his beard and long, brown, curly hair. I was never rude to him because I thought he was a good bloke, so I was quite upset when he threw me out of his class too. He intercepted me on my way to form class to tell me that Mr McCrystal wanted to see me, and when I got to R5 I was promptly told that I was never to return to my normal form class again and would register in R5 from then onwards. I hated Mr Bowles after that, because he never spoke to me again, not even to explain what I'd done wrong. I felt betrayed by him, he was one of the only teachers I respected and behaved for, but now that exclusive list was reduced to two people, Mr McCrystal, and his wife Mrs McCrystal who was a very caring teacher, and in all fairness, a very attractive lady, that many of the boys had a secret crush on.

Aylesbury was a big town and had several secondary schools, but most of my friends from middle school went to The Grange. Clever kids, who passed the "Twelve Plus" exam went to one of three grammar schools, The Boys Grammar, the Girls High School, or the Sir Henry Floyd Secondary School. A few of my good friends also went to a school in the neighbouring small town of Wendover called the John Colet, but because of the tribalistic nature of competing schools they quickly became the enemy. I turned against some good mates after the transition to secondary school, even attacking a few of them in the street without provocation. Conniving little shits would spread rumours that my old friends were slagging me off behind my back, and to save face I'd seek them out and confront them about it. It was probably all lies, but I never listened to their responses, instead issuing them with threats of violence or a punch in the face. Not taking decisive action would have made me look weak and compromised my reputation, but I wish I'd handled that differently now. I was a horrible little bastard sometimes.

Any fights that broke out at The Grange were always encouraged by a rapidly formed crowd of spectators who chanted "Fight! Fight! Fight! Fight! in unison to alert everyone else within earshot, so they could come and witness the forthcoming bloodshed too. One day I followed the noise of the battle-cry to an enclosed area between the metalwork workshop and the canteen to see two boys in a heated argument. One of them was a popular student called Paul and the other was a new kid called Stuart that nobody really knew, a quiet lad from Wales who'd only been at the school for a short while and kept to himself. Whether they wanted to get into a fistfight or not, the crowd had already whipped themselves up into a frenzy and decided it was happening, so it reached the point where backing down would basically be determined as a loss, or cowardice. The fight lasted about thirty seconds before a grown-up arrived on scene, obviously alerted by the chanting mob. Loud shouts of "Teacher!!" warned us all that a member of staff was about to spoil the fun, and everyone quickly dispersed in all directions before they could be captured for interrogation, including Stuart and Paul, who'd stopped fighting each other to blend in and escape with the crowd. I felt sorry for Stuart after that, as I watched him walk away on his own, compared to Paul who was surrounded by friends offering him reassurance that he'd won the fight. In my opinion it was a draw, but as the outsider with no support, Stuart was quickly being nominated as the loser, and I didn't think that was fair.

"Bullshit!" I said, interrupting a group of kids walking with Paul, congratulating him. "Nobody won that fight, it was a draw. Unless they do it again, it's a draw!" After that I approached Stuart and invited him to hang out with me and my group of friends. He accepted my offer, and over time his confidence grew as he came out of his shell. One day after school Stuart and I were loitering on the roof of a multi-storey car park in town, when we spotted another kid from our year walking on the pavement below. He was a nice lad who I'd known for a while, so I shouted down to him. "Simon you bell-end."

When he looked up and saw it was me, he smiled, waved, and carried on walking "Alright Steve?" he said.

As I waved back Stuart decided to join in the banter too, shouting out "Get your fucking hair cut!" However, those two weren't actually friends, so Simon didn't take kindly to that.

"Go fuck yourself you prick!" he replied angrily, sticking two fingers up to emphasise his disproval.

For me that crossed the line. It had gone from a bit of banter to an act of aggression, and it was time for Stuart to start getting some respect. I looked him in the eye and told him, "You can't let people talk to you like that mate. You need to sort that out." We ran down several flights of stairs and caught up with Simon on a paved area outside an office building where Stuart ran up to him and started ferociously punching him in the head. I hadn't seen that coming at all, and neither had Simon, who dropped to his knees as the punches repeatedly smashed into his face. I knew there was potential for a fight to start, but I was expecting a bit of posturing and an argument, not a brutal beatdown. I called for Stuart to stop and physically pulled him away from a dazed and confused Simon, who stumbled to his feet and walked away helplessly. A couple of days later I was arrested for grievous bodily harm (GBH) because Simon had been left partially blinded in one eye from the attack and thought I had also punched or kicked him during the onslaught. I hadn't, but I believe he genuinely thought I had, because he'd been totally overwhelmed, and it probably felt like he was surrounded. Fortunately for me there were witnesses from the office building, who confirmed that in reality I'd saved him from even more punishment and not laid a finger on him. Although my initial intentions were good, they were misguided. I thought I was teaching someone to stick up for themselves, helping the underdog, but what I really did was unleash a monster. Stuart's confidence rocketed and he revelled in the notoriety of being a wild child as he started to spiral out of control, drinking, taking drugs, stealing, and getting into more fights. One day, without provocation, he attacked a man with a tree branch, then danced on his head while he was unconscious. Within a year he was expelled from school and eventually sent to a young offenders prison.

I was arrested for actual bodily harm (ABH) as a teenager too, but not for fighting. I actually set off an exploding firework in a church hall while a ballet lesson was taking place in there, and the noise left some of the people inside with temporary ringing in their ears. My brother and I both received a caution for ABH because I held the door open while he rolled it into the class. The "Air Bomb Repeater" spun around on the wooden floor before stopping, pointing straight at the group of girls, and the piano suddenly went quiet when they all saw it. "Bang!" The first round fired, followed by a bright flash and a loud "Boom!" Everyone inside was screaming and we ran off laughing as the second round fired. "Bang!" "Boom!" It was supposed to be a prank, but understandably the girls didn't see the funny side, and when one of them told her boyfriend about it, he confessed that he'd been there, and snitched on the rest of us.

Launching fireworks at people while they filled up their cars with petrol was another of my great ideas as a youth. I'd wait in the shadows next to the petrol station until someone pulled up to a pump, then place a small rocket on the low perimeter wall pointing towards the target. Once the petrol was flowing I'd light the touch-paper and watch the reaction of the customer as the fizzing projectile screeched towards them, before making my escape over a high fence and disappearing into the dark, laughing my head off. After a few goes at that I decided to up the ante a little and snapped off three-quarters of the stick the rocket was attached to. The stick helped it fly in a straight line, so removing it made it completely unstable, and it would hurtle around unpredictably, bouncing off the forecourt roof, floor, or anything else it struck. To me it was hilarious to see the panic it caused, but to the innocent people at the pumps or in the shop it must have been absolutely terrifying. Luckily, nobody got physically hurt, but it could have been disastrous, and I only stopped after being chased by the police and almost caught. Idiot.

I spent a lot of time practicing martial arts in my teenage years and went through a stage of about two years where I practiced for several hours every single day. I'd spend an hour stretching, an hour on the punchbag, an hour sparring and an hour of weight training. My small bedroom had a punchbag, speedball, weights bench, squat stand, free-weights, spring-loaded resistance contraptions, and a pulley that I'd put my foot through and hoist up to the ceiling to practice high-kicks. I was, and still am a huge Bruce Lee fan, and I regularly took the train to London to visit the martial arts shops in Carnaby Street and China Town to buy books, posters, and weapons like Tonfas and Nunchakus. I even bought a pre-filled punchbag that I carried on my shoulder all the way home, and still have to this day. Two years of Taekwondo had taught me how to kick pretty well, and I loved all the dynamic jumping and spinning kicks, but my good friend and neighbour Karl taught me how to put kicks and punches together through a baptism of fire. Karl was a gifted, aggressive martial artist who won national and world titles in nunchaku and kickboxing, and he introduced me to a kickboxing club in Aylesbury that I attended with him for a while. However, the sparring sessions we did in my house were where I learnt the most from him. I'd formed some bad habits in Taekwondo and gotten used to "point sparring" where one clean kick or punch scored a point and meant both fighters returned to their start positions before continuing.

Several times after Karl hit me, I dropped my guard, turned my back, and went to reset. He warned me that if I did that in kickboxing I'd get knocked out, and after fair warning, when I continued to do it he gave me a proper punch in the face which really rang my bell. We didn't own any decent boxing gloves or shin guards back then, we sparred with cheap, wafer-thin, fabric mitts and foot-pads that had been handed down from one person to the next over many years and offered little protection to either of us.

"Don't drop your fucking guard!" he said.

I shook it off and we went at it again in the small space of my stripped-down bedroom. Once again he hit me, and my hands dropped. "Wham!" His instep smashed into my head and almost knocked me out. At first I was angry, but after letting me collect myself for a few seconds Karl spoke.

"I told you what would happen mate. If you drop your hands or look away, you'll get knocked out! Stop doing it!"

He was right of course. I learned a lot that day. It was a hard lesson, but it worked. Tough love!

On a neighbouring estate there was another kid who trained martial arts and was inadvertently building a reputation for himself as a hard-nut. Like Karl he was in the school year above mine, but he went to the Grammar School where the clever kids were, so our paths never really crossed. I knew who he was though, because I remembered him and his older brother going to an old Kung-Fu club on my estate as youngsters, which was ran from the same church hall that the ballet classes were held in. I'd seen them walking to and from the club in their kung-fu trousers and t-shirts many times. His name was Neil, and despite the fact we went to rival schools, when we did eventually meet we got on brilliantly. Whereas Karl was a fighter, who was excellent at martial arts, Neil was a martial artist, who was excellent at fighting. He absolutely lived for it, embracing the ethos and philosophies that came with it, and dedicating every spare minute he had to developing his skills and understanding. At that point in my life I went everywhere with a football and spent hours kicking it against a wall next to the shops. Neil and I decided that it would be great training to punch the ball instead of kicking it and created our own unique version of racquetball. It was actually really good, because you had to use both hands, and you had to move your feet fast to get into position. We played that game for hours. Because we were both fans of Chinese martial arts movies and people like Bruce Lee, Jackie Chan, and Samo Hung, we also played other games that involved kicking the highest brick on the wall, doing the most amount of kicks in one jump, and kicking multiple targets in one leap, trying to replicate what those awesome athletes did in their films. Neil was a great influence on me during that period and hanging around with him kept me on the straight-and-narrow, because he was a good person and I looked up to him. He didn't drink or smoke, he ate healthily, and trained religiously every single day. At fifteen or sixteen years old, two grown men tried to rob Neil on his way home from town, with one of them punching him and demanding his money. Using a finger-jab to the eyes, a kick to the groin, and a concrete pillar to smash one of their heads into, he destroyed those two unsuspecting thugs within seconds and made his escape. Nobody messed with him after that, and he went on to become a hugely successful fighter and coach in mixed martial arts and several other disciplines, including becoming a world champion in Filipino stick-fighting.

It got to a point in secondary school where I was spending my entire day in R5, or the Year Head's office because I'd been thrown out of every class except P.E. I think the majority of the ejections were probably justified, but a couple were definitely just teachers jumping on the bandwagon because of my reputation as a nuisance. I was wasting my time, and the time of the staff at the Grange, so Mr McCrystal reached out to the head mistress at a local specialist school for troublesome kids. Queens Park Secondary Support Centre was a small, discrete facility on the edge of town that only had three members of staff, Mrs Cannon, Mrs Carr and Mr Millea, and about fifteen students. However, there were only ever six to eight teenagers in attendance on any given day because of their unpredictability and potential for outbursts of violence, or disruptive behaviour. I settled in there very quickly, building good relationships with the other kids and the teachers, who treated us with respect and compassion, which in return they also got back from us. Even back then some people in the education system had identified the benefits of fitness and physical exercise for people with behavioural problems. At Queens Park we started our school day with fitness training, walking a short distance to the Reg Maxwell Swimming Pool in the town centre, where we had free access to a fully equipped weight training gym and fitness suite. After that we'd walk back to school and begin our lessons, working towards City and Guilds qualifications rather than the GCSE's done in mainstream schools. Classes were conducted much more informally there too, there was no school uniform, we had a teacher to student ratio of at least 1:4, we sat in a relaxed seating plan, and took regular breaks every 20-30 minutes so those of us with short attention spans wouldn't get too restless. During breaks the smokers would "sneak" outside to satisfy their cravings, moving only a token distance away from the windows so the teachers could turn a blind eye, but not far enough that we couldn't all hear them talking or see their exhaled puffs of smoke drifting past. We also had a small pool table in one corner of the open-plan building that we could use to decompress between lessons, but it was riddled with holes, rips, and tears, and tilted slightly to one side, so it took some getting used to. Our days ended with exercise too. We'd go to sports centres and play team games like basketball, hockey, or football. One day they took us to a swimming pool with a multi-stage diving board, and like typical cocky teenagers the first thing we did was climb straight up to the top platform. However, once up there it seemed a whole lot higher, and after nervously peering over the edge we immediately regretted it, laughing nervously as we stepped back and grasped hold of the hand rail. One lad, called Paul arrived a few seconds behind the rest of us though, and he had no such concerns. Without even taking a look, he sprinted straight from the top of the ladder through the middle of everyone shouting, "I can fly like a bird!" as he launched himself off the concrete platform and disappeared. That acted like a trigger for everyone else, and to avoid appearing weak we all followed on behind him, much to the annoyance of the duty lifeguard, who frantically blew his whistle as we crashed into the water in rapid succession like a bunch of ravenous seagulls dive bombing a shoal of mackerel. That afternoon we returned to the support centre to find a police car parked outside, and when we entered the building there were two police officers in the Head Mistresses office talking to her. I was gutted, but some of the others laughed out loud, because it was the same two coppers that had come in to arrest me for burglary the previous week, and we all assumed they were back for me again. Mr Millea went into the office briefly, then came over to where we'd all sat down.

"Are they here for me?" I asked him. I'd done lots of bad things and thought they must have found some new evidence against me.

"No. They're here for Paul this time." he replied despairingly, shaking his head and beckoning Paul towards him. Now we all laughed at Paul instead as he stood up, walked into the office, and got promptly arrested on suspicion of attempted murder.

Another afternoon Mr Millea organised a game of football between us and a different "naughty kids" school in a neighbouring town, and we drove to their site to conduct the match. Theirs was a much bigger establishment than ours, centred around a three-storey mansion in a grand old estate, with landscaped gardens and a sports pitch. This was more of a private boarding school, where rich people sent their spoilt brats, so someone else could deal with their temper tantrums and ADHD. There was a lot of testosterone in that match and the referee was kept very busy, regularly separating players, and giving out plenty of warnings for foul play. The game was halted before full-time so the teachers could calm down their respective teams before a brawl started, but we were beyond the point of return, and decided that as soon as play resumed we were going to physically attack the other team. A couple of their players had been gobbing off throughout the game and we'd had enough. Mr Millea realised what was going on and got us into a huddle.

"Right lads, I know these boys have been winding you up, but you can't get into a fist-fight with them, there's a lot more of them than us." he whispered.

He was right, we were on their turf, and with their friends spectating as well, we were well outnumbered. He had an idea though.

"In the back of the minibus are the hockey sticks from yesterday afternoon." he said with a glint in his eye. "If you were to go and get them, that would even things up a bit." It was a great plan, those wooden clubs were the perfect weapon. In that moment his kudos as a cool teacher rocketed into the stratosphere, and we all followed closely behind him, as he walked purposefully to the car park. We reached the minibus and Mr Millea opened the side door.

"Get in you bloody idiots!" he ordered. "We're going home." He'd tricked us all.

The three days a week I did in The Grange School were eventually halted altogether when I was expelled permanently. The final straw came when Mr Jones, the Head Master, and the Head of Year, Mr Redman were both reprimanding me for my bad behaviour one day and I snapped. Mr Jones had asked me how I thought I could possibly serve in the army if I couldn't even wear a uniform to school for a few hours a day.

"Don't you think people in the army have to wear a uniform boy?" he challenged me.

Mr Redman backed him up. "Exactly Mr Jones." he said. "He won't last long in the army if he can't even get dressed properly."

They had a good point, and I had no intelligent comeback, so I went on the offensive instead. "You fucking two are like Tweedledum and Tweedledee!" I told them, before doing an impromptu impression of them telling me off, trying to mimic their Welsh accents as I did so. I suppose I thought I was being clever, but I wasn't. I didn't even know who Tweedledum and Tweedledee were, in fact I still don't, I just knew it was an insult of some sort. On its own it wasn't that big of a deal, but it highlighted my total disregard for their authority, especially seeing as we were actually in the Head Master's office at the time, and they decided there and then that I was finished at their school. It was the right choice, and I don't hold any grudges with them about it, I'd have done exactly the same after all the chances I'd been given.

I walked out of The Grange and went straight to Queens Park Secondary Support Centre to tell the staff there what had just happened, assuming I'd now be attending there five days a week instead, but they were already oversubscribed. In the end they were able to give me one extra day, so for the last six months of my schooling I attended there three days a week and got up to mischief for the remainder. It was a shame really because I was excelling at Queens Park. The teaching style and informal atmosphere enabled me to concentrate, learn, and most importantly, ask questions. I sat my City and Guilds exams and passed them all comfortably.

CHAPTER TWO THE YOUNG MAN

I would have joined the army straight from school, but having a criminal record held me back for a while. Found guilty on charges of burglary and theft, I was given a 12-month conditional discharge by a judge in Aylesbury's Juvenile Court. My solicitor had stated to the court that I had aspirations to turn myself around and join the army in his appeal for leniency, and the judge had bought into it.

"I don't want to ruin your chances of a career in the military young man, so I am going to be generous." He told me, before warning me sternly. "But if you break my trust, and I see you before me again in the next twelve months, I will show you no such courtesy! Do you understand me?"

"Yes your honour." I replied respectfully. He meant business.

That conditional discharge, along with a compensation payment was about as good an outcome as I could have wished for. It meant I would have no criminal record once it was spent, and I'd be eligible to join the army as soon as it expired. My solicitor made a point of telling me how lucky I'd been and advised me that I'd probably get a custodial sentence if I offended again. I didn't deserve it, but I'd been given a second chance. That week, on the front page of a local newspaper was the headline *"Second chance for teenage burglar"* and a story about me. Luckily, because I was only sixteen years old, my name was omitted from the report, which saved my mum from too much further embarrassment. It wasn't the first time my criminal behaviour had been reported in "The Bucks Herald" or "Bucks Advertiser" though. In fact I used to purposely look through them to see if anything I'd done had made the news, even keeping the pages as souvenirs hidden in my bedroom. Another small report in the columns was titled "Petrol Shop Attack Man Hunted". My mate Dan and I had been causing a nuisance again, this time in a local petrol station shop, trying to impress a girl who worked there, when the manager asked us to leave. Being the obnoxious, obstinate little shits that we were we refused, and he became aggressive, trying to push us out towards the door.

"Get your hands off me before I knock you out!" Dan warned him.

The manager ignored the threat and continued to push Dan as we conceded and turned to the exit, but then put his hand on my back as well.

"If you push me, *I will* fucking hit you!" I told him.

He pushed me once more and as promised I turned around and punched him in the mouth hard, causing him to fall backwards, arms flailing, into some shelving, then onto the floor. He looked shocked and immediately got up and ran into his office, where we watched from outside as he picked up a telephone to call the police. He was shaking uncontrollably and repeatedly touching his face, then looking at the blood on his fingers. He shouldn't have pushed us, but he didn't deserve that.

The last crime I ever committed was actually whilst on bail for the burglaries. I spotted a £5 note inside a locked car and stole it. The vehicle was in the middle of a car park, so I'd obviously been looking for something to steal when I saw it lying on the driver's seat. It had probably fallen out of the owners pocket as they got out. I was with my old best friend Dan, and as opportunists we'd regularly carry a few tools around with us for just such events. Dan was carrying

attack man hunted

POLICE are hunting a man who punched a supervisor at a garage in Aylesbury. He is decsribed as being 5ft 10ins tall, white, aged between 15 and 17 with short, blond, spikey hair.

The victim of the assault ████, of ████, Aylesbury was hit in the face after he asked the offender to leave the garage in ████ Road last Sunday night.

a "centre-punch" that night, a spring-loaded tool designed for shattering vehicle windows. He handed me the tool and appointed himself as "lookout" while I carried out the work. He positioned himself on the pavement where he could see if anyone was coming, and I waited for the all-clear signal. Dan gave me a nod and I pressed the centre-punch into the driver's window hard, instantly shattering the glass with a dull thud. I quickly checked in with him once more, then punched a hole through the fractured window and snatched the money in one swift motion, before sprinting away from the scene, closely followed by my accomplice. Once we were safely out of the area and in a dark alleyway we split the haul. Dan had some change in his pocket, so he gave me £2.50, and I gave him the fiver. I looked at that £2.50 and it dawned on me that if I got caught, I might be sent to prison for it. It was pathetic, and for the next couple of days I was on edge, dreading a knock at the door from the police. I was on bail for burglary, awaiting trial, and trying to convince people I wanted to be a soldier. I was an idiot.

A few months after leaving school I enrolled in a government employment programme for teenagers called the Youth Training Scheme or YTS. I was accepted onto a bricklaying course at High Wycombe College and began my first full-time employment on a wage of £35 per week, starting with ten weeks of practical bricklaying training. There were a few theory lessons, but the vast majority of the course was spent building things using a sand / lime mixture instead of cement, so we could knock our projects down and re-use it. We learned how to build walls, piers, fireplaces, chimneys, and arches, and I really enjoyed it. After ten weeks we went to work for a building company, and I was found a place with an Aylesbury-based general builders'.

Just like back at school, my mum made sure I was ready for my first morning. She made me a packed lunch and taught me how to pre-warm a flask before filling it with tea so it would last all day, and we stood in the living room, watching out the window for a builders van to pull up. The men that drove up to my house in a green and white transit van to pick me up that morning were called Mark and Dave, and they'd worked together for a few years. Mark was in his late twenties, full of bravado and self-importance and clearly put-out by some new kid upsetting his exclusive partnership with his mentor Dave. Dave was a mid-fifties, overweight, bow-legged man who liked working with Mark, and had no interest in mentoring anyone else, especially not me. I know I was a little shit, but I never gave those two a single reason to dislike me. They knew nothing of what I did outside of work, and I was always punctual, hard-working, and polite to them. They however treated me with contempt and only spoke to me when they needed more bricks, blocks, cement, or help with the daily crossword they attempted.

"You should know this, you've only just left school." Mark would shout from the front seat, while I sat uncomfortably amongst the tools in the back. This was his way of undermining any correct answer I might give. "Type of Navy vessel that operates underwater. Nine letters, starts with an S?"

"Submarine?" I suggested, trying my best not to sound like a smart-arse stating the obvious.

They hated it when I knew the answer. They'd look at each other as they thought it through, before nodding reluctantly and writing it down.

The only other time they spoke to me was when one of them was away. Those were the best days on site, and I'd actually have a good time. It was like they were worried the other one would be jealous if they were caught talking to the new kid.

I used to fantasise about sabotaging the scaffolding when they were working at height. I'd look at the clips that held it all together and be tempted to loosen a few so the whole thing would collapse, and they'd fall to their deaths. I'd also think about "accidentally" dropping bricks or concrete blocks onto their heads when I was up high, and they were on the ground. Mark always had something to say about my work, but never gave me any constructive criticism or help, instead he'd just scowl and complain that the cement was too dry, or too wet, or his tea was too strong or too milky. Every now and then he'd try and have a bit of fun at my expense by sending me on a trick errand like fetching a left-handed screwdriver, or some tartan paint. To his frustration I'd heard them all before from my brother, who'd worked as a mechanic since he left school and had the same pranks pulled on him. One day he told me to go and get some equipment from another company member.

"Go and ask Nobby if he's got some pudlock holes we can borrow." he told me during a tea break.

Nobby was a great bloke in his early twenties, whose main job was delivering materials to the different building sites, and we got on really well. Pudlocks were short scaffold bars with a bladed end that fixed into the wall to help keep the scaffolding structure stable. I'd never heard that one before but knew it was a wind-up straight away.

"Pudlock holes?" I said with a grin. "That's a good one Mark, I like it."

He didn't appreciate that. I was spoiling his plan. "Go on then!"

he demanded. "Go and ask him!"

It was getting awkward now. To me it seemed pretty obvious that I hadn't fallen for the joke, but he was intent on seeing it through. "I know there's no such thing as pudlock holes mate. I do understand how they work." I explained.

Mark was visibly agitated as he told me one more time. "I want some fucking pudlock holes! Go and fucking get some from Nobby now!"

"Ok." I said and walked over to the tipper-truck that Nobby drove. "I've been told to come and ask you for some pudlock holes mate, even though I know there's obviously no such thing." We both looked towards Mark and Dave to see them laughing out loud and well pleased with themselves. To be honest working with those two helped prepare me for the harshness of recruit training, because it thickened my skin and got me used to being subordinate. If anything the treatment I got from them was actually worse psychologically because they treated me like shit for absolutely no reason. It wasn't character building, it was soul destroying, and to add insult to injury, I wasn't even getting paid by the company either. The YTS paid me £35 per week assuming I was developing my bricklaying skills, but in fact I was just a labourer, digging holes, mixing cement, and carrying bricks alongside grown men who were earning £100 a day for the same work.

The first time I walked into an Army Careers Information Office (ACIO) was in Oxford City. That was the nearest one that I'd heard of, so I caught the bus from Aylesbury bus station, arriving there about an hour later. By that point in time I was regularly reading everything I could find about knives, guns, survival, and the military. There was no internet, so I was buying magazines like "Guns and Ammo" "RAIDS" and "Combat & Survival" to educate myself. I also had a selection of books about the Paras, and a Royal Marine fitness guide. I walked to the ACIO and was greeted by a man in green camouflage clothing.

"How can I help you young man?" he asked.

"I'd like to find out about joining the Paras or the Marines please Sir." I said. I'd wanted to be a paratrooper since watching the documentary series about them at eight years of age and had also watched one on the Royal Marines at about fourteen.

The soldier smiled and nodded, I bet he heard that all the time. "Well the Parachute Regiment are in the army, and if you want to join them you need to talk to me, because I'm in the army." He paused, then pointed towards another man who was standing behind a desk immaculately dressed in a bright white shirt and trousers, with razor sharp creases in the sleeves and legs. "That gentlemen there is in the Royal Navy, and if you want to learn about the Marines, you need to talk to him, because the Marines are part of the Royal Navy." he explained.

I definitely did not want to talk to the man dressed like an ice-cream salesman, he wasn't exactly screaming out "murder death kill!"

"I want to join the paras." I stated confidently.

I spoke to that soldier for a long time about the process of joining up, and he gave me lots of information and booklets to take home and ponder over, some of which I still have. Before I left, as a quick fitness assessment, he also got me to do ten chin-ups on a bar they'd erected in a skylight in the ceiling. I did the exercise successfully, then I left there buzzing with excitement, I'd taken the first step to becoming a soldier. Walking through Oxford city centre after the careers office I stumbled across an army surplus store and went inside, exiting about ten minutes later with some essential equipment for my preparation; a camouflage net and a set of old 1944-pattern webbing, two items I had absolutely no sensible requirement for, nor knowledge of their employment, but I'd seen in Combat & Survival magazine.

My recruitment thereafter was taken on by the careers office in Bletchley, which was about five miles closer to home, but a longer journey because I had to change buses halfway in a small town called Leighton Buzzard. The soldier that dealt with me there was a colour sergeant from the Royal Green Jackets (RGJ), who immediately tried to convince me to join them instead of the paras. At the time they were the local regiment to my home town of Aylesbury, and he assured me that they were just as good, if not better.

"We invented camouflage." he told me proudly. "The Green Jackets were wearing green at the Battle of Waterloo when the rest of the British army were still wearing red coats!" It was kind of true because even though the RGJ had only been formed in 1966, they were descendants of many other historical regiments that had been amalgamated and disbanded over the years and could trace their history all the way back to the Battle of Quebec in 1759. My only knowledge of them up to that point was from something my mum said several years before, when our car was overtaken by a man on a motorbike going about 100mph in a 30mph zone. On the back of the motorcyclists green hoodie, in yellow letters was written "ROYAL GREEN JACKETS" and my mum said, "They're bloody mad them lot!" Apparently they used to run riot in Andover when she was younger.

Some of the colour sergeant's other statements weren't so encouraging though, telling me things like, "We get sent to Northern Ireland more than anyone else. In twelve years, I've been deployed there nine times." And "We've lost more men over there than any other regiment." I don't know why he would say that, even if it was true I'd have kept that one to myself if I were him. On my next visit to Bletchley I dealt with a different soldier, a staff sergeant who was from the Royal Engineers, because the colour sergeant was on leave.

"I've had a good think about the Green Jackets, but no offense, I still want to join the paras." I told him. He was fine with that and told me he'd worked with lots of different infantry units, but the paras were the best he'd ever seen.

"If I told any British infantry soldier to dig a trench and left him to it." he explained, "I'd come back a few hours later, and sure enough he would have dug a nice deep trench. But the difference with the paras is, if I told one of them to do it, I'd come back and he'd have dug the trench, built overhead protection, put out tripwires and flares, and he'd be alert on sentry duty watching for the enemy too."

I stuck to my guns and was allocated a place on the two-day Parachute Regiment, Potential Recruit Aptitude Course known as "Prac" in Depot Para, Aldershot. Walking away from the careers office after that visit I knew that it was definitely happening, I was joining the army, and the clock was now ticking. I had a date to start working towards, a fitness goal, and was extremely motivated. On my way home my usual short stop in Leighton Buzzard was extended to over an hour due to a breakdown, so I went for a walk to pass the time. On my route I passed a bicycle shop, and outside on the pavement were two used bikes with a price tag of fifteen pounds hanging from the handlebars. One of them was an old-school men's Raleigh racing bike. I didn't have a bike, and I didn't have a bus, but I did have fifteen pounds, and I did want to work on my fitness, so I bought it, tucked my trousers into my socks, and cycled the rest of the way home as fast as I could.

On 28 October 1992 I took the train to Aldershot where I was met on the station platform by a corporal from the Depot. Several other young men from the train were also attending the course and we were all quickly checked off his list and loaded onto a minibus that was waiting outside. He didn't talk to us, and we all sat in silence nervously until another train pulled in and more men were loaded onto the transport, filling it up before we departed for Depot Para, Browning Barracks, the home of Parachute Regiment recruit training since 1968.

Up to that point in my life, the following two days were the hardest thing I'd ever done. Twenty-one of us started PRAC and were allocated our numbered bedspaces in the accommodation block. I was number five and quickly found my bed in the first room I tried, placing my bags on the floor, and loitering apprehensively next to my bed awaiting further instructions. Like everyone else I was checking out the competition, comparing their physicality to my own and silently placing bets on who would pass or fail the course. I'd turned eighteen years old two weeks before and weighed about 175 pounds or 80 kilograms but there were younger and smaller men than me there. There were also some much bigger and older blokes too and it was easy to assume the big strong lads would be the successful ones. It didn't work out that way though, there was a mixture of ages and body types that passed, and I realised that looking the part was of little significance.

I learned a great deal on that course, including some regimental history, how to strip an SA80 rifle, and that you should never admit to a PTI that you are cold. We were lined up inside an old fashioned gym with wall bars folded against the wall and long wooden benches stacked in the corners. It was freezing cold and stood there in a black vest and running shorts I began to shiver. I wasn't the only one, plenty of the others were shaking a little too, as the PTI explained the exercises we'd be performing. Noticing our discomfort he addressed the course.

"Is anyone cold?" he asked sincerely. "Hands up if you are cold."

It seemed a genuine question, and I was genuinely cold, so naively I raised my hand in the air, much to the despair of someone standing behind me.

"Nooo!" he sighed under his breath, and I quickly learned why.

"Well we can't have that can we?" the corporal stated. "Let's get you lot warmed up!"

I'd fucked up.

"Press up position down!" he shouted abruptly. We all dropped to the floor obediently, adopting the nominated position, then began doing press ups on his command. "Lower, raise, lower, raise, lower, raise......On your feet up! Too slow, back down! Lower, raise, lower, raise.... On your feet up! Too slow, back down! Lower, raise, lower, raise......." and so it went on until he was content we'd gotten to our feet quickly enough. "Is anyone cold now?" he repeated the question.

My hand stayed firmly down by my side this time. Lesson learned.

Another time I drew the attention of the instructors was straight after two laps of the assault course. A bespoke course for airborne troops, it was designed to fatigue the legs with lots of high obstacles, jumps, and drops. I finished in the top five and felt exhausted but glad it was over, it was the single hardest thing I'd ever done, and I'd given everything. The officer in charge of the course was there to watch. He was an older gentleman, probably in the twilight years of a long career after going through the ranks, and he was unimpressed with our performance.

"Some of you are bluffing your case. Some of you were coasting on that test. So you are all doing it again, and you better do it faster this time, or I'll fail every single one of you!"

I couldn't hide my disappointment, my legs were like jelly, and I knew I couldn't possibly do it any quicker. I must have sighed, pulled a face, or muttered something under my breath because to my horror the next words I heard him shout were directed at me.

"Have you got a problem with that number five!?" He screamed angrily.

I think that's why I remember what number I was so clearly, because I can still remember that moment vividly to this day.

"No Sir!" I shouted back, standing up straight.

Before we went again the officer gave us the opportunity to quit the course, and a few took it, ending their chance of joining the paras right there and then. The remainder of us lined up and waited for the words we'd hear a thousand times more in Depot.

"Standby......Go!"

After the second obstacle we were stopped. It was a bluff, we weren't going again after all, they just wanted to see who had the stomach to do it again.

There were a lot of tests over the two days. We completed a two-mile running race, push ups, sit ups, chin ups, vertical jumps, the assault course, and parts of the Trainasium aerial obstacle course, where we climbed, ran, jumped, and swung across narrow planks on scaffolding high above the ground. One of the obstacles we had to conquer was the infamous "Illusion Jump", where you climb up onto a small platform that's about twenty feet high, then on the command "Go!" jump onto another narrow platform that's a few feet lower, and across an open gap. In reality it's not that far, the clue is in the name, but it is a good test of bottle that many fail. I completed all of the tests satisfactorily, unaware that I'd be doing them again about a year later on P-Company. On the last day of PRAC those of us who remained had an interview with the course officer to learn if we'd passed or failed. Of the twenty one that started, only seven of us were successful and subsequently offered a place as a Parachute Regiment recruit, and I walked out of there a very pleased and proud young man. I'd survived the first filter of my military career. That experience had such an impact on me that thirty years later I still remember not only my number, but the names of the two instructors that ran the course, Cpl Mansfield, and Cpl Ricketts the PTI.

The last job I had before joining the army was in a

warehouse for a garden equipment company on the Gatehouse Industrial Estate in Aylesbury. My original joining-up date had been 26 April 1993, but for some reason it was put back until 31 May 1993. I'd been laid off from the building company I worked for, so I applied for work with a temporary employment agency, and they found me a placement within a couple of days. The weekly pay was £3 per hour for the first 40 hours, then £4 per hour above that as overtime. On my first day at the Gardman factory I was shown to my work station and briefed on the complexities of the machinery I'd be using. My job was cutting strips of metal to a predetermined length, so it didn't take long. I had to slide the strip into the machine, then press a large pedal, which dropped a pneumatic cutter across it and deposited the cut piece into a metal container. Once I'd filled the container with strips I had to take them to another part of the factory where two men bent them into shape before passing them on again to two spot-welders, who made them into hanging basket brackets. To prepare myself for the army, I turned every task into a fitness training opportunity. I cycled the four miles to and from work as fast as I could and worked like a man possessed from seven o'clock in the morning until six o'clock in the evening, and within two days I'd produced a massive stockpile of cut metal lengths. On my third day one of the metal-benders failed to turn up for work and the manager asked me if I'd cover for him for the rest of the day. Before long I was into my own rhythm on that job, putting kinks and bends into those short strips like my life depended on it, quickly piling up the boxes next to the spot-welder I was supplying. The work wasn't physically hard, but I still managed to make it into a work-out by doing everything as fast as I possibly could, getting a good sweat on throughout the day. On my second day of doing that job the remaining metal-bender failed to show up too, and the manager told me I'd be supplying both of the welders until he was supplied with new staff. He was very apologetic and explained that he didn't expect me to be able to keep up with them but asked me to do my best. Challenge accepted! For the next five-and-a-half weeks I cut *and* bent the strips for *both* welders, and never fell behind once. It's safe to say I was a top chopper and an elite bender! When it came time for me to leave, the management were keen to keep me on, and offered me a proper job on the payroll. No wonder! My enthusiasm and work rate had been saving them two men's wages, but I declined. I had four weeks left before I started recruit training and wanted to concentrate on my fitness and preparation.

CHAPTER THREE
THE CROW

On the 31st of May 1993 my first day in the army was extremely nerve-wracking, but surprisingly calm based on my expectations. The instructors spoke firmly but weren't shouting and screaming like I'd expected. I was shown to my allocated bedspace in a ten-man room at the bottom of a long corridor, and informed I was now part of One Section, under an instructor called Corporal Fletcher. I wrote that down on the front cover of my newly purchased notebook, but even managed to get that wrong.

"Section One, Corporal Fletcher" I wrote in the top right-hand corner. I had a lot to learn. I was in One Section, not Section One!

Another mistake I made regarding the army numbering system was how I'd memorised my personal eight-digit service number. It felt like I couldn't do anything right. My platoon sergeant asked me.

"Name?"

"Steve Brown Sir." I answered.

"Don't call me Sir! I fucking work for a living!" he responded sharply, pointing to the three chevrons on his right arm. "I'm a sergeant. You call me Sergeant, or Sarn't. Do you understand?"

"Yes Sergeant!" I said.

"And you're not Steve Brown, you're Private Brown. I'm not your mate, I don't want to know your first name. Do you understand?"

"Yes Sergeant!" I repeated.

"What's your number Brown?" was the next question.

"Phone number or army number Sergeant?" I asked naively. Nobody had ever asked me for my army number before.

"Army number you mong!" he said despairingly. "Why would I want your phone number Brown? Why would I ever want to call you? You are not that interesting! Army number!"

I'd made a point of memorising the number I'd been given, thinking I'd get one step ahead of the game. "Two five O, two five four, O seven." I stated confidently.

Once again he was unimpressed. "O is a letter not a number! Zero is a number! Try again Brown, and this time using numbers not letters, and this time in two sets of four so I can actually understand what you are saying!"

I got there in the end, and it turned out I wasn't the only clueless person amongst the recruits. Others had called the corporals "mate" or "Sir" and the sergeant "Sir" or "Sarge", and several couldn't recite their army number correctly, so lots of us were receiving a quick education on army rank and number protocols. The first day was all about the admin of getting everyone booked in and accounted for, and that evening we were warned: "Get a good night's sleep tonight, and don't expect us to be so nice to you fuckers tomorrow. Tomorrow we start. Fucking brace yourselves gentlemen!" I don't think anyone would have accused them of having been nice to us, but in contrast to the following day they were fucking angelic, because there was a drastic shift in the way they spoke to and treated us from that moment onwards. Everything was given as a command, and everything needed to be done much faster and smarter than what we considered achievable. There was no excuse for walking anywhere casually, and even if you did someone else would push you out of the way because you were slowing them down. We ran and shuffled around from morning till night, reacting to every command instantaneously for fear of being branded "idle" or "jack".

Mornings in Depot were frantic. Upon waking there was no time for lying-in or pressing a "snooze" button. We'd get up immediately, make sure everyone else was awake then get cracking with our tasks. Everyone was told that shaving was to be done each morning, even the youngest, fresh-faced lads who hardly had a whisker, and we were all inspected first thing every day to make sure it had been done. Sinks, mirrors, toilets, showers, and baths had to be spotless, and the floors swept and polished to a high gloss. Beds were undressed, with the sheets and army-issue blankets folded into a perfect bed-block like we'd been shown by the corporals, and our immaculately pressed uniforms were donned quickly, with any last minute adjustments made to buttons, boots, and belts before inspection. Our black leather "Boots Combat High" were always expected to be highly polished, with clean, untwisted laces, and soles that were free of dirt or small stones. After a couple of weeks we'd have all this done and be ready to move within twenty minutes of waking up. I reckon a seasoned firefighter would have been impressed with how quickly we could get ready. My first morning was literally a massive wake-up call. Our section commander entered the room at exactly 0600hrs, and I heard a sound that every soldier learns to dread. Not the sound of him shouting at us to "get out of your beds!", because from that day forwards that was down to us. I mean the sound of the strip-lights on the ceiling kicking into life. First of all there is a buzz, followed by a flicker, then an audible click as the lights come on to end the peace and quiet of the dark, and signal the start of another day of intense training.

British Army recruit training had just been overhauled when I joined the army, with the disbandment of Regimental Recruit Training Centres and the formation of Army Training Regiments and role related courses. My first ten weeks were spent at ATR Lichfield in Staffordshire, where several other units from the army had also been relocated to. Fortunately the Parachute Regiment Recruit Company had retained its independence and continued to operate as a stand-alone unit within the barracks. I never actually knew what other units were there, we were under strict orders never to talk to the non-Parachute Regiment recruits and doing so would incur severe punishment. To be honest, anyone who wasn't Parachute Regiment was treated with utter contempt by the instructors, who robustly educated us on how we should now view other people, basically along the lines of:

- Civilians or "civvies" were disgusting creatures who didn't like soldiers, would never understand us, and had taken the easy route by not joining the army.
- Those who had joined the army but not the Paras were inferior to us. They'd obviously decided that our training was far too difficult for them to even bother trying, and they resented us for it. These soldiers were collectively called "Craphats" in reference to the large headdress they wore instead of berets when on parade, whereas paras only had one form of headdress, the maroon beret.
- Within the craphats there were other specific groups that received additional, special recognition:

  ◦ "REMF's" were Rear Echelon Mother Fuckers, or soldiers that weren't front-line, their units were also known as "Mess tin repair units".
  ◦ The Royal Military Police were called "Monkeys" and despised by everyone. Their sole purpose was to snitch on fellow soldiers, and even the real police thought they were scum.
  ◦ Others were classified as "Doss-bag Heads", "Cabbage Heads" and many more, depending on the shape or colour of their berets.

- The RAF were basically civilians in uniform, who stayed

in hotels instead of forests, drank wine instead of river water, and ate fine food instead of rations.

- The Royal Navy were strange people with ancient traditions. They wore flared trousers, drank lots of rum, and showered ten times a day.

All these people obviously had their own terms of endearment for the paras too, such as "The Parasite Regiment" or "Cherry Berets". Most of them also liked to think of us as intellectually defective Neanderthals.

Depot Para is sometimes referred to as "The Factory" because it's where paratroopers are made, and anyone who has been through it will never forget it. Most personal accounts are dominated by comical stories of beastings or hardships, normally told with a twisted, dark humour, but there are also many tales of brutality and subjugation. I never personally experienced it, but definitely saw examples of bullying by over-zealous instructors with their own views on disciplinary action, and I've heard plenty of stories of how it was apparently "harder in the old days". Personally I don't think my Depot platoon had it any harder or easier than anyone else's, either before us, or after us, we just did what we were told, when we were told. Sometimes it was brutally hard, intense, and relentless, but it was always for a reason; To prepare us for battle.

Recruit training physically broke us down by making it clear that we were nothing special. We were beasted beyond anything we'd ever experienced, with our weaknesses and shortcomings fully exposed to us, the other recruits, and our instructors. In civvy street I was regarded as tough, fit, and confident, but in Depot I realised I was none of these things outside of my own small social circle. What I also realised though, was that I had the potential to be all of them, and much more. Psychologically they broke us down too, through a mixture of de-civilianisation and dehumanisation. Collectively we were 583 Platoon, or Bruneval Platoon, and we all shared the same name of "Joe Crow". Individually we were addressed as Joe, Crow, our number, or our surname, and everything that happened to us was way beyond our control. We got up at "reveille", washed, shaved, made our beds, swept and polished the floors, cleaned the sinks, toilets, showers, and mirrors, got dressed, marched to breakfast, rammed food down our necks like starving, feral orphans, marched back to the block, finished cleaning, stood by our beds for an inspection, got beasted for tiny bits of fluff or dust in obscure places, then started our day. We were nobody special, but our instructors were, and we could be too if we worked hard enough.

In the early days of training there wasn't much in the way of positive reinforcement or encouragement from the instructors, and the methodology was definitely a lot more "stick" than it was "carrot". In fact, you'd find more carrot at a Texan carnivore's barbecue, and less stick in the Amazon rain forest. I remember the first time I actually felt like I was doing something right, and that as a group we were slowly becoming soldiers, and it wasn't when I first put the uniform on or got my hands on a rifle. It was the first time we marched in-step together as a platoon, and our boots made the audible "crump" of marching feet, as our heels dug hard into the ground in perfect synchronicity. I think it felt good because we were clearly doing something right as a team, and who else, other than soldiers, gets to do that?

Depot was intense to say the least, and you could say it was closer to an indoctrination process than a training course, but for me it was just what was needed; Routine, strong male role models, discipline, and respect. I listened intently to my instructors, hanging on to their every word. I tried to emulate the way they conducted themselves because they were everything I wanted to be; Fit, confident, capable, honourable. I couldn't imagine them having any weaknesses or even suffering from things like tiredness, cold, fear, or self-doubt. I genuinely thought of them as indestructible, it was like their para-smocks, berets, and parachute wings gave them superpowers, and if I could earn those prestigious things, I'd have superpowers too. I remember being freezing cold and feeling sorry for myself in the pouring rain one day and looking at one of our instructors, a terrifying man called Corporal Blacklock. The rain was dripping from his nose too, but he didn't look cold or uncomfortable at all. He stood upright, proud, and emotionless like always, and I honestly thought that his beret was keeping him warm and immune to the cold. It was crazy how I'd gone from a juvenile delinquent with no respect for anybody, to this reverent and inspired young man in such a short period of time, but those instructors truly turned my life around, and for that I'm forever grateful.

The standards were extremely high in Depot, and infractions would rarely go unnoticed by the instructors, who would mete out punishment as they saw fit. Push-ups were given out constantly and we'd do hundreds every day to shouts of "Lower!", "Raise!", "Half way up!", "All the way up!", "All the way down!", "Half way up!", and "On your feet up!" One of the other common punishments to receive was a "Show-Clean" where you had to parade at the guardroom at 2100hrs for an inspection, with your offending item remedied. Minor felonies leading to show-clean included heinous crimes like having a double-crease or "tram-line" in your shirt or trousers, not shaving properly, unclean boots, or an unfastened pocket.

"Paratroopers don't iron their kit, they fucking press it!" we were told. Ironing was the lazy man's version of pressing. The use of starch that was on sale in the NAAFI shop was strictly forbidden, deemed as a form of cheating or idleness. Our trousers, shirts, shorts, t-shirts, and combat jackets were all to be pressed, and those of us that didn't have the luxury of a steam-iron sprayed water onto our clothes instead, to make our own steam.

My first experience of ironing my own clothes was as an eighteen-year-old young man in Depot. Embarrassingly, up until then my mum had always done it for me, and probably without any real thanks or recognition from me too. Like a lot of teenagers, my clothes seemed to magically wash, dry, and iron themselves, before the invisible house fairy folded them up neatly and put them away in my cupboard for me. My mum suggested I learn how to iron before I joined the army, but I was dismissive, and declined her offer of a free lesson in equipment husbandry. How hard could it be anyway? I'd surely pick it up quickly enough when the moment came. Well, that moment came on day-two of Depot, when we were issued every piece of clothing we'd need for the next six months and told to have it immaculately pressed by the following morning. Corporal Fletcher gave us a perfect demonstration on how to press our shirts, shorts, t-shirts, trousers, and combat jackets, using either an ironing board or one of the square, wooden tables from the room. We had six pairs of trousers, including 2 x green lightweight denims, 2 x disruptive pattern material (DPM) camouflage, and 2 x barrack dress trousers, which all needed creases down the front and back. We had six shirts, 3 x green denim, and 3 x barrack dress, and they needed creases down the sleeves, and the collars pressed flat against the top of the chest. For P.T we had two t-shirts; one red and one green, and they needed creases down the sleeves too. Our two pairs of dark blue P.T shorts were required to have creases front and rear, and both our issued combat jackets also needed sharp creases down the length of the sleeves, with the pockets pressed flat. My second night as a recruit was spent ironing and cursing myself for not learning how to do it beforehand. Our ten-man room had four tables in it that were all quickly claimed by four people who'd had the foresight to bring along an iron, and they got ahead of the game by starting on their clothes as soon as we were stood down for the day. The rest of us went to the NAAFI and bought ourselves irons and ironing boards, alongside about thirty others, in what must have been a very profitable night for the shop. Some of the older lads managed to complete the mammoth task within a couple of hours and get their heads down at a reasonable time, but me and a few of the others were up well into the early hours, trying in vain to iron out the creases that didn't belong, and put new ones in in the right places. Every now and then a bedside light would go out, and the springs of a bed would squeak, as another bloke either finished or capitulated before calling it a night, and I finished in time to get only a couple of hours sleep before it all began again.

On the morning of day three our first formal locker inspection was an absolute disaster. Clothing was ripped out and launched into neighbouring bed-spaces, the corridor, and even outside through the open windows. It was extremely demoralising to see your hard work strewn across the floor in a crumpled heap that would need pressing again that night. And so it went on.

Fitness training in Depot was conducted at least once a day and there were never any easy sessions. We'd be given an impossibly short time to get changed into our P.T kit, then parade outside in our hideous, issued blue shorts, with razor sharp creases ironed into the front and back, and our red or green t-shirts with equally impressive creases in the short sleeves. Over time most people's P.T shirts ended up misshapen and ill-fitting, with gaping necks where they'd been dragged up a hill, over a wall, or through a river by the instructors at some point. When they were first issued to us we were instructed to sow a white patch onto the front and write our surnames on them, and that night we all cut the inside flap out of our issued, white cotton pillow cases and hand-sewed them on, before stencilling our names onto them in black permanent ink.

Our first P.T session was as disheartening as the locker inspection. We were taken to the gymnasium and lined up outside for the PTI's, who came out to introduce themselves, wearing traditional white vests with red markings. Both were relatively short men that looked like very fit individuals, one was English, and the other Scottish. Both were corporals who clearly detested Joe's, and after a short brief to inform us that we were going to get "beasted until our eyes bled" that "the ball was in our court" and that if we "worked for them they'd work for us" they took us for what they called a "steady-state run". However, within a few minutes it became clear to everyone that it was more of an eternal sprint, interspersed with partner carries and bodyweight exercises, rather than anything remotely steady. We ran harder and faster than I'd ever done in my life, so I was very happy when I saw the back gate we'd came out through and realised we were almost back to camp. But, instead of going to the gate we stopped at a football pitch just shy of it where the running continued, only stopping to pick somebody up and carry them, or conduct push-ups, sit-ups, burpees, long jumps, bear crawls, and another exercise I learned to hate, seal-crawls. I'd never witnessed someone be physically sick from intense exercise before that, but I saw a few that day. It was horrendous, and I was shocked at how hard I was finding it. I thought I was quite fit, but I was exhausted, and I genuinely wondered if I'd bitten off more than I could chew. I wasn't the only one though, it turned out everyone felt the same, and realising that made me feel a lot better. For a few of the lads, that first beasting was enough, and they threw the towel in there and then, opting to withdraw from training and go home to rethink their future.

As recruits we quickly had to learn how to dress correctly for a myriad of different activities and lessons. There was working dress, barrack dress, number two dress, shirt-sleeve order, long-sleeve order, smock order, PT order, marching order, fighting order, weapon training order and NBC order. In the words of the instructors, especially during the early days, we were also regularly accused of being in "Rag Order!" which meant scruffy / unsatisfactory / a disgraceful mess. Every time we got changed we made work for ourselves, because in our haste we messed up our perfect locker layout and created more washing and ironing for the next day. Because of this I absolutely hated "Quick Change parades", which were a series of clothing changes in rapid succession at the behest of the DS, sometimes used as another form of collective punishment. After a quick change parade your bedspace was destroyed, with clothes, footwear, and coat hangers scattered everywhere from the frantic chaos, as you rushed to get back outside within an impossible timeframe. During one of these parades I watched our corporal walk calmly past my door towards the staff room where his locker was kept. He'd told us if we could get outside in the nominated order of dress before him, the parade would stop, so when I saw him walking so leisurely while I was already half undressed I felt pretty confident it would be over quickly. However, what seemed like only a few seconds later, that same instructor walked back past my room in the opposite direction, fully changed, and as smart as a carrot. I did a double-take and stood still in awe for a couple of seconds, genuinely puzzled at how that could be possible, and once again reinforcing my belief that these men were superhuman.

Get outside!" he shouted as he walked towards the exit. "Don't let me beat you! Ten.. nine.. eight.. seven............"

By the time I got outside there were already several others there, stood in three ranks in varying degrees of distress, but nobody had beaten Corporal Riley who was looking at his watch disappointedly as we crashed through the door and sprinted to join the group.

"Press-up position down!" he ordered, as the last few stragglers appeared. "Lower!.. Raise!.. Lower!.. Raise!.. Lower!.. Raise!.. Lower! As we hovered with our chests an inch from the ground he briefed us on what he expected to happen next. "Some of you people are bluffing your cases!" he yelled. "Some of you are coasting, and we know who you are! When I say go, at the speed of a thousand gazelles, you will get to your feet, sprint around the block, get back inside, get changed into barrack dress, and get fell-in back here in three ranks before me! Do you understand?"

"Yes Corporal!" we shouted in unison, before receiving the next inevitable command.

"Standby....Go!"

I once heard an instructor from another regiment beasting his recruits and telling them to do something at the speed of ten gazelles. That made me chuckle, and further convinced me that our training was much harder than everyone else's. Only ten? Pathetic! We did things at the speed of a thousand! To be fair, I've only just realised while writing this, that it doesn't really matter how many gazelles there are, their top speed is still going to be about 60mph. A thousand does sound better though.

I thought there was even less chance of beating him this time, because he'd get a head start while we lapped the huge accommodation block, but when we got back to the door he was waiting for us with some additional words of encouragement.

"Hurry up! Don't be last!" he shouted, before following us into the block behind the last man. Once again I saw him casually saunter past my room while I was flapping like a headless chicken and ransacking my locker like a crazed burglar to get to my clothes. He got changed so quickly I started to think he must have a twin brother, and we failed on three or four more attempts before it finally ended. About nine years later I was telling this story to a good friend in Pathfinders called Nick Brown, an awesome soldier from 2 PARA, who'd previously been an instructor in Depot himself.

"Yeah, but you know how we do that in Depot don't you?" he said, assuming I'd long since worked it out. I hadn't.

"Do you wear the clothes underneath each other, then take them off in layers?" I guessed. I'd never suspected any trickery, I just thought my DS were very very fast.

Nick laughed at my naivety, then explained how all the other DS on a training team would wait in the staff room, ready with the next set of clothes, and the instructor taking part would simply walk in, stand still, and get de-robed and re-dressed by the others, like a Formula One racing car having a tyre change at a pit-stop. That blew my mind. Ingenious. Nick was a fantastic soldier and great bloke, who always had a hilarious story for any occasion. Sadly he was killed during a special forces mission in Iraq in 2008 while serving with special forces.

Everything in Depot was done under pressure, some self-induced, but mostly system-induced by the staff. Firstly there was always an unrealistic time limit on every task we were given. We'd come back from the assault course soaking wet and covered in mud, then receive our instructions for the next lesson.

"When I say go, you lot will get inside, get showered, change into barrack dress, and be back out here in three ranks ready for inspection." they'd tell us before delivering the killer blow. "You've got three minutes, do not be late! Standby.... Go!!!"

We'd sprint to the locked entrance door, frantically enter the three-digit security code, fight against the surging crush of the blokes to get the outwardly-opening door open, bound up the stairs, through another fire door, down the corridor, and into our rooms. I was always jealous of 3 and 4 Section during these periods, because their rooms were a little bit closer to the entrance than mine, giving them an overall time advantage of about six vital seconds. On entering our rooms we had to open the ammunition container that held the keys to our padlocked lockers, and scramble to find them amongst the other nine sets belonging to the other occupants. We'd then open our lockers, get undressed, grab our towels, and sprint to the ablutions, which had two showers that could each just about fit two men in at a time. We'd take turns to get in, get wet, get out, lather up with soap, then get back in again to rinse off, the whole time making a mess of the place we'd spent ages immaculately cleaning the night before and that morning. There wasn't much talking while we rushed around, just the odd word or pointed finger to warn someone that they still had mud on the back of their necks, or in their ears, or just quickly get it off for them like wild gorillas picking fleas off each other. Within seconds we were out of there and back in our rooms getting dressed again, trying our best not to sweat into our clean clothes, because our bodies hadn't had the opportunity to cool down yet.

It's surprising how fast you can do things when under pressure, and how you can find shortcuts in everyday tasks. We'd have our shirts already placed inside our woolly jumpers, and as we pulled them over our heads, to save a few seconds, we'd be simultaneously putting our feet into our boots. Once our laces were tied we'd secure our lockers and start heading back outside, tucking our shirts in, and adjusting twisted collars or sleeves as we went, and by then the instructors would usually be shouting at us to hurry up. We'd also check each other's clothing before lining up in three ranks, making sure pockets and zips were fastened, belts, collars and laces weren't twisted, and berets were spotless.

"Outside!" They'd yell down the corridor. "Don't be last!" The real panic started when the DS began the dreaded countdown. "Ten... Nine... Eight... Hurry up you fucking people!... Seven... Six... Don't be last!... Five..." You could feel the vibrations through the floor, and hear the pounding of feet, as the entire platoon rushed from their ten-man rooms in a bid to get outside before the person in front of them. Being last always incurred some kind of punishment, ranging from fifty push-ups, a lap of the accommodation, or a show-clean, all accompanied by a verbal beasting. When the countdown reached number three or four was when the motivational slaps to the back of the head and kicks up the ass to encourage us to move faster would begin. "Four... Three... Two...." I never found out what it was like to still be inside after the countdown had finished, but I assumed you'd be either mortally wounded, dead, or wishing you were dead because of the pain you were suffering at the hands of the infuriated DS.

Inevitably someone is always going to be last, but when that someone is repeatedly the same person, they quickly become very unpopular. Firstly it would be the DS that tired of their relative lethargy or perceived lack of a sense of urgency. They'd award their punishment as they saw fit in an effort to deter the offender from ever being last again and forcing everyone else to wait for them. Initially, for the rest of us recruits, those blokes were the gift that kept on giving, their slowness made us look faster, and kept us out of the spotlight. However, the DS knew exactly how to deal with that situation, and after a while they'd punish everyone who was on time until everyone who was late turned up. That method made those of us who were on time resent those who were late, and those who were late feel very bad about themselves, as they were made to watch us run around or do push-ups. Sometimes for extra effect, the last person would be made to point and laugh out loud at us, or we'd all have to shout out "Thankyou Smith" or whatever their name was, on the execution of every push-up or sit-up we completed. People causing extra P.T for the platoon were not liked, and after a while they'd be robustly encouraged to pull their finger out by the remainder. It worked though because none of those recruits made it very far before being weeded out.

Para recruits were strictly forbidden from talking to recruits from other regiments or corps. We weren't even allowed to look at them, and they certainly weren't allowed to look at us either.

"Look away you fucking creatures!" our instructors would shout at them if they even dared to glance in our direction. "You are not worthy of looking at my killing machines, you disgusting little wretches!" As much as they seemed to dislike us, our DS absolutely despised other recruits. If ever we were out running or tabbing, and any were spotted ahead of us on a road or track, no matter how far away, we'd always have to overtake them. And if ever we were on the same pathway but moving in opposing directions, we'd be ordered to continue forwards without giving away any space, sometimes resulting in us smashing through their ranks like a freight train.

To an outsider the mindset that our instructors slowly instilled in us might seem arrogant and egotistical. Maybe it is, but it's also much more than that. In an age where elitism is frowned upon, and any suggestion that one group of people can be better than another is met with indignation, soldiers still need to believe that they are the best. I suppose that soldiers in every regiment or corps are told that they're the elite too, and if not their instructors are doing them a disservice. We were constantly reminded of what it meant to be a paratrooper and that's why we stuck with it through all the adversity and hardship of Depot, because we believed wholeheartedly that our chosen regiment was the best of the best. I suppose you could liken it to the mentality of sports fans, where people are fiercely loyal to their chosen teams, convinced that they are the best, and that anyone who disagrees is their adversary. I later learned though, that despite these rivalries, just like football fans will join forces to support their national teams during international competition, the military will also put their superficial differences aside on operations, to work together towards a common goal or objective. Essentially it's just healthy competition, with the odd brawl thrown in.

There were a few exercises in Lichfield, beginning with an overnighter called "First Venture" that was basically a bit of crazy camping, where we learned how to carry out basic tasks in the field. We put up shelters, dug latrines, and washed, shaved, cooked, and ate from our small, metal mess tins. It was a good introduction, and yet another reminder to me that I knew nothing. The next exercise was imaginatively named "Second Venture" where we stayed out for a few days, learned some basic infantry tactics, and got "bugged out" for the first time. This is when you get attacked by an enemy force and have to conduct a fighting withdrawal, and this became a recurring theme on every single exercise we did from then onwards. Exercise "Steel Eagle" was a week long pass-or-fail exercise where we carried heavier kit and were assessed on our fitness and basic skills. The biggest hurdle in Lichfield was an exercise called "Basic Wales" which was a week on the Sennybridge Training Area in Wales, which finished with two back to back endurance marches over the Brecon Beacons that used to be part of P-Company. Like Steel Eagle it was a pass or fail exercise, and failure would mean getting "back-squadded" which meant being removed from 583 Platoon and joining a platoon behind us, most likely 584, or 585 depending on how much re-training the DS decided was required. We had a couple of recruits in our platoon who'd been back-squadded to us, and we picked their brains for any information on upcoming events that they'd already experienced. Prior knowledge didn't help much though, everything was a beasting either way. I really didn't want to be back-squadded, and just the thought of going through any of the training twice was motivation enough to work hard and pass the first time. Basic Wales took me to a new benchmark of hardship. For a week we were cold, wet, tired, and under pressure. I learned that inside the forest it continues to rain even if the Sun is shining outside of it, and that water drips with pinpoint accuracy from branches into the small space between the material of your collar and the skin of your neck. I also found out that the Sun will never warm your body while you are still inside the woods, and that the human body will never warm the ground beneath it when that ground is made of wet mud. However, I also learned that a platoon of soldiers can move silently through a thick forest in complete darkness, and that our bodies could perform great feats of endurance, even with minimum rest and food.

At the end of the ten weeks in Lichfield our parents and families were invited to the barracks for our passing-out parade, but most of us didn't want to do it. By the books we'd passed basic training and were now moving on to advanced training, but that meant little to me and the others in our platoon, because we weren't even half way through yet. We'd survived ten weeks there, but had another sixteen weeks to go in Catterick, it was far too early for celebration. The staff put on a good show for the guests though, with a parade, abseiling, and unarmed combat demonstrations, as well as equipment displays and briefings on what we'd done so far.

After some summer leave we started the Combat Infantryman's Course at the Infantry Training Centre in Catterick, North Yorkshire, another four months of training with a new group of instructors from the Parachute Regiment Recruit Company. The downside to this two-phase training concept was that we were immediately teleported back to day one, week one with our DS. We'd long established who was fit, keen, and hardworking, as well as who the less motivated recruits were, but our new training team had no idea, to them we were all equally irrelevant, useless Joes, until we could prove otherwise.

Catterick had plenty of its own benchmarks too, including a defensive exercise called "Mole Mania", P-Company, Live Fire Tactical Training, and the Parachute Course.

Exercise Mole Mania, also known as Exercise Dynamite Mole, required us to dig full-size fighting trenches for the first time. For two days we used picks, shovels, and our bare hands to dig deep into hideous ground, working through the night, with no rest. During that exercise was the second time in my life I experienced hallucinating because of tiredness, and I remember looking through a telescopic night-sight and seeing what looked like a heavily camouflaged man signalling to me. I can still see him now, on the edge of a forest block, with the upper half of his body poking through the trees at a forty-five degree angle. The sight picture was shades of green and black, but I could see the features of his wild eyes and manic grin clearly as he waved at me. It was very surreal, I thought I was probably hallucinating, but at the same time wondered if it could be a soldier on the enemy force warning us of an imminent attack. Maybe it was someone who'd been back-squadded from our platoon and still trying to do his bit for 583.

CHAPTER FOUR
NUMBER FIVE

P-Company or Pre-Parachute Selection Company is one of the most famous courses in the British military because of its arduousness and high failure rate, and passing it is a rite of passage for any soldier that wants to earn their parachute wings and the right to call themselves airborne. The RAF and the Royal Marines have their own courses to determine whether or not someone is suitable for airborne operations, but the Parachute Regiment and staff of P-Company remain the standard bearers for the army. They ensure that every soldier can pass the well-established series of tests within P-Company before being allowed onto the parachute course at RAF Brize Norton. All serving soldiers that are not in the Parachute Regiment but wish to be part of an airborne unit must first pass P-Company, and normally this is preceded by a few weeks of intense training within their own units. For me as a recruit P-Company was yet another daunting event that I both looked forward to and dreaded in equal measure. It was a massive milestone, and opportunity to take a significant step towards becoming a paratrooper, but it was also a huge psychological and physical hurdle that could become the most demoralising experience of your life if you were unsuccessful. Getting beasted was nothing new to us, it was part of everyday life as a Joe in Depot, but the added pressure of knowing that each performance on P-Company could determine whether we earned our maroon berets, or got back-squadded to another platoon, where we'd have to do it all again weighed heavy.

Our P-Company was conducted on week sixteen of Depot and included ten events which were the log race, the steeplechase, milling, the assault course, the trainasium, the stretcher race, and four loaded marches; the ten-miler, the ten-kilometre speed march, and two cross-country endurance marches which were twelve and eighteen miles long.

The Assault Course

I have to admit, the assault course in Catterick wasn't as demanding as the one in Aldershot but it was still a beasting because it was an individual effort. A NATO standard design meant there were still plenty of climbs, jumps, scrambles, and water obstacles though. We had a bloke called Chris West in our platoon who was the bookies favourite for that event. He already held the record for it, and sure enough, after two laps he won impressively. I was nowhere near as quick as Chris, but I did pretty good, and was happy I'd scored well too.

The Trainasium

Because a new trainasium hadn't been constructed in Catterick yet, we had to take a coach trip all the way to Aldershot to conduct the test there, a round trip of over five-hundred miles and about ten hours driving. Failing the trainasium meant an immediate fail on P-Company and withdrawal from the course, so it was an essential serial that had to be carried out. We departed Catterick early in the morning with a haver bag meal from the cookhouse for our lunch and left for Browning Barracks, Aldershot. On arrival, we quickly debussed and watched the DS perform a flawless demonstration of the entire apparatus. At varying heights between twenty and forty-five feet the obstacles included the illusion jump, ramp-jump, balance bars, shuffle bars, cable-crawl, see-saw jump, rope swing, and superman jump, all with very little safety equipment, and nothing to stop you from falling off the sides. Wearing green denim trousers, combat jackets, and helmets we started off by climbing about thirty feet up the corner of the scaffolding to the start point, where we waited for the DS to address us.

"Name and number!?" they'd shout from below, and we'd come to attention before replying.

"Number five, Brown, Staff!" was my reply.

"Okay number five. Standby..................Go! they yelled.

Just like when I did PRAC, I was once again number five, and once again sprinting around some rickety old scaffolding like an absolute lunatic. The event ran like a well-oiled machine, and before long we were being loaded back on the bus with another haver bag meal for our dinner. Not a single person failed that test.

The Log Race

The log race was a 1.5 mile team event, where eight men carried a heavy telegraph pole across arduous terrain by short lengths of rope that were wrapped around their wrists. Regarded by many as the hardest event of the week, it was absolutely horrendous, with steep climbs and descents, water-filled ditches, and the relentless screams of the DS telling us to go faster, work harder, and stop coasting. Three men came off our log, one at the front, one beside me, and one behind me. Two of them were withdrawn by the DS for not working hard enough and the other fell through exhaustion, each withdrawal making the log heavier and heavier. I gave everything I had on that race, working anaerobically from the start, and with the finish line in clear sight I stumbled forwards, face-planting into a deep puddle on the gravel track before the DS dragged me off to the side so I didn't get stampeded by the teams behind us. Exhausted, I mumbled incoherently and tried to get to my feet to re-join the log, but I was done, and within a few seconds the remainder of my team had crossed the finish line. The staff put me in the back of a Land Rover and took me straight to the Medical Centre on camp where it was quickly established that my blood-sugar level was very low. To get it back up they gave me two packets of glucose tablets from the old ration packs to eat immediately, washed down with a pint of water, followed by another pint of water, five minutes of observation and a "Get away you horrible little creature!" as I was discharged. Often, coming off the log will result in an immediate fail on the course, so I was absolutely devastated, thinking that I'd be back-squadded to do it all again. Fortunately my graft had been acknowledged by the DS and I was permitted to continue the course. The two blokes who were withdrawn weren't so lucky though, they were both failed on the spot. While writing about this I did a quick internet search on the causes of low blood sugar and the following came up as risk factors; lack of sleep, anxiety, and insufficient calorie intake. Sounds like a summary of 24hrs in Depot.

Milling

Milling is best described as a boxing match, where you are not allowed to actually box. Instead you must stand still and throw straight punches at your opponent's head as hard and fast as you can, while he does the same to you, with neither of you attempting to dodge or block the punches coming your way. On the morning of the milling we were lined up in the corridor in two opposing rows and told to stare the person opposite us in the eyes while our instructors got us fired up with some motivational speech.

"That person in front of you wants to take away everything you've worked for! They want you to fail so they can win! They want to hurt you! They want to punch your fucking teeth out of your head! Are you going to let that happen?"

"No Corporal!" we all shouted in reply.

This went on for a while with some of the recruits clearly buying into it and getting visibly vexed, but it didn't really work on me. The bloke stood across from me was a good friend, and even when they got us to slap each other across the face several times really hard, I just found it funny. Those guys were like brothers to me, I couldn't even imagine wishing them harm. Once suitably wound up we were marched to the old fashioned gymnasium where the P-Company staff took control of us.

After being weighed, we were matched up with someone of roughly equal weight then sat down on the long, wooden gym benches in order, with the lightest at the front of the queue, and heaviest at the back. The benches we sat on formed a small square in the centre of the gymnasium, and that square denoted the boxing ring. The first bout was between the two smallest blokes in the platoon called Tiddy and John H. Tiddy was a former schoolboy boxing champion from Manchester with an air of intensity, confidence, and swagger about him, whereas John was more of a jovial, chilled-out southerner from Brighton, and I think most of us assumed Tiddy would easily win. However, it turned out John was hard as nails too, and those two put on an awesome display of guts and determination that set the bar for the rest of us and earned them a draw. My bout was against a recruit called Brookes, who was bigger than me, but only by a few kilograms, and I felt quietly confident. I'd probably done hundreds of hours of sparring in my youth, and the gloves we were using were huge compared to the lightweight ones I was used to. I knew it was important to get the first strike in, and as long as I could do that, I'd do well. Mike Tyson is famed for saying *"Everyone has a plan, until they get punched in the face."* and he's right, because Brookes beat me to the punch as we both threw at the same time, and he caught me with a solid right-hand to the head. I tucked my chin and returned fire, with the majority of our punches deflecting off each other's arms and fists, until he telegraphed a wild left hook which I ducked under and countered with one of my own that landed cleanly.

The referee stepped in between us shouting "Stop!" then turned towards me to issue a warning. "This is not boxing, this is milling! Do you understand?"

I didn't really understand but answered obediently, yelling "Yes Staff."

Stepping back he gave the command for us to recommence fighting, shouting "Mill!"

Brookes threw another haymaker right hand, but this time I instinctively slipped it and caught him flush with a counter right.

"Stop!" The referee intervened again, this time giving me a stern warning. "This is not boxing! If I have to tell you again, I'll disqualify you! Do you understand me?"

This time I got it, and when he shouted "Mill" again I just clenched my jaw, tucked my chin, and threw and absorbed hail-Mary punches until the bell went. To be honest, I was relieved when we were also awarded a draw, because I thought the warnings might go against me.

The Ten-Miler, 10km Speed March, Twelve-Miler, and Eighteen Miler

There were four test-marches on our P-Company where we carried weapons and bergans at speed, across the Catterick and Warcop training areas. The ten-miler, with a cut-off time of 1hr 51mins is the bread-and-butter test of British airborne forces, and in my opinion, barring injury, all paratroopers should be able to comfortably complete it at any given time during their service. The 10km speed-march was a short and sharp test at an even faster pace than normal, coming in in just over one hour. The twelve, and eighteen mile endurance tests were slower, but longer, and conducted on cross-country routes in the mountainous Warcop Training Area of Cumbria. I stayed with the DS for all of these events, so was confident I'd passed them.

The Steeplechase

The steeplechase was a cross-country race with obstacles thrown in, that mostly involved jumping, or running, into deep, freezing cold puddles and streams. Like the assault course it's an individual effort, and you are not allowed to encourage or assist anyone else along the way. Your goal is to overtake the man in front, not help him. The DS want to see aggression, not compassion. Again I was happy with my performance on that event.

Leading the way out of a water obstacle on the Steeplechase

The Stretcher Race

This team test was the final event on my course and involved teams of about eight men carrying a stretcher for six-miles over the undulating terrain of the Catterick training area. The stretcher itself was constructed of scaffold poles and metal sheets and weighed 180lbs. The event is designed to simulate a casualty extraction under pressure, and like the log race it's a race to the finish against the other teams. It doesn't matter how fit you are, those tests are exhausting, and the DS run alongside their team's stretcher shouting and screaming the entire way. Only four men can carry the stretcher at a time, with the remainder running next to them, waiting for their turn to take over. Dictating when the change overs happen, the DS order people on and off the stretcher, while they also control the pace shouting "Standby!........Sprint!" over and over again. When carrying the stretcher it bounces hard off your neck and shoulders, as you all try to keep in-step to shouts of "Left, right, left, right, left, right, left!" But the uneven ground, inclines, declines, potholes, and puddles make that extremely difficult to maintain. You look forward to the moment you are relieved from carrying it, thinking the break will give you time to catch your breath and re-energise, but it doesn't. Somehow running alongside seems equally as difficult, and before you know it you are back underneath it being ordered to "Sprint!" Like most infantry courses psychology plays a huge part on P-Company, especially during team events. A simple comment by the DS like "Some of you people are not working!" casts doubt on everyone's mind and makes them push themselves even harder. Of course they'd say that anyway, but the slightest thought they could be referring to you is incentive enough. We lost a few blokes on the stretcher race but crossing the finish line meant the end of P-Company, and I hoped I'd never have to do it again.

When P-Company was over I really didn't know if I'd passed or not, and there are people out there who will be genuinely angered to learn that I did, knowing that I didn't finish the log race. In keeping with tradition, after the course we were lined up outside to be told our results by the Officer Commanding P-Company. When my number was called I came to attention, shouting "Sir!"

"Pass." he said.

"Sir!" I acknowledged, standing at ease once again. I was relieved more than I was happy.

The parade ended and our platoon sergeant addressed us one last time as a group, before those who'd failed were back-squadded to another platoon to do it all again. Pointing at his beret he told us.

"Just because some of you fuckers have got one of these now, don't start thinking you're special, because you're not! You are still just a bunch of crows! The hard work starts now!"

It wasn't exactly a congratulatory speech, but it was as close as we were going to get. Prior to that we'd been told we were nobody special until we earned our berets. Now he pointed at the parachute wings on his right shoulder.

"If and when you get a set of these," he said, "then, and only then, will you be paratroopers."

Shortly after P-Company we were sent to the Parachute Training School at RAF Brize Norton in Oxfordshire. Once there our Depot staff relinquished control of us to the Parachute Jump Instructors, a collection of RAF corporals and sergeants. Brize Norton was like a holiday camp compared to what we'd become accustomed to, and the food was like Michelin star cuisine, where we were actually given sufficient time to eat it. Also on the course were soldiers of all ranks from the rest of the army who'd passed the "All-Arms" P-Company. Our first parachute decent was made from a metal cage that hung beneath a big old barrage balloon. The balloon was filled with helium and tethered to a huge mechanical winch on the ground by a thick metal cable. Four men at a time would get into the cage along with one PJI who shouted, "Up eight hundred, four men jumping." The winch operator would then release the brake and let the balloon ascend to eight hundred feet, from where the parachutists would jump out, one at a time.

The day of our first jump we arrived at Weston-on-the-Green drop zone by military bus just as someone was leaping from the cage. Everyone on the bus rushed to the left-hand side to see the parachute open nicely and watched nervously as the soldier hanging beneath it was guided through his drills by an instructor with a megaphone. Unfortunately his landing technique wasn't very good, and as soon as he hit the floor he started shouting "Medic!" The medical team on the DZ must have heard him scream, because they were racing across the flat grass in their ambulance within seconds, not realising that the next parachutist had already been dispatched and was slowly drifting down from above their heads. He landed right in front of their vehicle, causing them to brake hard before swerving around him and carrying on to the casualty. It was a crazy introduction to parachuting, you couldn't make it up, and we hadn't even got off the bus yet. If anyone was nervous before, they were terrified now. By definition the balloon jump was actually a BASE jump, like jumping from a bridge or building, because the cage was still attached to the ground by the cable. It was a strange experience, quietly ascending to eight-hundred feet above the Oxfordshire countryside. Below us was the large open expanse of the drop-zone, with its prominent circular sand-pit in the centre, and to the east was the busy M40 motorway. It was eerily silent up there though, and the only person with much to say was the PJI, who joked that from up there we could see the graveyard where they buried people whose parachutes failed. One at a time we were called forward to stand in the small doorway with our PX4 parachutes on our backs and reserve parachutes clipped onto our fronts.

"Both arms across your reserve!" The PJI ordered.

Just like we'd rehearsed in the hangar dozens of times we folded our arms over the top of the reserve parachute container.

"Go!" he said.

Months of responding to the command "Go!" ensured no hesitation when it came to my turn, and I jumped into the void immediately, plummeting vertically about two-hundred feet before the parachute opened above me. There was no time to enjoy the experience, the ground was approaching fast and

PJI's on the ground shouted instructions at us through loud-hailers to ensure we landed safely. Back on the bus everyone was buzzing with excitement, we'd all done the exact same thing, but each person had their own personal experience. After seven more descents, where the added complexities of equipment, weapons, and night-time were added to the mix we qualified as military parachutists.

The day we received our wings on the drop zone our platoon sergeant gave a rousing speech about what it meant to be a part of our chosen regiment. He talked about the hard-earned reputation that our forebears from World War Two had forged on the bloody battlefields of Arnhem and Normandy, and the tenacity of the men that had upheld it on subsequent operations, all the way through to the Falklands War of 1982. It was a rare moment of uplifting praise from a man who seemed to genuinely detest us, but he quickly brought us back down to earth before we got any delusions of grandeur.

"Don't start thinking you're special yet though you crows! This is just the beginning. When you've done a bit of time in battalion and done some proper soldiering, that's when you'll be real paratroopers."

The goal posts had moved yet again, a theme that seemed to happen at every milestone throughout my career. There was always another course or job to be done, no matter how long you served or how hard you worked. Nobody has ever "completed" the army.

Adding "foreign wings" to your collection is a favoured past-time for paratroopers all over the world. Each country will set their own criteria, but normally it's just a case of conducting one or two jumps with their parachute system, and once awarded you can wear them on your para-smock, above the right chest-pocket, but only one set at a time. I never wore any of them, but during my career I received my French, Belgian, German, Swedish, South African, and Jordanian wings.

To be honest, during my time at Depot I always hoped I'd be sent to 1 PARA. My first section commander, Corporal Fletcher was from 1 PARA, and to me he was the ultimate paratrooper, I wanted to be just like him; switched-on, professional, fit, funny, approachable, and ferocious at the flick of a switch. All three battalions were represented brilliantly by my Depot staff, but Corporal Fletcher, he was the one who impressed me the most. There are very few men that I've idolised in my life, but he is definitely one of them. I guess it was the same for all the recruits, unless you had a friend or family member in one of the battalions, your preference was influenced by your personal experience of the paratroopers you'd met up until that point. If I hadn't gone to Pathfinders, I think I'd have wanted to go to Depot as an instructor for a couple of years. My instructors were such a huge influence on me, I'd have loved to have that kind of positive effect on a bunch of recruits.

The young men that pass Depot and get sent to the para battalions are often regarded as maniacs, lunatics barely under control with a penchant for violence, and as a proud veteran I kind of agree with that assessment. In my opinion anyone that thinks the need for soldiers like this is obsolete or unnecessary in modern warfare is detached from reality and living in cloud cuckoo land. It's delusional to think our enemies won't have troops capable of real ruthlessness and savagery, and we need the ability to match and defeat that aggression head-on. The soldier that passes out of Depot will, on command, and without question or hesitation, leap out of an aeroplane, run towards an enemy machine gun position, post a hand-grenade into it, jump into the trench, and ferociously kill everyone inside with bullets, bayonet, headbutts, knees, elbows, and fists. And that is why the relatively small British army, especially the paras, will always be such a credible fighting force that's respected throughout the world.

On 17th December 1993 I passed out of Depot with 583 Platoon and went on Christmas Leave as a proud member of the Third Battalion The Parachute Regiment.

CHAPTER FIVE THE NEW BLOKE

On 10th January 1994 my first day in 3 PARA began with us fourteen, fresh-faced recruits getting off the bus under the "covered way" of Bruneval Barracks, Montgomery Lines, in Aldershot. The covered way was an area behind the main stores of the battalion, where equipment could be loaded and unloaded under the shelter of a large, high roof. It was the standard rendezvous point for collective briefings, inspections, and physical fitness training. Within a couple of minutes of arrival we were allocated to our respective platoons, and it was quickly obvious that they'd simply gone down the list of names in alphabetical order. The first name called out was my friend John, who I'd shared a room with from day one of Depot.

"Private Austin." The sergeant major shouted out.

"Sir." Replied John, smartly coming to attention.

"One Platoon, A Company." He was directed.

"Sir." Answered John.

And so it went on..

"Private Brown."

"Sir."

"One Platoon, A Company."

"Sir."

"Private Bullock."

"Sir."

"Two Platoon, A Company."

"Sir."

"Private Cullen."

"Sir."

"Three Platoon, A Company.

"Sir."

Private Young was last to be told, and he went to Nine Platoon, C Company.

When I got to my platoon it didn't take long to realise that there wasn't a great deal of imagination on the intakes previous to mine either. In One Platoon there were several other privates with names starting with A and B, including Privates' Andrews, Astle, Atherton, Black, Bloodworth, and Boyd. A month later we were joined by Private Bennett who'd been back-squadded in Depot because of an injury. Once again I was sharing a room with John, this time on the bottom floor of A Company block, and we were the only occupants of that four-man room, both choosing the bed-spaces furthest away from the door. We'd learned in Depot that the closer you were to a door, the closer you were to the shitty jobs. Sleeping next to a door also meant continually be woken up at night by people coming and going, as the light from the corridor illuminated your bedspace and the cold draft wafted across your blanket. Our platoon sergeant was a Falklands War veteran from Wales called Sergeant Williams, "Taff" to his friends. He was soon to be posted to another platoon, so he didn't invest too much time in us, but he was a good bloke and gave us a decent welcome brief. However, the only thing I remember from it was his warning on some do's and don'ts.

"Two things I fucking hate, and won't tolerate, are theft and drugs!" he warned us. Just as he said that a big burly bloke with an impressive, well-groomed 1980's moustache walked past.

"If I ever catch either of you two taking drugs or stealing from the blokes, I'll lock you in a room with a few lads like him" he continued, pointing at the passing paratrooper. "And I tell you one thing for sure, you won't be fucking walking out!"

He wasn't joking. It was clear that he really despised those two crimes, the intensity in his face and words was palpable. Fortunately those days were well and truly behind me by then, the army had put me back on the straight and narrow and those kind of activities were not something I'd even consider.

My early days in 3 PARA were great, and thankfully most of the horror stories we'd heard in Depot, about what happens to Joe Crow in battalion turned out to be nonsense. Being a good crow wasn't difficult, I just kept my head down, spoke when spoken to, volunteered for every crappy job that came up, and tried my best at every task I was given. As far as initiation ceremonies went, all me and John had to do was buy a load of beer, and dance naked in a crowded pub in Aldershot town at the weekend. Some of my friends who went to a different company were made to go into town naked to buy a takeaway for everyone. One of them told me that he'd ran into town late at night, bought a load of food from the infamous "Tony's Fish Bar" with his own money, and by the time he got back most of the blokes had either left or gone to sleep. One of the few that remained gratefully took his food then asked, "Where's my change Joe?"

My mate was a little confused. "There isn't any change Corporal, nobody gave me any money, I paid for it myself." he explained to the drunken soldier.

The corporal wasn't interested in lame excuses. "Where's my fucking change Joe?" he repeated, this time louder and more aggressively.

My mate handed over the loose change he'd got from Tony and left.

"Well done Joe, that's a good airborne scoff that is." he heard as he went to his bedspace.

Apart from getting naked a couple of times and getting sent to the NAAFI to buy the odd brew, my induction to One Platoon was very civilised. We were still "Joe Crows" though and wouldn't drop that unenviable title for a while, but each time a new batch of recruits turned up we climbed the pecking order a tiny amount, striving towards becoming "Toms," the informal name given to private soldiers who'd established themselves in battalion. One day I was talking to one of the other privates who'd already served a few years and attained the well-respected unofficial title of "Senior Tom."

"You were lucky to get One Platoon Steve." he told me sincerely. "This is the best platoon in A Company."

Apparently Two Platoon had a few angry blokes in it, and Three Platoon had some super-strict NCO's in it. It seemed I'd landed on my feet, especially seeing as though I'd already been told that A Company was by far the best company to be in in 3 PARA. Our sergeant major, WO2 Gough was an ex-pathfinder, and our Officer Commanding, Major Lawrence was firm but fair, and they left the blokes alone as long as we were performing well. From what I'd been told B and C Company were constantly harassed and messed about by their hierarchy. In Depot our instructors that came from 3 PARA had also briefed us on how the third battalion was the superior one of the three, citing historical achievements on operations, sporting events and exercises as way of proof. A couple of weeks after my arrival the whole battalion went to Sennybridge Training Area in Wales to conduct two weeks of live firing, and I was put into Two Section, under command of Lance Corporal Wilcocks. One of the other senior toms also in Two Section briefed me on my latest good fortune.

"Todd is probably one of the best soldiers in A Company." he told me respectfully. "Listen to him, and you'll learn a lot. This is the best section you could ever get, especially for your first exercise."

It dawned on me at that point, that I was in the best eight man team in the entire British Army. We were the best section, in the best platoon, in the best company, of the best battalion, in the best regiment in the British Army. And the British Army was the best in the world. So in fact I was in the best section in the whole wide world. Maybe it was true, maybe it wasn't, but I reckoned I wasn't the only one receiving this morale boosting information. No doubt my mates who'd gone to the other platoons in A, B and C Company were given the same brief by their proud peers too.

In my early days at 3 PARA I learned that our camp was visited by a refreshments van. It sold sandwiches, pies, soft drinks, and snacks, and the blokes would form a small orderly queue when it pulled up under the "Covered Way" in Bruneval Barracks, Aldershot. I was talking to another private soldier from my platoon called Stu Black who'd been in 3 PARA for about three years already. Stu noticed the van outside the window and immediately stopped talking to me to shout "BUN SLAAAAG!" at the top of his voice. His announcement was repeated by soldiers on the floors above us, and by blokes in the other accommodation blocks, echoing around the battalion lines, informing every one of the arrival. "Bun Slaag!"

"Why do you shout that?" I asked him. I was keen to know everything.

Stu pointed out of the window to a white transit van that had come to a halt behind the company stores. "The Bun Slag is here." he said. A woman got out of the driver's seat and walked round to the side of the vehicle to open the side door.

"Is she a bit of a slag then?" I enquired.

"No mate, she's a mega chick!" Stu informed me. "Her scoff is quite good, pretty cheap, and she's a good laugh. She's sound."

I was a little bit miffed. "So why does everyone call her the Bun

Slag?" I said.

Stu didn't seem to share my confusion. "That's just what she's called." he clarified, shrugging his shoulders.

In the battalions there is a small group of men called the Provost Staff, and their job is to maintain law and order among the soldiers in camp. Consisting of a sergeant and three or four corporals, they work directly to the Regimental Sergeant Major, enforcing his rules and policy on all matters, such as dress code, haircuts, out-of-bounds areas, and tidiness etc. As a new bloke in Aldershot I kept as far away from them as possible, and when I did have to walk past them, I avoided eye contact. One Provost Sergeant was affectionately known as "Harry the Bastard" and he'd walk around with a black marker-pen and a pair of scissors in his pocket. If he saw someone with a beret that was shaped outside of the accepted standard he'd tell them to remove it, then cut it in half and hand it back to them. The marker-pen was deployed when he caught someone with non-regulation sideburns. Apparently, if you're keen enough to look long enough, it's written somewhere in the Queen's Regulations that sideburns must be no longer than mid-ear. Harry the Bastard would draw a black line with permanent ink across the cheekbone of those he found breaking the law and order them to report back to him with their sidies trimmed above the demarcation line. Sometimes, you'd be walking through camp and a group of other young privates would come sprinting past urgently. "Harry the Bastard is coming!" they'd warn you, and you'd start running as well. It was brilliant and must have been hilarious for the old sweats to watch.

The Provo Office was located in one corner of "Red Square" in the battalion lines. Red Square was a red, tarmac parade ground that was seldom used, and for some reason, strictly out of bounds to us soldiers. Along one side of it were the company armouries, and along another, on a raised walkway were the company stores and offices, so there were always people walking along its boundaries. As a young private making that walk was extremely hazardous, because if you dropped your guard for a second somebody would push you sideways onto the sacred ground. That red tarmac might as well have been made of lava the way we avoided touching it, and blokes would pull off gravity-defying acrobatics to keep off it. They'd be on one leg, leaning at impossible angles, with their arms swinging in circles, as they fought to stay upright, and everyone would watch with sadistic anticipation until they inevitably touched down on the square, before bouncing back up like it was a sprung floor. Then you'd hear it. The unmistakeable sound of the Provo Office window sliding open with a thud, followed by the haunting sound of the Provo's voice echoing across the square.

"You! Get over here now!"

The offender would run quickly to the window to learn his fate while spectators would suddenly disappear around corners and into doorways before they were also summoned. The standard punishment awarded by the Provo Staff was a beasting on "The Shell", a sixty-pound, brass, anti-tank shell filled with concrete. The shell was from the old 120mm WOMBAT, recoilless rifle that was used by the anti-tank platoons before it was replaced by the MILAN missile system. Defaulters would be made to march and run around the square with the shell over one shoulder, performing halts, turns, and marking time at a pace that was completely impossible, as the Provo screamed "left, right, left, right, left, right, left!" as fast as they could. A shell session could last anywhere between twenty minutes to an hour, and that sixty pounds soon got very heavy when you were running around with it above your head or doing sit-ups with it on your chest.

After only a couple of weeks in 3 PARA the entire battalion went to Sennybridge Training Area in Wales to conduct live firing training, in preparation for an upcoming exercise in Kenya. It was a great opportunity to work with my platoon and learn the ropes, and also a good way to prove myself to them as a good Joe Crow. It was interesting to see how the three platoons of the company worked together too and work out who the different characters were. A couple of the corporals were wired extremely tight, taking everything very seriously and shouting a lot at their section. I'd later realise that they were chasing promotion, and only socialised with people of equal or senior rank to their own. Their style of leadership created an "us and them" hierarchy which can be highly effective in some situations, but not healthy overall. Others took a more relaxed approach, and they seemed to enjoy themselves much more, turning the aggression on and off as required. As a Joe it made little difference to me, I just did as I was told and accepted that I'd be beasted if I messed up. The super-keen soldiers were easy to identify. Always the first to apply camouflage cream, extremely fast at loading ammunition into their magazines, and always soaking wet. A lance corporal called Jay Bown was unbelievably enthusiastic, and he'd return from every range drenched from head to toe and covered in mud, even when others would come back clean and dry. He'd joined Junior Para Company at sixteen years old, straight from school, and loved his regiment more than anything in the world, he was truly army barmy. Most of the humour was provided by the young privates who'd been in the company long enough to know everybody and understand the boundaries of banter. Stu Black was the natural entertainer in One Platoon. He was very confident, hyperactive, loud, and liked by everyone, like the funny kid in school who drove the teachers mad. I reckon he was probably an early candidate for ADHD before it was even a thing. Wherever Stu was laughter followed and I looked forward to the days when I could act like that. Those days never came though, I'd never be an extrovert like him, I was far too reserved.

Live-firing packages involve a large amount of hanging around while you wait your turn to go down the range, so there is always some kind of concurrent activity to keep the soldiers busy. Corporals would take lessons on things like improvised booby traps, trip flares, foreign weapons etc, and it was great to learn new things from the experienced soldiers of the company. One day the activity was an old confidence course that was close to the range we were using. Whilst blindfolded we had to negotiate obstacles like wire bridges, tunnels, jumps, and balance beams. The first obstacle was a wire traverse over a river, and the corporals instructed me what to do.

"Right Brown, in front of you at head height is a wire. Reach out and take hold of it." they told me.

I quickly found the metal cable and held onto it with both hands.

"At knee height, directly underneath that wire there is another wire. Find it, and step onto it with both feet." they said.

I stepped onto the lower cable and steadied myself as both cables wobbled under my weight.

"Now shuffle along to your left until you are told to stop."

Staying relaxed, I moved sideways across the cable until ordered to stop, then held on tightly as the corporals shook the wires violently in an attempt to get me off and into the river below. Unsuccessful, they told me to continue, and I got to the other side where I was told to step down.

"Can you see through that blindfold Brown?" a voice asked me.

"No Corporal, I can't." I replied.

"I know you can see Brown!" he insisted, before throwing several punches towards my face. I could hear the snapping of his clothes and feel the wind from his fist as he barely missed my head. I didn't flinch like he expected because I really couldn't see. It may have looked like I was being over-confident or cocky, but I wasn't. I was just very good at following instructions and trusting my superiors. Depot had taught me that.

The ranges didn't go without incident though. One man, a corporal from another platoon was seriously injured when he was accidentally shot in the back during a company attack. That wouldn't be the last time someone was shot on a range I was on in Sennybridge either.

In February, shortly after returning from Sennybridge, the battalion deployed to East Africa on a six-week training package in Kenya called Exercise Grand Prix 3. It was a fantastic experience, and my first exposure to soldiering in extreme heat and jungle environments. We saw wild elephants, gazelles, zebras, giraffes, and plenty more while training in the Dol Dol, Mpala Farm, and Archers Post training areas, and met Maasai tribesmen who'd magically appear in the middle of nowhere, dressed in their traditional red robes and carrying spears, with colourful, beaded jewellery around their necks, wrists, and ankles. One day in our tented camp at Dol Dol I was talking to one of the older private soldiers called "Scouse" Wilson who'd already been to Kenya once before. I was asking about the other training areas and what I should expect from the rest of the exercise. He told me that we'd be visiting Mpala Farm next, which was another good place to go, with even more wildlife to see. I asked him where it was, and he pointed into the distance.

"See that ridgeline on the horizon?" he said.

In the fading light of the evening I looked towards what looked like a far-away mountain range.

Scouse directed me onto one particular hilltop that resembled a shark fin. "That's Mpala Farm. It's about thirty-two kilometres from here." he told me.

"How do we get there?" I asked, assuming it would be by truck, but hoping it would be by helicopter or even better, parachute. I still had a lot to learn.

"We walk." was his answer. "How do you think we get there?"

Of course we walked. We walked everywhere, covering long distances every time we went on exercise, transport was a luxury seldom afforded to us. Regardless of the weather conditions or terrain, we put our heavy bergans on our backs and walked, always being reminded that it was good for us, that it was character building. In truth, as much as we joked about it, it really was character building, but at the time it just felt like another gratuitous beasting.

That exercise was also my first exposure to jungle warfare, spending a week in a forest area in the foothills of Mount Kenya called Kathendini. Training there was conducted by the Jungle Warfare Instructors of the battalion and included some excellent lessons on jungle-specific tactics, navigation, and survival. After that experience I knew I wanted to spend more time in the jungle and found out there was a jungle warfare school in Brunei that conducted Jungle Warfare Instructor, Tracking Instructor, and Long Range Reconnaissance Patrol courses.

Kenya was also my first taste of overseas adventure training. There was a selection of activities to choose from including an excursion up Mount Kenya, paragliding, and cycling. I opted for mountain biking, partnering up with my good friend from 1 Platoon called Joe Dzioba. It was a good choice and involved cycling to the tourist destinations of Lake Baringo and Lake Bogoria over a few days. We stayed in hugely discounted lodges, ate good food, drank plenty of beer, and relaxed. It was awesome. John, my friend from Depot chose paragliding, and unfortunately suffered a nasty accident that broke his back and landed him in Nairobi hospital. We'd only been in battalion a couple of months, but that was the end of his soldiering career and after a long recovery he was medically discharged from the army in 1995.

John wasn't the only casualty 3 PARA sustained on that exercise either. A terrible mistake on the final battalion attack resulted in some soldiers from the Anti-tank Platoon being shot, and their officer, Captain Kelly fatally wounded. In 2000 I was on exercise in Kenya again when two more soldiers were killed in a horrific road traffic accident. It's strange when people are wounded or killed on exercise or operations. Even if you don't know them it still affects you, because for all you know you could have been sat next to them at scoff the day before, or they might have held a door open for you or helped you out in some way. It also highlights your own mortality, especially in an accident where it could just as easily have been you. There often seems to be no reason for it to happen to one person over another, it's down to fate, luck, destiny, or whatever else you believe guides the universe.

On return from Kenya we were introduced to our new platoon sergeant, and I recognised him immediately from two well-thumbed episodes of a military magazine called RAIDS that I'd bought in December 1992 and January 1993. Sergeant Roy Charters had just left the Pathfinders after spending about nine years there, and prior to that he'd been in the Falklands War with 2 PARA in 1982. To me he was like some kind of celebrity super-soldier, and I felt honoured to get the opportunity to serve with him.

June 1994 was the 50th anniversary of the D-Day landings of World War Two, and I was blessed to be part of the commemoration celebration in France. On the 5th of June about one thousand, three hundred soldiers from 5 Airborne Brigade boarded eighteen C130 Hercules planes and a single C47 Dakota at RAF Lyneham and flew across the English Channel to Normandy. I was in the first Hercules, number thirteen on the starboard side, and as we flew towards France I was awestruck to look out through the lowered tail-ramp and see the other seventeen aircraft lined-up behind us. To this day that remains the most spectacular jump I ever did. There were two passes over the drop zone, each dispatching almost seven-hundred men, and when I landed I quickly took out my camera to capture the moment. It was a beautiful day, with white clouds dotted across the bright blue sky, hardly any wind, and fields full of tall, green grass that made the landing soft as snow. It was nothing compared to the massive airborne invasion of 1944 where over eighteen thousand wartime paratroopers filled the skies, but it was still awesome.

I eventually became the British military's lead instructor in it, but my first experience with escape and evasion was in 1994, when 3 PARA were tasked with providing the "Hunter Force" for the UK special forces course. We spent a week chasing, ambushing, and harassing candidates on SF selection, as they tried their best to evade us whilst navigating long distances across rural Wales. At our disposal were military working dogs, 4x4 vehicles, and helicopters, including the old Wessex and Sea king. With the help of occasional tip-offs from the DS we captured several of the soldiers on the course and handed them over to their instructors for some "special treatment" before they were released into the wild again, now more motivated than ever to avoid capture. Once the evasion phase was complete a smaller number of us were required to assist with the interrogation phase and I volunteered enthusiastically, keen to see what happened next. As the "Guard Force" we were responsible for moving the "prisoners" around and making sure they were in the right place at the right time, but we also got to witness their interactions with the interviewers and interrogators. It was interesting to observe how the candidates coped in various ways, and how their attitudes and behaviours affected our own towards them. Those who appeared weak, making noises, and fidgeting with the discomfort they were being subjected to annoyed us because we were constantly sitting or standing them up straight. In contrast, the men who were able to compose themselves, and remain strong or stoic, they gained our respect and admiration. I remember one bloke in particular who didn't show a single sign of weakness or vulnerability throughout the entire exercise. He was a foreign soldier, Danish I think, and although he wore a blindfold the entire time you tell by his stern expression that he was completely focussed and determined not to buckle. Another candidate, who wasn't impressing people quite so much was an English officer. I delivered him to an interview room where he was taken inside and told to remove his blindfold. In place of a door there was just an ill-fitting hessian blanket hanging from the frame, and I could see inside. Making sure the interrogator couldn't see me spying on them I watched through a gap as the questions started to come thick and fast, fascinated by the scenario. Maybe it was nerves, or maybe he had some kind of twisted sense of humour, but for some reason the candidate started to smirk, clearly suppressing a desire to laugh, and I shifted position slightly to see how the interrogator was reacting. He was doing his best to disguise it, but it was pretty obvious that he too was dying to laugh, even though the language and posture he presented was extremely aggressive.

"You think this is fucking funny do you?" he snarled, trying to get a grip of the situation. His eyes were deceiving him though, creasing at the edges as he fought against the impending laughter.

The officer could obviously see it too, and his shoulders started bouncing up and down uncontrollably as he chuckled his response. "I can not answer that question Sir." he replied, with tears running down his cheeks.

Suddenly one of the DS appeared from behind me and stormed into the room. He'd been monitoring the situation via CCTV and was not impressed. "I'll give ye somethin te fuckin laugh aboot!" he said in a strong Scottish accent, then smacked the officer square in the face, sending him reeling backwards through the hessian and into the corridor next to me. The DS followed after him and hit him several more times in a furious flurry of blows, as the candidate curled up in the foetal position on the ground to protect himself. "Not fuckin laughin noo are ye ya fuckin prick!?" he shouted as he dragged the shocked man back to his feet roughly. That quickly put a stop to any more tom-foolery I can tell you.

Towards the end of my first year in 3 PARA, my company, A Company went back to Africa for another six weeks, this time to Botswana in the south of the continent. I was settled in by then and had made some good friends, plus a few other platoons of Joes had arrived since mine, so I wasn't the new(est) bloke anymore, which was great. The training area was a vast expanse of undulating bush-land, with rocky hills and knolls that were home to neighbouring troops of baboons, who watched us suspiciously. I was completely ignorant to how dangerous they could be, and thought it was great when they got close to us, searching for food and water. They were fascinating to watch, because they moved in a very similar way to us, patrolling their territory in formation, and conducting obstacle crossing drills just like we did. Other animals in abundance included scorpions and camel spiders, and we'd always have to check our kit before putting it on and shake out our boots, in case one had crept inside. The biggest scorpions I've ever seen were in Botswana.

That exercise was the first time I did anything with the Pathfinders, who'd sent a team of four men on the trip to conduct their own training alongside A Company. The PF blokes generally kept to themselves and spent most of their time out on long patrols honing their skills, but one day they offered to give us some demolitions training, using PE4 plastic explosives. It was only basic stuff, but for us youngsters it was great, and we all got to make our own small "confidence charge" and detonate it inches away from where we took cover behind a fallen tree. I liked the way they operated, nobody was posturing, shouting, or talking down to us, and they all seemed to really enjoy their work. They got left alone too, seemingly able to focus on what they wanted to achieve without interference.

We also got to do some training with the Botswanan Defence Force, including a foreign weapons day, where we exchanged weapons with their soldiers. Their rifles were old British Army Self-Loading Rifles that the MoD had replaced with the SA80 in the 1980's, and for some of the old sweats it was a nice opportunity to reacquaint themselves with it, they preferred it to the new model, and missed it. The BDF used the same 7.62mm General Purpose Machine Gun as us that we were already familiar with, but they also had Uzi 9mm sub-machine guns and RPG 7's which were pretty cool. I was lucky enough to fire one of the rocket-propelled grenades at an old tank, and just before firing, to add some pressure, was told that missing with a rocket or missile meant buying a crate of beer. Luckily I hit it.

Botswana was a great way to round off my first year in battalion. As well as there I'd been to Kenya, France, and best of all Wales (twice). I'd jumped out of planes, blown stuff up, fired lots of guns, seen wild elephants, giraffes, gazelles and baboons, and forged friendships that would last me a lifetime. It was awesome, and I was still only twenty years old.

My second interaction with the Pathfinders was when I attended an Escape and Evasion course they ran called "Exercise Valkyrie Chase". My platoon sergeant Roy Charters secured a handful of places on it through his mates in PF, and along with some other extremely keen blokes I volunteered immediately. The course was part of the Pathfinders selection programme and involved a week of practical survival training, followed by a week of escape and evasion on Dartmoor, then finished off with 24 hours of resistance to interrogation. After two days of lessons in Aldershot we were taken to a small forest in Hampshire where we spent several days building shelters from natural materials, lighting fires, collecting and treating water from a local stream, setting traps and snares, and eating anything we could find or catch. An ex-butcher who was in PF and was another one of the recruits in the

480 Platoon documentary, taught us how to kill and carve up chickens and sheep, and we made a smoker to cook the meat in so it would last longer. Military dog teams taught us how to evade tracker dogs and defend against attack dogs, finishing with a demonstration using the biggest, angriest, German Shepherd I've ever seen in my life. The dog was terrifying, and it chased a man in a protective suit, knocked him to the ground then savagely mauled at his neck and groin until the handler pulled him away. That beast was absolutely mental, and we were all quite disturbed to learn that it would be hunting us down during the evasion phase. To make it worse they told us the dogs would not be muzzled and would be released if we failed to stop on command, stating they had been given special dispensation for the course. It seemed unlikely, but the mere thought was enough to make us very nervous.

After a week of survival training we were driven to Dartmoor National Park in Devon to begin the evasion phase. Using sketch maps that we'd made ourselves we navigated back and forth across the vast, rugged landscape, criss-crossing the rivers, moors, marshes, and forests for five days and nights, until we were finally double-crossed at a checkpoint and taken captive. After several hours of blindfolded stress positions, verbal abuse, and a long drive in the back of a truck, we arrived at a detention facility where the interrogations started. Over the next twenty-four hours we were exposed to physical and psychological thuggery, skulduggery, and detailed threats of buggery as our captors tried every trick in the book to get us to talk. I met several interesting characters during that 24 hours. There was Mr Nasty, Mr Psychopath, Mr Shouty, Mr Repetitive, Mr Nice, and two young ladies, Ms Made-You-Jump and Ms Your-Penis-Is-Pathetic. The interrogations were quite stressful, but at least they gave us a break from the stress positions we were forced to stand or sit in. I'd been told the interrogation phase would last 24 hours and when it felt like that time was almost complete I began to get restless, but

I was way ahead of myself, and it had probably been about 18 hours when I started to anticipate the end. Time flies when you're having fun, but it drags when you're cold, tired, blindfolded, and listening to white noise, or being told you're a worthless piece of shit who's about to have their throat cut. The last two times I was taken into a room for interrogation I was convinced I was going to be told the exercise was over. It was pretty devastating when the sandbag was pulled off my head and I was confronted with yet another snarling nut-case. When finally it did end, I was surprised to learn that it had indeed only been 24 hours, it felt much longer.

CHAPTER SIX
THE TOM

In the summer of 1995 my battalion moved from its spiritual home of Aldershot to the south-eastern port-town of Dover, in Kent. I had left A Company and was now a "Tom" in the Signals Platoon in D Company, after successfully completing the signals cadre. 3 PARA were leaving 5 Airborne Brigade and joining the Allied Command Europe (ACE) Mobile Force, Known as AMF, where we'd specialise in arctic warfare and spend two or three months a year in the snow-covered mountains of Norway. Many of the Dover inhabitants were not impressed to learn we were coming to their town, and raised a petition to protest it, but we settled in eventually when they realised we weren't all that bad. It was a completely different atmosphere to Aldershot, with no military training area for us to use, no regimental history, and shockingly no Woolworths shop. What it did have though was plenty of big, steep hills to keep us fit, and lots of pubs. I never liked the town itself, but I had the best time of my life during those years in Dover. We worked hard and played hard.

D Company 3 PARA was a great place to be in the mid 1990's, with loads of big characters and blokes with notorious reputations within the battalion. My platoon, the Sigs, were accommodated on the middle floor of D Company accommodation block and was mostly known for its high level of fitness and the deviant sexual exploits of some of its members. Because we specialised in communications it was also sometimes mistakenly known for its ability to fix peoples televisions and stereos. Among our ranks we boasted celebrities such as "The Chinese Elvis", "Stan the Sheep Shagger", "Borneo", "Big Scotty", "Little Scotty", "Bosh", "Nine-Two", "Chod", "The Fonz", "Worm", and the infamous "Shitto Man".

On the floor above us were Patrols Platoon and up there were some of the keenest soldiers in NATO. They got a fair bit of stick for being sickeningly enthusiastic about soldiering and thinking they were something special. To be fair, they were special, with an absurd amount of them moving on to special forces within a short period of time, including my good friend Jon Hollingsworth, who was tragically killed on operations with the SAS in Iraq in 2006. I went to see a mate up there one day and interrupted him camouflaging his tent pegs with light green, brown, and dark green spray paint. The small aluminium spikes were laid on some newspaper on the floor of his room next to his small, hand-painted camouflage fridge.

"What's the point in painting them when they only get buried underground anyway you pest?" I asked him.

He didn't even answer, he just laughed and shook his head like he felt sorry for me. I was obviously too stupid to understand the tactical necessity. The nicknames in Patrols Platoon included "The Hammer", "Sigfried", and "Wang-Eye".

Below us, on the ground floor was Recce Platoon a.k.a "Recon" or "Rolling Thunder" because they had a fleet of Scimitar armoured fighting vehicles. This was highly unusual for the Parachute Regiment but was a part of the battalion remit in our arctic warfare role in the AMF. Recon, like the Sigs, was blessed with a high number of reprobates with a tendency to get drunk and cause havoc wherever they went. For a couple years our platoons would ambush each other at random if we caught someone from the other platoon out on their own and vulnerable. Pub toilets were damaged on a few occasions as blokes fought to stop themselves being dunked in the toilet bowl, and people were thrown in the Dover town centre fountain more than once as well. It was all just a bit of fun though, we were all really good mates outside of the banter. Recons' characters included "Trauma Lormor", "The Dom-inator", "Big Nose" and Noah. Noah was a laid-back and relatively quiet bloke, who surprised us all when he appeared naked in the "One for the Ladies" section of a British adult magazine with the words "Noah from Redcar" next to his picture. Apparently his step-dad was ex-Para Reg too, and also a real character whose name was Billy Moonmagic. Sadly Noah was killed by a roadside bomb in Iraq in 2006 while working as a security consultant. Another huge character in Recce Platoon was a long-serving corporal called Keith Butler. Keith was a veteran of the Falklands War and highly respected and liked by everyone in the battalion. In all my years I have never met anyone as adept at tying knots as he was, and I have many friends that are keen climbers and survival enthusiasts. Keith's skill wasn't with rope or cordage though, his speciality was with clothing, and he could tie multiple, extremely tight knots in the sleeves, trousers, and laces of any item left unattended in seconds. I watched him tie someone's jacket sleeves up right in front of them once, without them even noticing. Their coat was draped over a chair behind him, and he carefully sabotaged it behind his own back whilst engaged in a group conversation with them, showing not a hint of guilt or deceit on his face as he did it. He was a very funny man. Unfortunately, while working for a security company after retiring from the army, Keith was also killed in Iraq, when the convoy he was protecting came under attack in 2004.

In military towns everyone knows which pubs the soldiers, sailors, marines, and air force chaps frequent, and that will hugely influence the local population's decision of whether or not to go there themselves. Often, large numbers of the blokes will adopt one pub as their own and drink there almost exclusively. They will know everyone in there, and everyone will know them, and if ever they are being sought after, that place will be a sure bet every Friday and Saturday night. In Aldershot that pub was "The Trafalgar Inn", known to patrons as "The Traf". If ever a paratrooper speaks of "The Traf" there is no confusion as to where he means, he means "The Traf" in Aldershot. In Dover it was the "The Elephant and Hind" or "The Ellie" to the blokes. When 3 PARA were there we generally used the right-hand side of the pub, where the pool tables and juke box were located, and the bar was longer. Local civilians tended to use the left-hand side. One Saturday afternoon I was in The Ellie with a few mates and returning from the bar with a drink for my good friend Scotty, who was talking to a girl I'd never seen before. I knew most of the local girls, but she was new. I handed Scotty his pint and carried on with my game of pool. Eventually he introduced his friend.

"Lads, this is Becky" he announced "We went to school together. In school we used to call her Becky Bucket."

I stood up straight from taking my shot and looked her in the eye. "Why did they call you that?" I asked, fairly confident that I could have guessed the answer.

Without a hint of embarrassment she replied matter-of-factly, "Because the boys said I had a fanny like a bucket." With that, she grabbed Scotty's hand and thrust it down the front of her trousers.

"She still has!" he laughed.

We all nodded in acknowledgement and carried on like it was perfectly normal behaviour, leaving them to it. To be fair, it would have taken a lot more than that to shock any of us lot. Dover had more than its fair share of classy ladies like that, and 3 PARA had even more classy gentlemen ready and willing to entertain them. Nicknames assigned to women over the years were as brutal as the one's the blokes gave each other. They included:

Female Nicknames	Reason
All-Round-Defence Head	Large eyes that were very wide apart
All-Round-Observation	Had crossed eyes
Amplivox	Wore a large hearing aid. Amplivox was the name of our issued ear-defenders
Axe Head	Profile view resembled the shape of an axe
BJQ	Blowjob Queen
Blackfoot Sue	Girl who was always barefoot because the blokes used to hide her shoes
Budgie	Because she loved seed
Danny DeVito	Looked like the actor
D Company Debbie	Popular with soldiers from D Company
Diesel	One of the blokes called his wife this because she was an old boiler
Googley Eyes	Large eyes that darted from side to side
Marvellous Maxine	A talented lady
NBC Suit	Lost her clothes after a night in camp and was loaned a nuclear, chemical, and biological warfare suit to go home in
Playstation	Everyone had a go
Rocking Horse	Had a hunched back
Rod Stewart	Looked like the singer
Snaggletooth	Had bad teeth
Speed Freak	Big eyes made her look like she'd been taking the amphetamine Speed

The Exorcist	One of the blokes called his wife this because she'd come round your house and all the spirits would disappear
The Fat Adidas Gobbler	Girl with specific skill who always wore the same tracksuit top
The Folkestone Four	Four extremely promiscuous girls that used to regularly visit Dover from Folkestone
The Horse	Looked like a horse
The Pony	The Horse's younger sister
T Rex	She had short arms
Trig Point	Everyone had been over her. A trig point is a small concrete monument located at the top of large hills, used as a navigation waypoint
VD Verna	Rumoured to have venereal disease
Zelda	Resembled the alien character from the 1980's kids TV show Terrahawks

Officers can be easy targets for the soldiers to have a dig at. Ultimately they are deemed responsible for any shitty jobs or "dickings" that come the blokes' way and have to prove themselves worthy to a very unforgiving audience. Collectively they are called "Orifices' or Ruperts', but individually their popularity can be gauged by the name they are issued by the "other ranks." I had an excellent boss in the Pathfinders called Major Champion who was liked by the men and the officers, and his nickname to everyone was "Champs." I think it's safe to say he was a good bloke, and he could sleep at night. Another officer I worked with was not so popular, he somehow saw himself as special, better than us mere soldiers, despite the numerous amount of fuck-ups he'd made, including negligently discharging his rifle in front of a bunch of us. He unashamedly told people that his nickname was "The Adonis" because of his good looks, but in reality his nickname was something far less complimentary, unsubtle, and P.C, it was in fact "The Spastic". The harshest nickname I ever heard for an officer though, was for the CO of one of the battalions, a highly unpopular Lieutenant Colonel. A friend I'd been in Depot with called Adam was telling me about him and how he was absolutely detested by the officers and men alike. I was in Pathfinders and well out of the loop, but I did know the officer from my time in 3 PARA when he was a major.

"You know what his nickname is don't you?" Adam asked me. "You must have heard about him?"

"No mate." I said. "What is it?"

Adam's answer said it all. Even as a soldier it was quite shocking and left no doubt about this officer's personality. "He's called Joe the C*nt." he told me.

When an unpopular officer denied one of the soldiers in 3 PARA compassionate leave to visit his ageing grandmother in hospital, the rest of the blokes were pretty pissed off. It was well known that the young lad was very close to her, and he was deeply upset. Sadly the old lady died before he got to see her, and word got round the entire battalion in no time at all. From then on the major became known as "Harold Shipman" in reference to the prolific British serial killer Harold Frederick Shipman, who was at the time accused of murdering several people, mostly elderly women.

"Cobanicus Panfaticus" was the name awarded to a young officer who was originally just called "Panfat" because he was as much use as pan fat. After he climbed the ranks to major and became a company commander his nickname developed to Cobanicus Panfaticus because he was the Commander of Bollocks and Nonsense (COBAN) and still as useless as pan fat.

"Baby Seal" was the unfortunate nickname given to another officer because everyone wanted to club him to death.

An officer with an above average sized head was simply known as "Ed the Head"

Acknowledging his ability to create a morale vacuum by sucking any sign of it from the atmosphere with his mere presence, one officer was given the moniker "Dyson", after the powerful vacuum cleaner.

In recognition of his poor map reading skills the name "Captain Compass" was dealt to another man, and upon promotion he became known as "Major Map".

Being called "The Prince of Darkness" must have told a 1 PARA officer what his blokes thought of him.

Soldiers Nicknames	Reason
Big or Mis-shapen heads	
Box Head	Head was big and square
Cock Nose	Nose looked like a penis
Easter Island Head	Head was like the huge stone monuments on the Polynesian island
Helluva Head	Hell-of-a-head
ISO Container Head	Head the size of a shipping container
Lego Head	Head like a Lego block
Medicine Ball Head	Big and round head
MFO Box Head	Head like a type of extra-large box
Moon Head	Big and round
Nik Nak Head	Mis-shapen head, like the potato snack Nik Naks
Optical Head	Bloke wore thick glasses
Peanut	Head shaped like a peanut

Sangar Head	Like a fortified defensive position
Sausage Head	Long and thin
Torpedo Head	Long and thin
Alien Lookalikes	
Mars Attacks Head	90's alien comedy film
Mekon Head	Arch enemy of comic book hero Dan Dare
Odo the Shapeshifter	Star Trek character
Predator Head	The Predator is an Arnold Schwarzenegger movie alien
Animal Lookalikes	
Bison Head	
Cod Head	
Dog Face	
Dog Head	
Dolphin Head	
Hyena Boy	
Man in Pigs Body	
Meercat	
Moose Head	
Pelican Head	
Pilot Whale Head	
Sheep Head	
Sheep's Teeth	
The Cat	
Turtle Head	

50/50	
Meagle	Half man, half eagle
Mantress	Half man, half mattress
Mant	Body of a man, head of an ant
Moid	Body of a man, head of an asteroid
Other nicknames	
BUM	Battalion's Ugliest Man
Butt Plug	Soldier accused of having his head up the OC's ass
Dang Dang	Looked like he'd been hit in the face with a frying pan
Drill-bit	A small boring tool
Ed First	Because his name was R. Slater
Empty Head	Man of below average intelligence
FONO	Friend Of No One. Extremely unpopular person
Fred West	Uncanny resemblance to the infamous serial killer
Harry the Spoon	Previously known as Harry the Knife, but he lost his edge
Pie Face	Round and crusty
Pluke Farm	Bloke had bad acne
Rentboy Ray	Pretty-boy called Ray
Sperm Bank	Real name was Brooksbank
Thrush	Irritating prick
TK Max-Dermott	Real name was T. McDermott
Upside-down Legs	Calves were fatter than his thighs

White Sifter	Also the name of a piece of electronic counter measures equipment that interfered with everything and fucked things up

CHAPTER SEVEN
THE SOLDIER

Our first battalion deployment to Norway was in February 1996. Selected officers and men had already completed Arctic Warfare Instructor and Military Ski Instructor courses with the Royal Marines' Mountain Leaders, and it was up to them to pass on their knowledge to the rest of us. Everyone had to attend the Arctic Ski and Survival Course, where we learned the basics of cross-country skiing and living in the extreme cold. It was a good introduction to our new role and completely different from anything most of us had done before. Operating in the Arctic was dependent on your ability to survive the cold, and the environment was your greatest enemy. The desert and jungle are both hostile places, but the Arctic can be a relentless battle. The cold can kill you, but you don't want to get too warm either because your sweat will turn to ice and that will kill you. On another trip to the Arctic several years later a Swedish instructor would yell at us, "If you sweat, you die!" In theory you are surrounded by water, but water can freeze in your bottles, and it takes a lot of effort to melt snow or ice. Rations are dehydrated and need a lot of water and time to prepare them. The cold will freeze the fuel in your lighter, drain your batteries, turn chocolate bars into jaw-breakers, numb your hands and feet, and turn your hard-earned brew cold in seconds. We didn't sleep on the floor under ponchos in Norway like we were used to. Now we carried tents everywhere and learned to live in them, with anyone who was clumsy or messy inside them being labelled a "Tent Rhino".

The Mountain Leaders and Norwegian officers that supervised our training were brilliant skiers that made it look easy, the Norwegians had been doing it since they could walk, and the ML's were the British military's foremost experts. Most of us were absolutely terrible at it, and the initial learning curve rapidly ran away from us. It felt like on day one we were being taught which end of the ski was the front, and on day five we were skiing uphill, in the dark, with rifles and eighty-pounds of kit on our backs. Everyone stuck with it though, and after a few weeks we were efficiently moving entire companies of men across the mountains and valleys.

A couple of weeks after returning from the freezing snowscapes of Norway I found myself in the sweltering tropics of Brunei, where I spent a month on the Long Range Reconnaissance Patrol (LRRP) Course.

"Let's just fucking kill him!" Pete shouted insanely. His rifle was pointing at the sitting Bruneian soldiers chest.

I was just as exhausted and frustrated as he was, but that cheered me right up, he'd completely lost the plot. "You can't kill him Pete." I told him, laughing loudly, "Come on mate, pick him back up."

We were both dripping with sweat and gasping for air in the humid heat of the jungle, but I was doubled over with laughter not exhaustion. Pete was literally spitting as he shouted at the poor bloke on the floor. "How the fuck can someone so small be so fucking heavy!?" he ranted. "We should just kill the prick and fucking leave him here!" To be fair, the bloke was shockingly heavy for someone so short. All the Bruneians' on the course were small in stature, but this one was the stockiest by far.

The best part was, the bloke wasn't even our enemy, he was actually our casualty, and we'd been carrying him up a steep jungle track on an improvised stretcher while being chased by a group of Gurkhas. It was the final serial of a four week jungle course in Brunei and all we had to do was get to the top of this one last hill so we could be extracted by helicopter. Our personal kit was heavy enough on its own but trying to carry that man as well was horrendous. When the DS first nominated him as an unconscious casualty during our fighting withdrawal his own blokes had carried on running and left him behind, which left us to evacuate him. Two of our team quickly cut some long straight branches with their machetes and we fed them through the holes of a hammock to create an improvised stretcher. Hoisting him onto our shoulders, Pete and I carried him along the narrow jungle track as fast as we could, but the long poles were difficult to manoeuvre through the trees and vines, getting stuck and tangled up while our feet slipped on the steep, wet, muddy ground. It was brutal work and to make it worse we had the DS screaming at us to "hurry up!" and shouting, "he's going to die if you don't get moving!" It had been an extremely hard four weeks, we'd all lost about twenty pounds in weight (except for this one Bruneian bloke), were tired and dehydrated, and he wasn't even in our team. I was snapping as well, but Pete was way ahead of me on the anger scale, and when we got stuck between two trees for the umpteenth time he just dropped the stretcher off his shoulders, dumping the casualty on the floor.

"Fuck it, let's just fucking kill him!" he screamed.

The rounds in our weapons were blanks, but Pete was so enraged I couldn't be sure if he wanted to actually kill him or just fire some blank rounds at him to simulate killing him. Either option wasn't really going to work. Murder was illegal in that particular part of Brunei, and even worse still, we'd probably fail the course. The poor Bruneian soldier looked quite worried, he didn't speak English, but he didn't really need to to understand what was happening. Pete was seething, and pointing a weapon at him, it was one of the funniest things I've ever seen, and I think my laughing might have helped him calm down.

"Come on mate, pick him back up." I said, taking up my position at the rear of the stretcher again. Still ranting, Pete went to the front, and we picked him up once more, slowly traipsing up the steep hill to the helicopter landing site where the helicopter duly landed, and the exercise ended.

The Brunei LRRP course was the hardest thing I ever put my body through, including Depot and the PF Cadre. The heat and humidity were like nothing I'd experienced before and hit me like a brick the moment we stepped off the plane at Bandar Seri Begawan Airport. I started sweating profusely and didn't stop for the next four weeks. We arrived at Medicina Lines at about midnight and were shown straight to our rooms on the first floor of an accommodation block. There were no glass doors or windows in the building, just mesh sheets to keep the mosquitos out, and the bedding comprised of only two white sheets, one to go on the mattress and one to use as a blanket. Fans hung from the ceiling and two rows of standard issue, metal-framed beds lined the walls. One of the blokes dropped his bergan on a bed making the springs squeak loudly, and suddenly there were voices calling from outside.

"Boys."............"Boys."............"Boys!" they shouted, getting louder each time.

We looked at each other awkwardly. We'd all heard the stories of who hung around the perimeter fence but didn't expect a welcome party at that time of night. It had been a long day already, so we ignored them and got our heads down as quickly as possible before the course began in the morning. On the way to breakfast I met two of the fence-dwellers, who were very bright-and-breezy for the time of day and dressed like they were just on their way out to a party. Both wore high heels, short dresses, and impeccable make-up, and waved at us while giggling shyly as we walked past. I'd never seen a ladyboy before, so it was quite a shock to me, and I just kept on walking with my head down. Over the next few days the ladyboys became much more aggressive in their flirting tactics, trying to entice the blokes to engage in sexual activity, either through the fence or back at their houses, but the louder they got, the deeper their voices got too. They were harmless enough though, and a few of the blokes from the course had a bit of banter with them.

Our course photo was taken on the first morning at about 1030hrs, and in that photo my eyes are actually closed, because I was already on the verge of fainting from dehydration. An officer from the Gurkhas was stood next to me and noticed.

"When was the last time you had a drink?" he asked me.

"At scoff this morning Sir." I replied. I'd drank a few cups of orange squash with my breakfast at 0700hrs.

"Quickly go and get some water inside you and keep drinking all day." he told me. He was posted to Brunei permanently and used to the intensity of the heat.

There's an autobiographical book about jungle warfare that was written by former British Army officer Colonel Freddie Spencer Chapman in 1949. He fought the Japanese in Malaya for over three years, surviving captivity, illness, and injury, then documented his experiences in "The Jungle is Neutral". That title is regularly quoted by soldiers who've worked in jungle environments because they've seen how it provides you with everything you need to survive, while also wielding the potential to kill you, and it doesn't discriminate. However, if you don't put in the graft and stay switched on, I'd suggest the jungle quickly drops its neutrality and turns against you. Like every extreme environment, understanding and respecting its nuances is vital to your survival, and training is the only way to prepare for it.

I believe that one of the best teachers a person learns from is suffering. Pain and misery etch themselves deep into our brains and are hard to forget. Just like Depot, I learned a lot on that course through those mediums, and never allowed myself to forget. I was very fit at the time, and even managed to overtake the "front marker" on the fitness test we did on the first day, but the rapid weight loss from the combination of heat, humidity, workload, and insufficient calorie intake was something I wasn't prepared for. As the patrol signaller, on top of the usual water, food, spare clothing, shelter, hammock, machete, and ammunition, I had the additional weight of the PRC320 High-Frequency radio too, about an extra twenty pounds. For the final exercise I ditched everything I didn't deem essential to reduce the weight I carried until there was nothing in my kit but vital equipment. I tore most of the sheets of my notebook out so there were only a few left, used a shortened pencil to write with, and kept a tiny eraser so I could re-use the pages. I worked out the minimum amount of food I could survive on and took only that, rationing myself to a boil-in-the-bag meal for breakfast, a packet of biscuits for lunch, and another boil-in-the-bag meal for dinner. As a treat, I also carried a boil-in-the-bag dessert for every other day too. Despite the name we didn't actually boil our rations though because we couldn't risk the smell of cooking compromising our position, instead we ate everything cold. When other blokes started pulling out chocolate bars and tins of meat paste for their biscuits I was the most jealous I've ever been in my life. Sometimes they'd offer me some, but I'd never take it, pretending I wasn't hungry. In Depot I was told "Never eat another man's rations!" and I've always stood by that since. Sacrificing food for weight was one mistake I never made again, I was starving.

Operating in the jungle is sometimes made out to be some kind of black art, but it's not really. If you learn and apply the basics of good soldiering it will still be hard graft, but you'll be alright. If you don't, and you try to cut corners or bluff your way, you'll get caught out, and you will suffer. The LRRP course was supposed to be arduous, and it was, but it taught me a lot about myself and my own strengths and weaknesses. I was pushed to new levels of fatigue, lugging my heavy bergan up steep climbs and across rivers day after day, while my empty stomach screamed out for food, and my blistered feet craved to be dry. It also set a benchmark that I could use as a reference for the rest of my life, and for me personally, for many reasons, it remains the hardest course I ever did.

Me, Si, Daz, Ian, and Pete at the end of the Brunei LRRP course 1996. Our sixth man Moggy had been withdrawn due to injury.

In July 1997 I deployed to Belfast, Northern Ireland on my first operational tour. After landing at the city airport our plane taxied to a discrete corner of the airfield where we were transferred into the back of some civilian lorries. Sat on top of all our kit we were briefed to keep still and stay quiet during the short journey to Girdwood Barracks so our presence would not be compromised to the public. Two men were nominated for security detail and given loaded weapons, and they sat closest to the shutter door at the rear as we were driven to camp. We sat in silence throughout the transit, balancing ourselves on top of the bergans and bags as the driver negotiated the normal urban obstacles of traffic lights, roundabouts, and lane-swapping, and it was strange to hear people talking to each other on the other side of the thin metal bodywork when we stopped, oblivious to our presence. Sat there I wished it was me that had one of the weapons, we were extremely vulnerable in that lorry, and if it was attacked we'd be sitting ducks. The drive went without incident though, and the next time the rear door was rolled up we were inside the perimeter of Girdwood Barracks. As a member of the Signals Platoon my job was to man the radios of the ops room, pass information between the watchkeepers and the troops on the ground, and help maintain the communications network for the battalion. Although very important, for me that was quite boring, and I wanted to get out on patrol as much as possible. After a couple of weeks the novelty started wearing off for the blokes going on patrol, so I'd volunteer to swap with people and go out on patrol between shifts in the ops room, allowing them to take some time off and me to get out on the ground.

The situation in Northern Ireland was a very complex set of circumstances to get your head around as a young soldier, and I'd heard lots of stories from the older blokes in battalion, who'd spent many months and sometimes years there on previous tours. There were so many different racial, political, ideological, and religious demographics to try and understand. There was loyalist v's republican, protestant v's catholic, unionist v's nationalist, British v's Irish, and to complicate things even further there were numerous armed paramilitary groups on each side too. Those on the loyalist side included the Ulster Volunteer Force (UVF), Loyalist Volunteer Force (LVF), Ulster Defence Association (UDA), and Ulster Freedom Fighters (UFF). These groups were protestants, who were loyal to the United Kingdom, and they could be identified by the display of things like union flags, the red hand of Ulster, and Glasgow Rangers football shirts. Catholic groups, on the republican side, who were seeking a united Ireland included the Irish Republican Army (IRA), Provisional Irish Republican Army (PIRA), Real Irish Republican Army (RIRA), and Irish National Liberation Army (INLA). They could be identified by the presence of Irish flags, Glasgow Celtic football shirts, and the way they threw projectiles and spat at passing police or military vehicles. All of these groups on both sides had their own unique flags, insignia, and murals on display in the streets they controlled.

One of 3 PARA's other responsibilities during that tour was the security of HMP Maze Prison where convicted terrorists from both sides of the troubles were detained. In March that year an underground escape tunnel had been discovered in one of the wings. It was said to be 40ft long and fitted with electrical lighting, so had obviously been worked on for a considerable amount of time. Large mounds of rubble and earth had apparently been piled up inside the cells but somehow gone unnoticed by the staff. One day, along with a small group of others, I was given the opportunity to visit that wing and a prison officer guided us around. He showed us some cells, a common area, a gym, and showers, but declined from showing us where the tunnel was, stating it was out of bounds. We were all thinking it, but one bloke said it out loud. "Not being funny mate, but how did nobody notice all the mud and earth that they must have pulled out of that tunnel?"

We'd walked around most of the wing and there was absolutely nowhere that you could have hidden it. There was no outside allotment or garden space, and the interior was very minimalistic. The officer answered honestly.

"Gents, when ten men from the IRA stand in front of you and tell you you're not going any further down the corridor, you don't go any further down the corridor." he confessed. I suppose those blokes were in an impossible position really, the threat of reprisals against them and their families must have been a huge factor in how they conducted themselves at work.

The Maze was a notoriously rough prison, but in comparison to our accommodation in Northern Ireland it was a relative palace. Each cell had its own TV, with far more space and privacy than we had in camp. Annoyingly, each wing had its own gym, they had plenty of showers, and they even had windows. Plus they obviously didn't get mucked about with inspections either. It was quite frustrating to think they lived in such comfort when they could have been in there for murdering our friends, comrades, and innocent civilians.

Shortly after returning from that tour I was at home on Christmas leave when a member of my family confided in me that they were being bullied and harassed by a man in their home town. They'd been threatened, assaulted, and suffered a smear campaign against them and their partner. They were obviously upset and desperate, and it must have been a difficult thing to discuss with me seeing as though they'd known me since I was a baby.

"Do you know anyone who could help me out?" they asked.

I knew what they meant. They wanted someone to stick up for them and deter the bully from continuing their vendetta. I'd seen enough intimidation to last me a lifetime in Belfast.

"Yeah, I know someone who'll help you." I said. "Me. I'll sort this fucker out!" It was sad to see someone feeling so helpless, I had to do something. I didn't have a car back then and used to get around by train or borrow my mums car, so I arranged to borrow her old Proton the following weekend. Not really knowing what I was getting into I thought it best to get a bit of back-up and called my good friend Jonah. I had a few initial ideas of how I saw it playing out and knew it would be easier with an extra pair of hands. I rang him up, told him that my relation was being bullied by a thug, and that I was going to drive to a town in the Midlands to confront them. "I'm thinking I'll either burst into their house and do it there or follow them on foot until they're in a quiet street or alleyway."

I explained. "I'll warn them off, and if they kick off or start fighting I'm taking a hammer, and I'll use that to break their fingers! We might have to chuck them in the car boot and take them to a woods if we grab them off the street, but we'll recce all that beforehand mate." There was very little detail in my "plan", but I intended to get there in plenty of time to have a look. Jonah was completely unfazed by the madness of it all.

"Okay mate, I'll come." he said. "How are we getting there?" He was a great friend and was probably more concerned with keeping me in-check than meting out vengeance on someone he didn't even know.

"I'll pick you up on Saturday morning." I answered. "Have you got a balaclava?"

"No mate, why would I have a balaclava?" Jonah chuckled.

"Don't worry, I've got a spare one, I'll lend you it." I said. For whatever reason, I happened to have a few.

The next weekend I borrowed the car and began the drive to collect Jonah, stopping at some shops early on to get something to eat and drink on the way. Returning to the car with my supplies I turned the key in the ignition and the Proton spluttered pathetically, refusing to start. I tried again several times, no doubt making the situation worse with every attempt, until eventually the engine completely stopped responding. Having absolutely no mechanical skills whatsoever I decided to call my brother from a nearby phone booth. He was a vehicle mechanic by trade and offered to come to my assistance within the next couple of hours. The next person I called, to tell them I'd been delayed was the relative I was helping out.

"That's ok Steve, you don't need to come now anyway." they told me. "Something's happened."

I didn't own a mobile phone back then, so they'd been unable to inform me of an interesting development.

"What's happened?" I asked.

"The bloke was in a car crash last night and he's badly injured in hospital." they said.

It was a blessing really because that situation could have got extremely out of hand.

"Oh well, he was probably going to end up there one way or another anyway." I replied. I was a bit disappointed, I'd been thinking about punishing that coward for a week, and I know it would have been very satisfying. At the same time though, in all honesty I was relieved. I had no idea how far it might escalate, and I lived a long way from my relative, so I couldn't protect them from any repercussions or reprisals quickly.

I phoned Jonah to tell him and thank him for the support and we kept that story to ourselves.

Today, as a much older, arguably more mature person in my late-forties, I fully appreciate how insane all that might sound, but at the time it seemed perfectly reasonable to consider breaking and entering, threatening, kidnapping, and maybe even torturing someone in the name of justice.

Straight after Christmas leave I attended the Junior NCO Cadre, a five-week course that would qualify me for promotion to Lance Corporal. In the paras this course was known as "Drill and Duties" or "D&D's" and mostly conducted at the Household Division and Parachute Regiment Centralised Courses (HDPRCC) in Pirbright. The first two weeks were spent learning how to teach recruits foot-drill, which is how to march, turn, halt, and salute etc, with and without weapons. Notoriously poor at drill, this was the part that most paras dreaded. Few will ever use it, and many will probably try their best to forget it. It's extremely boring, and to make it even worse the training was given by sergeants from the Household Division who'd spent thousands of hours during their careers on ceremonial duties, looking impeccably smart, conducting massive parades in perfect synchronicity, or standing completely still outside places like Buckingham Palace and Windsor Castle, and for some inexplicable reason they actually seemed to enjoy it. For us it was two weeks of hell, shouting all day, stamping our feet into the parade square, and swinging our arms shoulder high, but although we hated it, it was good for our confidence to start teaching and coaching other groups of soldiers. One thing it taught me, was how the military could over-complicate the simplest task and turn it into an epic. For example, coming to attention is a very simple movement. In a nutshell, it requires the slamming of your left foot into the ground next to your right foot, ensuring your left thigh is lifted parallel to the floor before being driven back down. We spent hours learning the detailed instructions in the drill pamphlet word-for-word, then delivering that lesson to each other on the drill square, critiqued harshly in microscopic detail by the DS for every slight deviation or imperfection. In my opinion, you could teach a one-year-old schizophrenic chimpanzee with ADHD how to do that in a couple of minutes, without reading any instructions. In Depot, we were first taught this simple task while waiting outside the clothing store to be issued our uniforms. One of the corporals took the opportunity to conduct some concurrent activity while we stood in the queue. He demonstrated the action a few times, got us to copy him, and within a few attempts we were basically half way there. He emphasised a few of the finer points such as keeping our heads up and our arms pinned into our sides, and it was good enough for a quick off-the-cuff lesson. It was our first full day at Depot, and I liked his style of teaching. To get us to stamp our feet harder he said angrily, "Imagine you're stamping on the head of some scumbag that just raped your mother or sister!" That did the trick and set the scene for the next few months as we all started stamping aggressively on the ground shouting "In!" as we did so. Violent scenarios and analogies would play a big part in our training.

The second phase of D&D's was infantry tactics,

learning how to command a section of men in the field, and at this point we were joined by soldiers from the Guards regiments, who obviously already knew how to do drill, they're the best in the world at it. For this part of the course we were split up and put into new sections, which meant my least favourite part of any course needed doing again, introductions. Each of us was told to prepare a two minute talk about ourselves that we'd deliver to the section the following day. I was teamed up with some good mates from 3 PARA and that night we discussed what we would be talking about in our presentations. They had some good ideas, but I had no clue what to speak about, especially for two minutes. I slept on it and decided to make it up on the spot instead of overthinking it. When my turn came I stood up, walked to the front of class, and cuffed it.

"My name is Private Steve Brown, I'm from 3 PARA, and I'm a bowling world champion." I said sincerely. I saw my good friend Stu raise an eyebrow and chuckle, he was almost as surprised as me to hear those words come out of my mouth. To clarify my status I told them my title was from lawn bowling, not ten-pin bowling, and I explained how I'd recently defeated a famous Russian bowler at the world championships in Finland. I made up names, dates, and places to fill out the time and add credibility.

"You have probably often wondered how it is we make the ball curve the way we do. Well, it's all in the wrist." I told them. There was a bit of time remaining, so I moved the lectern aside and bluffed a demonstration, finishing on one knee with an exaggerated twist of the hand. Holding the pose I looked at the rest of the section.

"Are there any questions?"

There were no questions, but there were a lot of blank faces as I stood up and returned to my seat. What I didn't realise, was that apart from my 3 PARA mates, everyone thought I was serious. To me it was obviously a joke, but due to my distinct lack of facial expressions and serious persona I'd just convinced a room full of people that I was a bowls world champion. After the presentations were all finished, we went outside for some fresh air before the proper lessons started and that's when I realised how convincing I'd been. One of the 2 PARA soldiers from my section called Pat was talking to some of his mates, when I noticed him pointing towards me.

"See that 3 PARA bloke there?" he said. "He's a fucking world champion in bowling!" There were a few sniggers and raised eyebrows and I knew I had to nip it in the bud.

I moved next to him to talk. "Mate, you know I was only joking right?"

He looked surprised. "What? Seriously?" he replied.

I explained that I'd never played bowls in my life and didn't know anything about it.

The rest of the course was intense but very well taught, and we learned lots about leadership and command before moving to the Sennybridge Training Area to conduct the final test, in the form of an exercise. This week-long consolidation and assessment package was designed to test our soldiering and leadership skills under arduous conditions, and it did just that from the moment we crossed the cattle grid, which denotes the boundary of the training area. To many infantry soldiers that cattle grid, and the sound of wheels rumbling over it is synonymous with suffering and misery. Situated at the top of a steep uphill climb that army trucks ascend laboriously, it marks a unique, precise point on Earth where the temperature inexplicably drops by ten degrees, heavy rain falls even when there are no clouds in the sky, and morale is sucked out through your eyeballs by an insidious invisible force. Legend has it that it only actually rains once a year in Sennybridge, but that downpour starts on January the 1st and ends on December the 31st. On the first morning of the exercise we had barely crossed the cattle grid when the transport stopped, and we were ordered off. Our DS pointed to a forest in the distance, told us to start patrolling in that direction, and within a few hundred metres we were engaged by the "enemy". The soldiers nominated as Section Commander and Section 2i/c (second in command) were then assessed on their command skills as they organised and executed their section-attack on the enemy position. Once the enemy was destroyed, we quickly reorganised, then reshuffled the roles in the section as directed by the DS, and started again, repeating this process for the rest of the day, covering several miles of treacherous terrain in the process. During attacks ammunition is regularly redistributed among soldiers to ensure nobody runs out and everyone has roughly the same amount. It gets passed around in numerous containers, including boxes, bandoliers, sandbags, or magazines. On that course, for two different reasons, I learned that handing over your own magazines was not always a good idea. Firstly you rarely got your own magazines back, and nine times out of ten the ones you did get back were dirty or rusty, because the person who owned them hadn't bothered to strip, clean, and oil them. I reckon I'd cleaned half the magazines on the course by the end of it and still ended up with dirty ones on the last day. Secondly, using a magazine that's been filled by someone else runs the risk that it may not have been done to the same standards that you'd expect from yourself. On my course, this is exactly what happened, and resulted in a soldier being killed when live rounds were accidentally mixed with blank, and inadvertently fired into a young recruit. Whoever originally owned or filled that magazine was never determined, it would have been impossible, they'd been passed around for a week in daylight and darkness, and always under stressful, time-pressured conditions. The soldier who fired the fatal shot hadn't even realised he'd done it until after the casualty was pronounced dead a few hours later.

That exercise was hard work. We grafted all day and night, and everyone suffered from sleep deprivation, catching an hour or two here and there and the occasional, accidental snooze for a few seconds during a lesson or briefing. People were falling asleep the second they sat down, especially if they leaned against a wall or tree. We'd nod off while standing, and some even managed it while walking, waking up as they stumbled forwards. Scrawled notes written during lessons with numb fingers, were indecipherable when revisited. Starting fairly neat, the words became smaller and smaller until they flatlined, then plummeted downwards and off the page where the author had succumbed to his fatigue.

At the end of the course I had developed numbness on one side of my face and was struggling to speak properly. Unable to purse my lips, I couldn't pronounce my "P's" or "B's" and when I blinked, only one eye closed, making it look like I was winking at people all the time. On return to camp I visited the Medical Centre and explained to the medics how I hadn't really slept for five days, and my face had gone numb. After prodding and poking me for a few minutes they called the duty doctor and he explained that it wasn't tiredness, it was a medical condition called Bell's Palsy where one side of the face becomes paralysed. I asked him how long it would last.

"It could be two days, it could be two years." he said. "We don't really know what causes it or what cures it, but more often than not, it goes away after about two weeks."

I could handle that. To be honest it wasn't even bothering me that much, apart from the winking. He carried on, obviously trying to manage my expectations.

"Do you know the reporter Kate Adie?" he asked me.

I'd watched her on the news for years, so knew exactly who she was. "Yes. Why?" I replied.

"She's had it for about twenty years." he said.

That wasn't so good to know. Fortunately, mine did only last two weeks.

Returning to 3 PARA after the course finished was great. I hadn't seen most of my mates for over two months because of Christmas leave and the Drill and Duties cadre and was looking forward to spending time with them again. On my first day back at Connaught Barracks we were lined up outside the company office, waiting to be briefed by the sergeant major. He did his usual Monday morning routine, asking if anyone had been in trouble with the police and checking we were all there, then asked for a volunteer for the Army Physical Training Instructor course. Someone had dropped out, and it was starting that morning. In fact, whoever volunteered was already late, because it had just started. I'd always wanted to do the course, but I'd just finished D&D's and wanted to have a few beers with the blokes, so I kept my head down. Unfortunately, there was no hiding place, everyone knew I was very fit and had wanted to do the course for a while. One of the corporals walked straight over to me.

"Steve, you should get yourself on that." he told me. "Come on Airborne, are you up for it or what?"

It was bittersweet. "Yeah, go on then, I'll do it." I told him. After the briefing I went back to the block, re-packed my kit, and was in the duty car, a red Vauxhall Astra, heading towards Aldershot within about thirty minutes to start another six-week course. By the time I got there I was only a few hours behind everyone else and hadn't missed much. To my surprise there was a 1 PARA soldier from my D&D's course there and we both laughed when we saw each other. Jim was a great bloke who I got on really well with, and it turned out he'd only been told that morning too. Also on that course was a good friend of mine from my platoon in 3 PARA called Shaun, and Wang-Eye from Patrols Platoon. Shaun was a keen runner and very enthusiastic, but Wang-Eye was an absolute maniac who just bull-dozed his way through everything with zero finesse, and not a single care given about it. He was the morale for the next six weeks. Wang-Eye's real name was Matt, but everyone knew him by the moniker he'd been designated in 3 PARA. He didn't care, he was nuts, but most of us were far too polite to call him Wang-Eye, at least to his face anyway, so we politely called him Wang instead.

For mainly historical and traditional reasons the PTI course had a lot of gymnastics in it. We were required to perform a number of classic agility exercises with poise, grace, and elegance, but they were three attributes Wang was completely devoid of, so he struggled on that element. There were a lot of tests, ranging from simple exercises like chin-ups and handstands, to more advanced ones like neck-rolls and head-springs, and the head-spring was Wangs' Achilles heel. Basically the test was to start from a standing position, and in one fluid movement, drop forward into a headstand, then flip yourself over, landing on your feet. On the last day of the course Wang still hadn't executed one to the required standard of the instructors and was at risk of failing the entire course because of this completely irrelevant exercise. A group of us pulled out some heavy, green, gym mats and persuaded one of the DS to give him one last chance, and he stood and watched with his clipboard in-hand while Wang attempted it over and over again. He was terrible, landing flat on his back, on his ass, or face-planting straight into the mat, but each time we'd all look at the assessor expectantly, trying our best to influence / intimidate him into giving it the nod of approval. Wang was bright red, sweating, and no doubt very dizzy when he finally landed on his feet, and we all cheered triumphantly. It was still rubbish, but we surrounded the DS like a pack of hungry wolves in a bid to convince him it was acceptable, and he finally capitulated, awarding the pass. I bet that remains the only head-spring Wang-Eye ever landed to this day.

In August 1999, in preparation for the upcoming Pathfinder Selection Cadre I managed to secure myself a place on a course at the NATO International Long Range

Reconnaissance Patrol School in Pfullendorf, Germany. Several of my friends had attended courses there and rated it highly, so I applied for the Basic Patrol Course which was ten days long and right before my cadre. Students were attending from all over the world so the first day was purely arrival procedure and a heads-up on what was happening in the morning. Finding out we had a fitness test first-thing surprised some of the students, making a few very nervous, but for the Brits on the course it was expected, our courses always started like that. One bloke, a musclebound U.S Marine in the room opposite mine, was so perturbed that he didn't even bother unpacking his kit.

"I can't run three miles!" he told me. "I'll be going home tomorrow anyway!" He was stationed in Germany, so home wasn't far away.

The test was only a three mile run carrying thirty pounds of equipment and a rifle, but he deemed that as too difficult and accepted he'd be sent packing after his inevitable failure. To his credit he was right. The route was two laps of a 1.5 mile circuit, the first led by an instructor, and the second as a race. My fitness was very good at the time as I was getting ready for the PF cadre, and at one point I was so far ahead of everyone else I started to think I'd gone the wrong way, because I looked behind me and couldn't even see anybody. Luckily I hadn't gone wrong, just very quickly, and I was pleased with the result when I finished first. My preparation was working.

The course started and we were put into teams of six men, supervised by instructors from NATO elite forces. My team's DS was a captain from the German paratroopers, the Fallschirmjager, and my team included me, another private from 3 PARA called Dave, two Royal Engineer lance corporals, a corporal from the U.S Army, and an Italian army captain. It was a good couple of weeks, and despite my junior rank I was appointed as patrol commander for the final exercise, where we were assessed on things like navigation, patrol skills, tactics, and close-target reconnaissance. It was excellent preparation for the PF cadre.

CHAPTER EIGHT
THE CANDIDATE

Returning to Montgomery Lines for the Pathfinder Selection Cadre on the 3rd of October 1999 brought back some good memories of my time there with 3 PARA. Unlike Dover, Aldershot was a proper military town where you felt like you belonged. Even the signage as you crossed the town boundary said, "*Welcome to Aldershot, home of the British Army*". Back in Dover there were still two pubs with signs on the door that said, "*Out of bounds to airborne troops*". I parked my car, went into the guardroom where I'd spent many days on duty as a young Joe, collected my vehicle permit, then went to the Pathfinder Platoon compound. I'd been there before on the escape and evasion course, so I knew where to go, plus there was a big PF flag flying above their HQ displaying the motto "First In". After a bit of admin I was sent to the accommodation block where I met another candidate called Paul, an Irishman from 1 PARA. Paul was softly spoken, quite serious, and army barmy like me, and we got on well from the very start. Also in our room was another private called Gaz, a brilliantly funny Welshman also from 1 PARA, whose first language was Welsh. Another soldier came into our room on that first day to visit Paul. They were obviously good friends who hadn't spoken for a while and when he left Paul told me his name was Gareth.

"Is he an officer?" I asked. Gareth was confident, well-spoken, and smartly dressed in a shirt and chino's, typical officer attire.

"Yes mate, he's a mega bloke. One of the best officers I've ever met." Paul told me.

Along with the majority of people in the world at the time, officers were another demographic that I chose not to like or trust. "I fucking hate officers!" I said dismissively.

Paul was slightly younger but much more mature and level-headed than me. "Gareth is awesome mate." he said. He was right, Gareth was a great bloke. Highly intelligent, extremely fit, motivated, humble, and a natural leader, everything an officer should be. Over the following weeks, through shared hardships and experiences we would all become close friends. Also on the cadre were soldiers from the Royal Engineers, the Royal Tank Regiment, the Royal Anglian Regiment, the Princess of Wales Royal Regiment, and a few other units.

The first couple of days on the cadre were based in Aldershot and focussed on military skills and fitness. We completed numerous theory tests on subjects like first aid, map reading, and military knowledge, before being called forward one at a time for the weapon handling test on the SA80 rifle. One of the first people assessed was a candidate from the Royal Tank Regiment, who was only gone for about ten seconds before returning with his tail between his legs.

"They told me to get someone to go through the drills on the rifle with me." he announced dejectedly. He was a decent bloke, and everyone offered to help him out.

In a weapon handling test the first thing you're normally asked to do is take control of a weapon that's on the floor. The weapon is always deliberately left in an unsafe condition, and it's up to you to render it safe by completing a full unload as soon as you pick it up. He explained that he'd entered the test area, picked up the rifle, put the bolt forward, removed the magazine, and pulled the trigger, while the weapon was pointing towards the instructor. Had that rifle been loaded with live ammunition a round would have been fired. The DS had immediately ejected him from the classroom with a firm warning that he had one more chance to get it right or he'd be removed from the course that day.

"If they want me to show them the drills on the 120mm gun in a Challenger 2, I'll do that with my eyes shut!" the soldier declared frustratedly.

"That's great mate, but there's not much need for that in the PF, they don't have tanks!" Paul told him.

We took him through some drills, and he scraped a pass on his re-test.

The fitness was intense, but I was well prepared and managed to actually enjoy most of it. I beasted myself every day in 3 PARA anyway, it was normal routine. We did an eight miler, a ten miler and a two-miler on the Aldershot training area carrying 40lbs of kit and weapons and it quickly became apparent who the fit people were and who'd massively overestimated their physical ability. During the opening address from the PF sergeant major, one soldier had even asked if there was a gym he could use in the evenings. Clearly he was either super fit or super naïve. It was the latter, and he was one of the first to fail and be sent home. On completion of the fitness tests we packed our kit and headed to Sennybridge for the next phase.

Walkabout Week

The second phase of the cadre was "Walkabout Week" where we went out on the hills of the Brecon Beacons in small groups and were assessed on our ability to navigate over arduous terrain by the DS. With bergans weighing at least forty pounds, plus water, food, SLR rifles, and a twenty-pound safety radio that we took turns carrying, we covered between twenty to thirty kilometres each day. Alternating between fast walking and running we needed to average a speed of four kilometres per hour across the steep-sided valleys, boggy marshes, and well-trodden trails of the stunning Welsh mountains. It was hard work, tabbing for about eight hours a day, but the DS taught us some top-tips on navigation, and it prepared us for the forthcoming test marches. Unfortunately Gaz took a nasty fall on one of the days, injuring his leg, and getting medically withdrawn from the cadre. There was a lot to learn and not that much time to learn it, so in the evenings after dinner we returned to the classroom for lectures and lessons until about 2000hrs. Although the vast majority of the DS were decent blokes, there were a couple that I found extremely irritating. Their lessons were sloppy, and their attitudes towards us candidates was dreadful, interacting with us with utter contempt at every opportunity. I failed to understand why they'd put themselves on such high pedestals and struggled to keep my mouth shut and my hands in my pockets. They wore no rank, addressed us by our surnames only, and seemed to revel in the power they held over us while we addressed them respectfully as "Staff." My legs were fatigued and aching like everyone else's, but to spite those people I'd run to and from the shower block with a spring in my step every day, passing the DS accommodation on the way. Walkabout week finished with a long night march that started at the Talybont Reservoir and finished at the Lower Neuadd Reservoir near Pen-Y-Fan. Navigating in poor weather and limited visibility was essential for the upcoming test marches, especially "Endurance" which was sixty-four kilometres long and started at midnight.

As a young soldier I was known for my good level of fitness and along with loads of other blokes in 3 PARA I trained like a professional athlete when we were in camp. Everyone in airborne units trained at 0800hrs, but I'd normally train in the afternoon or evening as well, often cracking out three good sessions in a day. I've been prone to ankle injuries since tearing the ligaments in Depot, but when I stayed injury free I'd maintain an excellent fitness standard. On the pathfinder cadre my ankles were strapped up tightly into stirrups with strong adhesive zinc-oxide tape to stop me rolling over on them, because numerous sprains and connective tissue injuries had drastically weakened their lateral stability. On the even surfaces of tracks and roads I was fine, but off-road, across country I was very prone to ankle twists and falling over. Psychologically I was extremely fit, in my mind I didn't think that anyone could be that much fitter than I was, so whenever I started to feel tired during an event, I knew that everyone else was too, including the DS on my cadre. There were faster runners and tabbers than me of course, and there were plenty of stronger people than me too, but as an all-rounder I knew I could hold my own, and that was a great mindset to possess.

Prior to the cadre I'd read in a book that if you wave or say hello to an imaginary person, it releases the same chemicals in your brain as if you'd just seen a friend, making you feel happy. I started doing it while out tabbing in the Brecon Beacons preparing for Pathfinder selection, and it worked. Obviously waving and talking to people who aren't there might seem a bit odd, so to avoid looking like some kind of nutcase I waved and spoke to animals instead. It felt a bit weird at first, talking to the sheep that roamed the Welsh hills, but I soon got used to it even though they were ignorant bastards that never once replied. During the PF cadre I told one of the other candidates to try it, because he was struggling on one of the routes and I could see that he was getting overwhelmed, staring unblinkingly at the floor, and panting heavily.

"Mate, calm down. Try thinking about something else to take your mind off it." I advised helpfully. "Look at the trees and the animals and pretend you're just out for a walk."

It wasn't helpful to him at all, he could hardly lift his head up, he was in a world of pain. We tabbed past some sheep that were stood still, staring at us judgementally like they often do.

I raised my left hand and quickly waved in their direction, focusing on one that was chewing on some grass as it watched us. "Alright mate?" I called out. I'm pretty sure those sheep sometimes shook their heads at me in disdain, they can be very negative little buggers. "Try waving at the sheep mate, it makes you feel better." I explained, grinning broadly. It really did work. He didn't take my advice and shortly afterwards fell behind, never to be seen again. His cadre was over. Another day, on another beasting, I was telling a different bloke about my method. His name was Ginge, and he was from 9 Parachute Squadron, Royal Engineers a.k.a "9 Squadron". We got on really well, he was fit, keen, and like most soldiers in 9 Squadron, extremely airborne.

"What the fuck are you talking about you absolute mentalist?" was his immediate response.

We were tabbing fast down a long straight road on the training area, and nobody was talking. I get bored very easily and assumed others would be bored too. I waved at a sheep, had a little chuckle to myself, then told him to try it.

"Fuck off you idiot!" he said. "I'm not waving at sheep!"

I persisted, and eventually Ginge gave in and did it, before turning to me with a big smile on his face, trying his best not to laugh, but failing.

"See, I told you it works!" I said triumphantly.

Ginge still wasn't having any of it. "I'm laughing because it's stupid, and I feel like a mental person!" he told me.

It was hard to prove either of us was right, but I took it as a win. "You waved at the sheep, and it made you happy mate. Admit it, I was right."

I reckon there were a few blokes doing that by the end of the course, personally I'd advanced onto conversing with birds, rabbits, and cattle by the end of it. I even said hello to some civilians that I saw hillwalking once. Once.

Another side-effect of the pathfinder cadre was subconsciously counting your paces everywhere you went.

On the hills phase and while patrolling on exercise we were constantly asked what our pacing was by the DS. It was the best way to keep track of distance travelled during navigation, and not knowing the answer meant a red mark against your name. The problem was, after two weeks of spending eight hours a day counting every step, you couldn't stop doing it. I'd be walking through camp then realise I was either silently counting or counting very quietly to myself. "Fifty five, fifty six, fifty seven, fifty eight......." I wasn't the only one, we were all doing it.

A physical memento of the cadre was numb feet. All of us suffered with that in varying degrees. I couldn't feel my toes for about four months after it finished, and others couldn't feel theirs for up to six months. Our feet were destroyed from a combination of all the running, tabbing, coldness, water immersion, and long periods of lying or sitting motionless while cold and soaking wet.

Test Week

Test week of the PF cadre comprises four loaded marches, three in the daytime, and one that starts at night and continues all the way through into the following night. The routes vary every time, and can be conducted over the Brecon Beacons, Black Mountain, or Elan Valley. Regardless of the location the rules remain the same for all candidates:

- An average minimum speed of 4kph must be achieved over the route.
- The use of GPS is forbidden.
- Bergans will be weighed at the start, finish and at random checkpoints.
- Food and water does not count as part of the weight in the bergan, it is additional.
- Roads and vehicle tracks are out of bounds.
- Weapons must be held correctly at all times.
- At checkpoints candidates will use their maps to identify

their exact location to the DS and then show the exact location of the grid reference they are given as their next checkpoint.

- Candidates will inform the DS of their bearing, distance, and proposed route to the next checkpoint before departing.

- Any candidate who wants to voluntarily withdraw from the cadre or receive medical attention while on a test march must alert the DS at the earliest opportunity.

Our first test was a well-known 27km route that's also used on UK special forces selection because of its undeniable arduousness. "Point-to-Point" is a fantastic test of navigation and fitness, and if you can complete that on time, while carrying weight on your back, you can definitely class yourself as a very fit human being. For soldiers who've spent a lot of time in the Welsh hills the checkpoints known as 642, Bryn, Beacons Reservoir, Torpantau and The Fan are all places that need no further explanation. I'd already done Point-to-Point during my own personal training, so I was confident in my knowledge of the area and ability to pass and came in well under the 6hr 45min time limit.

Test march two was another 32km, this time around the Black Mountain on the western side of the Brecon Beacons National Park. Like every other time I've been there the visibility was poor due to low cloud and fog, and with very few paths to utilise it was hard going. Apart from the DS I didn't see anyone during the whole test which always makes you start questioning if you've gone the wrong way, but I hadn't, and finished comfortably within the 8hr time limit.

The third test march on my cadre was a route named "Scorpion" because of the shape the route makes when drawn on a map. One of the mountains included in the route is a lesser-known feature called Fan Gyhirych in the Forest Fawr region of the Brecon Beacons. Standing at an impressive 725m in elevation Fan Gyhirych is smaller than the renowned neighbouring mountains of Fan Fawr and Pen-Y-Fan, which peak 734m at 886m respectively, but once you've climbed her steep western slope, you will never forget it. That morning I woke up feeling pretty rough and at first I put it down to fatigue, although my legs felt fine. I ate my breakfast and by the time we paraded at the trucks to depart for the Brecon Beacons I'd already been sick several times. We drove out to the start point, and after a short wait I was set off to find my first checkpoint, a spot-height called 619, and on the way there I was sick another seven or eight times, pausing momentarily to vomit onto the wet grass. Approaching the checkpoint one of the DS exited from the small tent he was sheltering in to greet me.

"You alright mate?" he asked, looking a little concerned.

"Yes Staff, I'm good thanks." I lied. I felt pretty rough, but I didn't want to be medically withdrawn from the course.

I didn't know at the time, but the Welshman had been told to check on me by another DS who'd watched me throwing up from a distance and radioed ahead. What I also didn't know was that several members of the PF had also been ill with suspected food poisoning.

"Don't carry on if you're in shit-state." he advised me. "You don't want to go down on these hills, it's pretty rough up there!" He nodded towards the cloud covered mountain top of Pen-Y-Fan, the highest mountain in the Brecon Beacons. I assured him I was ok, and he gave me my next set of coordinates. I finished the test on time and that afternoon the sergeant major announced that the final test march "Endurance" was going to be delayed. It should have started that night at about midnight, but there were so many people unwell he couldn't afford to risk it. Our test-week was over, albeit incomplete, and for those of us remaining on the course there was a welcome couple of days off to rest and recover before we began SOP week.

SOP Week

Every military unit has its own set of standard operating procedures or SOP's, and PF is no different. Learning, understanding, and practicing these is the only way to ensure that everyone is singing from the same song sheet and has a good understanding of what everyone else will be doing in any situation. Fitness training continued with runs every day and plenty of bodyweight exercises thrown in for good measure, but the focus was on patrol tactics, and we received many lessons on how to operate in small teams. We learned things like tactical movement across open and close terrain, how to cross different types of obstacles, observation post (O.P) construction and routine, cache laying and retrieval, claymore mine deployment, and ambushes. However, the subject we spent by far the most amount of time on was contact drills, which are the drills carried out by a patrol if they come under fire from an enemy force. With each man expending thousands of blank rounds and conducting dozens of drills, by the end of the week we were pretty good. The DS were hyper critical over every mistake we made, but for the most part it was constructive and well-intended. One DS in particular, a corporal called "Dolly" from the Parachute Regiment was an awesome instructor and as a course we were all in agreement that he was the best of them all, very strait-laced, but totally professional, and passionate about soldiering.

SOP training finished with a 48hr exercise over the weekend on Sennybridge Training Area. More of a test than an exercise, we were assessed on all we'd been taught up until that point, and everything we did was scrutinised in detail by the ever-watchful DS. They were relentless, asking loaded or leading questions that made you question every decision you made.

"Do you think that's a good place to take a knee?" They'd ask when the patrol paused, and you got down on one knee to lower your profile.

"When was the last time you re-applied your camouflage?"

"Do you think that Claymore mine is deployed effectively?"

"Does this position provide you effective cover from enemy fire, or do you think you'd be better off if you moved somewhere else?"

You never knew the intent behind the questions. Were they offering advice? Were they testing your loyalty to the patrol commander? Or were they just interested in your opinion? There was no way of telling, but it definitely kept us on our toes. Other questions were less veiled, and you knew you'd messed up if you didn't have the correct answer.

"What's the bearing and distance to the ERV? was a firm favourite that we were asked repeatedly, along with "What's your pacing?" Knowing exactly where you were and the location of the emergency rendezvous at all times was essential.

Range Week

The week-long live-firing package was another beasting, and because we hadn't yet completed Endurance it was decided that we'd tab to the range every morning to compensate for it. Each day the transport would halt shortly after crossing the cattle grid and we'd de-bus with our bergans and weapons, then speed-march along the metalled roads and tracks for an hour or so until we reached the ranges. One day the route was only ten kilometres, so the DS gave us all a General Purpose Machine Gun to carry which weighs about twenty-five pounds. I remember that tab well, because we went like the clappers from start to finish, led by a PF corporal from 216 Parachute Signal Squadron called Daz, who possessed an insane ability to sprint down steep hills. With the extra weight of the GPMG's none of us could keep up with him when he let himself go, so we'd have to catch him up on the flat or uphill parts, basically running the entire route with almost seventy pounds of kit on our backs. Because there were only a small number of us left on the cadre the ranges came thick and fast, with short breaks between the practices. Normally on range packages you have to wait your turn, sharing the ranges with other teams, but we were the only one's left, so as soon as we finished one practice, we'd get a hot debrief from the DS, refill our magazines with ammunition and go again. It was a fantastic week of live-firing where we all expended thousands of rounds of ammunition on the pistols, rifles, sniper weapons, and machine guns, threw dozens of hand grenades, and fired anti-tank rockets. The way the PF ran the ranges made them much more exciting than anything I'd done before. Without compromising on safety they made them more challenging, realistic, and spontaneous, and they gave us the opportunity to move freely, without an over-zealous safety supervisor giving us instructions or critiques at every turn. Often on range packages you know before it even starts which way you will be attacking or defending because of the way it's laid out. If there's a river on the range it's a given that you'll be getting in it, and if there's a tunnel on the range, you'll definitely be crawling through it, regardless of whether or not you actually think it's the best option. On the cadre, so long as we were safe, the DS let us make our own decisions, allowing each practice to play out, and when it was over they gave us feedback, both positive and negative. If we made a tactical error, rather than interrupt, the DS would let us suffer the consequences, and watch on as we struggled through marshes, or steep sided valleys. We were all mature enough to know when we'd made mistakes, but the pressure of the cadre, and the ever critical DS magnified our frustrations when we did. We practiced instinctive shooting, pairs fire and manoeuvre, contact drills, attacks, and ambushes, so when Range Week finished that Friday afternoon the four of us that remained were pleased to get on the transport and go back to camp for some rest.

Final Ex

The final exercise was one last week in Sennybridge,

where we were assessed on everything we'd been taught on the entire cadre, and it started with a horrendous thirty kilometre insertion march carrying full equipment. We were dropped off by helicopter near the Usk Reservoir, well outside the southern boundary of the training area, and began our long march north, negotiating hills, marshes, woodland, and the A40 trunk road before we even reached the familiar army training estate of SENTA.

I learned a lot of new things on that cadre via different means and media. I learned by listening to great lessons, watching well-rehearsed demonstrations, experiencing new things, and repeatedly practicing drills over and over again until they became instinctive. But that night I learned through the mediums of pain and regret that you should never, ever, under any circumstances, try to tactically navigate through a valley of recently deforested woodland in the dark, while carrying over one-hundred pounds of equipment and a rifle. We weren't allowed to use roads or tracks, but in hindsight, I'd rather patrol naked through a mile of gorse bushes than go through that again. It was horrendous, like an hour of walking through tripwires, booby traps, and grease covered logs to cover about four hundred metres. In daylight it would be easy, but in complete darkness it was a nightmare. I never did that again.

Our mission was to observe and report on a suspected enemy position inside a forest, where a high-value target was thought to be hiding. The day we were given the coordinates I'd immediately recognised the location from my Drill and Duties cadre. It was the very same farm building I'd been tasked to watch on that course almost three years before, so I had a good idea where to go without the need for a detailed map study. Military training areas are littered with trenches and excavations where troops have constructed observation posts and defensive positions over the years. It took us two nights of walking to reach the target area, concealing ourselves in some thick forest during the daylight in between, but when we got there the ground was exactly as I'd remembered it, and we were able to utilise the old ditch for our own observation post, saving us hours of digging.

For the next few days we didn't move much, just watched and reported on what was happening at the farm. A platoon of soldiers from the Royal Engineers were acting as an "enemy force" and performed a series of tasks for us to observe to create a scenario and give us something to report back to HQ. Being in an O.P was boring, cold, and extremely uncomfortable, and we alternated between sentry, scribe, admin, and rest in the small confines. Being on "hard routine" meant we talked in whispers, ate cold food, drank cold water, field-cleaned our weapons, and carried out toileting needs into bags and bottles, all without leaving the cramped space. The only time anyone got to leave was when we needed to erect an antenna for the radio, collect water from a nearby stream, and once to retrieve a buried cache of rations for resupply. Those tasks were a welcome break from the inactivity of the O.P and an opportunity to get the blood flowing through our cramped-up limbs. The worse part was we knew we were doing Endurance the same night the exercise finished and shivering in a ditch for a week was the worst possible preparation for that. The DS had tried to keep it a secret, but we'd overheard two of the drivers talking about it one night and encouraged them to spill the beans.

On the final day of the exercise I was on sentry duty with Paul when we saw the high-value target arrive at the farmhouse. Both agreeing that it was him, we turned on the radio and alerted the HQ, requesting an artillery bombardment to take him out. To their credit, unbeknown to us, the engineers had dug some low-explosive battle simulations into the ground around the farm in preparation, so when they exploded beyond the building to simulate the artillery shells landing off-target, we called in our adjustment.

"Drop four hundred!" I ordered over the radio.

The next explosions were short of the target.

"Add two hundred!" I said, and the next explosion was bang on target. The engineers were obviously monitoring the radio too and detonating the charges themselves. It was great training.

"Fire for effect! I said, and after a short wait dozens of loud blasts erupted all around the farm, with bits of earth and smoke flying in all directions.

It went quiet for a few seconds before the farm kicked back into life, and armed men started pouring out of the doors into the courtyard. They'd obviously been told where we were because they immediately started running in our direction, pointing towards us, and shouting loudly. All four of us put our bergans on our backs and agreed to meet at the emergency rendezvous if we got separated. We waited patiently until the advancing enemy entered the killing area of the Claymore mines we'd placed to our front, then detonated them using our hand-held firing devices. To simulate those going off we threw two "Thunderflash" battle-noise-simulators at our attackers then started our withdrawal. Moving in pairs and firing blank ammunition we made our escape up the steep hill behind us, but the enemy were apparently bulletproof, and didn't stop for the explosions or the rifle fire directed at them, soon catching up with us and taking us captive. Clearly their orders were to ignore our fire, they needed to get hold of us so the cadre could continue as planned under the control of the DS.

When I was caught along with Paul my weapon was taken from me and a sandbag was placed over my head. I was gasping for breath after trying to sprint up that hill with all my kit and the sandbag made it difficult to breathe. I got claustrophobic and panicked.

"Get this fucking sandbag off my head, I can't breathe!" I snapped.

Thankfully they were a good bunch of blokes and lifted it up over my mouth and nose to help me out.

"Thanks mate." I said. I still couldn't see, but at least I wasn't suffocating any more.

I was marched down to the farm and I could hear the others being moved around too, so I knew we were all together. We were in the courtyard we'd been watching, kneeling on the cold concrete in silence, and all I could think about was Endurance. My knees were already smashed to bits from the cadre, and I figured I'd be needing them pretty soon for that monster beasting, so when I heard someone walk past I made my request.

"Any chance you could go easy on our knees mate? We're doing Endurance tonight." I said. There was a bit of whispering, then we were sat down. I was expecting some type of interrogation, but it didn't happen, and about ten minutes later the sandbags were removed. The final exercise was over.

Endurance

I've got a few mates who've done Endurance several times, but only because they've had to. The only person I know that has done it just for fun is my good friend Cam Williams, one of the fittest human beings I've ever met, and the only person I know who is literally addicted to fitness. As the PF platoon sergeant I actually had to order him *not* to do Endurance on a couple of occasions when he wanted to do it as a safety supervisor on the PF cadre. We always had a few DS acting as "sweepers" on our test marches, just in case someone got injured or lost, but they'd only do half, or quarter of the route on Endurance, before handing over the responsibility to someone else at a pre-determined checkpoint. Cam would always volunteer for the whole thing, but to protect him from injury, I'd tell him he couldn't. He was always one of the older blokes in the PF, in his mid-thirties, and he'd picked up several injuries from the years of beastings he put himself through on a daily basis. He had nothing to prove to anyone. As far as I know the only courses that use Endurance as a test are the PF cadre and UK Special Forces Selection, and I certainly wouldn't recommend doing it to anyone who doesn't have to, at least not in one go anyway. The route is 64km long and criss-crosses the Brecon Beacons, taking in most of its highest points on the way. Officially the test must be completed alone, a solo effort with no outside help or motivation for the individual, but most people will partner up with someone else at some stage while they're moving in the same direction at the same speed. On my cadre I met up with Gareth early on, and we stayed together for about 45km, splitting up as we approached checkpoints, then discretely re-joining each other shortly afterwards out of sight of the DS. I'd already covered every section of the route before, either during my own preparation training or on the cadre, but Gareth's knowledge of the area was even better than mine, and between us we hardly even touched our maps. Approaching a checkpoint known as 642, which is a trig point that stands at 642 metres above sea level, we split up again, agreeing to rendezvous a few hundred metres away afterwards. Gareth went first, and I watched from a distance until he left the DS's tent and headed off again. After receiving my new coordinates a couple of minutes later I also ran off, but couldn't find Gareth, so cracked on by myself. Probably due to fatigue we'd misunderstood each other and gone to completely different rendezvous points, and he continued solo as well. I reached my penultimate checkpoint before dark and cracked on as fast as I could, hoping to get through a forest while there was still some daylight. The final leg was the only part of the route that I hadn't visited during my recent preparation, having last been there a few years before with my mate Jon Hollingsworth when we were doing some hill-walking together. I remembered it well enough though and was confident I'd be able to find the best route without needing my map. However, by the time I exited the forest it was pitch black and the clouded sky afforded no ambient light whatsoever. The obvious track that I remembered was now indistinguishable amongst dozens of others that had been carved by walkers and livestock, so I chose the one that seemed most prominent and continued with a sense of urgency towards the Talybont Reservoir, where the final checkpoint was located. Shortly after setting off I began to doubt myself. The track had slowly become less and less apparent, and my compass was telling me I was heading in the wrong direction, but I carried on for few hundred metres, hoping I'd still find the track junction I was looking for. I didn't, so I stopped and got my map out for a navigation check, knowing I was close, but not knowing in which direction. After a bit of searching I realised I'd definitely missed the track and had been walking the wrong way, so instead of wasting any more time focussing on that, I set my compass to north and decided to crack on. I knew roughly where I was, so I knew the forest to my north had several good tracks in it that would take me where I needed to go. I headed across some open moorland before starting a steep decline towards the pine forest that stood out as a dark mass on the landscape. Once I hit the tree-line the thick vegetation slowed me down drastically, and I crashed through it noisily, trying to find the best route in the darkness, while maintaining my northerly heading. I was very conscious of the time I'd added on because of my mistake and feeling angry with myself for not taking the time to conduct a proper map study when I'd exited the forest, but I was committed to that route now, and paying the price. Eventually a track appeared in front of me, crossing from left to right, so I double-checked it was heading north-east, drank some water, brushed the pine needles off my head and neck, and started running. I'd covered about fifty-eight kilometres by then and had been tabbing for about sixteen hours, over arduous terrain, carrying my 60lb bergan and rifle, but I knew I was on the home straight, and wanted to regain some of the time I'd lost, so I ran all the way to the finish point. When I reached the final checkpoint I was greeted by the PF sergeant major, WO2 Wags Wardle.

"Ah Brown." he said. "What took you so long? I had money on you being first. Did you enjoy that?"

"Yeah I loved it Sir. Can I do it again please?" I replied, still trying my best to look unfazed by the rigours of the cadre.

"Get in you silly fucker." Wags told me, pointing to the back of the Land Rover. "Your mate Gareth finished ages ago, and he's back at camp already."

That was the final hurdle of my cadre, and when it finished there were four of us left. Gareth, Paul, Ginge, and I were interviewed one at a time and told we'd passed.

The next day I phoned my mum to tell her the good news and she congratulated me. However, she also had some news that wasn't so great. To her credit she'd known for a while but waited until the end of the cadre to tell me, because she didn't want me to be distracted or withdraw myself from the course to go and support her. In the same conversation that I proudly told her I'd been successful, she told me she had cancer.

From an early age I'd been the man of the house, the confidant, the stable one, and I knew she wanted me there to support her. The PF cadre was over, and all that was left was a formal presentation ceremony and some admin. I made my way to the PF HQ, told them the situation, and they immediately stood me down to go home. I was one of them now, and they made sure I was alright. My mum had already beat cancer once, and fortunately she beat it again.

A couple of years later I was in Sennybridge again, this time instructing on the PF cadre, when I received some more bad news from my mum. My brother had been sectioned and committed to a psychiatric hospital after attempting to take his own life. Once again I left SENTA and headed to Northampton to be with my family. Shortly after arriving at my mums, we drove to the hospital together, and on the way she told me what had happened. After not hearing from him for a few days, she'd gone to the rented house where he lived and knocked on the door, her mother's intuition telling her something was wrong. After some persistent banging my brother unlocked the front door and slowly opened it.

"Oh my God! What have you done?" my mum said immediately on seeing him.

He was confused, pale, withdrawn, and his clothes were soiled. My mum called for an ambulance and waited in the house with him until the paramedics arrived. In his living room, photographs of his son were spread across the floor, and in the centre of them, a samurai sword was placed on the ground, wedged upright between some books, clothing, and a small table, with the tip of the blade pointing upwards towards the ceiling. He later explained to me that he'd placed it like that in the hope that he would fall on the sword after taking an overdose of pain-killers, washed down with lager. Sure enough, he had indeed collapsed, but had fallen beside the sword on top of the photos of his son. In the two days since doing that he had no recollection of anything. Potentially he'd been unconscious the whole time, until my mum knocked at his front door and woke him up.

"I can't even fucking kill myself properly!" he told me solemnly. Seeing my big brother in there was really sad. I don't know whether it was the effects of the overdose, the subsequent medication from the doctors, or just his mental state at the time, but he was definitely in the right place, because he *looked* like a mental patient. His eyes were wide open, quickly flitting nervously from side to side and up and down, and he looked scared, he looked vulnerable. I remember looking around the large room we were in and being reminded of a classic Jack Nicholson film I'd watched years before.

"This place is like the hospital in "One Flew Over the Cuckoo's Nest" I said, deliberately trying to make light of the fact we were in some kind of lunatic asylum. My brothers expression told me that he hadn't seen the film, and my mum's told me she thought it was an inappropriate comment. I never knew he had such terrible demons until that day. He told me he was hearing voices in his head and had regular thoughts of driving his car off a bridge. I didn't know how to respond or reply to that.

"You don't need to feel like that Ian, we're here for you." I said. "We love you mate." Speaking like that was not the norm between my brother and I, or anyone else in our family for that matter. Emotions and feelings were always kept under wraps, but it felt natural in that moment after he'd tried to end his own life. I reminded him that he had a young son that also loved him and would be devastated if he died.

In his younger days Ian was a lot of fun, the life and soul of the party, acting daft and making everyone laugh. I think most people who knew him back then would agree that everything changed after he was involved in a terrible motorbike accident which killed his good friend Ross, who we'd both known as young lads. My brother's physical injuries had long since healed from the incident when I first realised that he was still suffering psychologically. I was back in Aylesbury enjoying a weekend off from the army, and we were drinking in a popular nightclub called The Rectory when he told me that he thought the accident was his fault, and that he was to blame for Ross's death. Three of them had gone for a ride that day, and Ian had suggested they stop at a quiet place he knew for a cigarette break. On the way there, while waiting to turn right into another road, a van struck them from behind at speed, launching them into the air, scattering them and their motorbikes across the road.

"If I hadn't suggested we went that way, Ross wouldn't have died. He'd still be here today." my brother told me.

He'd never spoken to me about the accident before, so I was surprised to hear him say that, and shocked to think he was blaming himself.

I did my best to try and reassure him that it was a tragic accident and not his fault, but he was having none of it, and I was left feeling helpless and worried about him when he ended the conversation with an awful statement.

"Have you ever watched one of your mates screaming in pain as they bleed to death in the middle of a road?" he asked me angrily.

"No, I haven't." I answered.

"Well I have." he said, looking me square in the eyes. "And it was all my fucking fault."

It wasn't his fault. I don't imagine anybody else thinks it was, or has ever even suggested it was, but he carries that horrendous burden with him every day. I think that misguided guilt destroyed my brother, because he was never the same again after that crash.

I bet there are hundreds, maybe thousands of soldiers living with these feelings of guilt or culpability, because decisions made by a commander at any level could easily be misconstrued by them as the causation for someone's injury or death. Hindsight will always make us question our choices and actions, as we try to comprehend any tragic event or failure that might possibly have been avoidable. Tactics employed, commands given, selection of key personnel, delegation of tasks, assets used, deconfliction, preparation, and personal skills will all come under scrutiny as we try to apportion blame and credit where it is due. A good friend of mine in 3 PARA was on leave in the UK when one of his soldiers was killed in Afghanistan, and I could see that he felt guilty about it. We only ever spoke of it once, but I could tell he was wondering if it might have been different had he been there. He was an excellent leader, loved by his men, admired by his peers, and respected by his superiors, and he'd done absolutely nothing wrong. If anything he was the person least responsible because he was thousands of miles away. I hope he is at peace with that now.

CHAPTER NINE THE PROBATIONER

After the PF cadre I returned to 3 PARA, packed up my kit, had a few interviews with my commanders, and one last night out with the blokes before leaving my battalion and starting a new chapter in the Pathfinders. For soldiers who pass the cadre the first twelve months in the unit is a probationary period. During this time they are closely monitored and expected to complete numerous modules of continuation training. First of all is the induction cadre, where they will be introduced to some of the specialist weapons, equipment, and skills employed by the patrols. The PF is very well equipped, with its own stores, vehicle fleet, and armoury, so most of the training is conducted organically, and every year all available soldiers attend several cadres. The air cadre, mobility cadre, communications cadre, medical cadre, and demolitions cadre, are all organised and run by one of the senior soldiers, usually a sergeant or corporal. At the end of the first year all soldiers will have a good understanding of the niche capabilities and probable tasks that they might undertake in their new role.

My first year at PF was very busy, but as a young, keen soldier it was awesome, and it flew by. I completed the month-long military freefall (MFF) course in Arizona, spent another month in Sweden on a winter patrol course with the Swedish special forces, deployed on operations to Sierra Leone, competed in an international military competition in Germany, went to Kenya on exercise, and completed the first half of a twelve-week promotion course in Wales. Along with helping out on selection cadres and other commitments I spent the vast majority of that year away.

My first day began at the PF compound in Montgomery Lines in Aldershot, where I'd originally served with 3 PARA, but I was only there to help load up some stores as the PF were relocating as a unit to Wattisham Airfield, near Ipswich. Within a few hours I was on the road to my new home in the county of Suffolk, and we drove in convoy all the way to the new compound, which was situated in a quiet corner of the camp, next to the bright yellow Sea King helicopters of B Flight, 22 Squadron, R.A.F Search and Rescue. Once the stores were secured, we were shown to our accommodation which was the bottom floor of a wing in the sergeants' mess. Little did we know but putting us in there as mere privates and corporals had caused quite an upset to some of the mess members. Even though we weren't allowed anywhere other than our corridors they were furious that we were in their sacred sanctuary, especially the one's who'd had to vacate their rooms to make way for us. To be fair, they had a point, they'd worked hard for the privileges of the mess, and they paid a higher accommodation rate for it, whereas we were junior ranks, who only paid a standard fee. It wasn't our fault though, someone well above our paygrade had failed to realise that we'd need somewhere to sleep as well as somewhere to work, and there wasn't anywhere else to put us. Besides, we only slept there, we still ate and drank in the junior ranks' bar and cookhouse. They were so offended by our presence they even had a fence built to cut us off from the rest of the building, and we had our very own tradesmen's entrance which prevented us from accidentally entering places reserved for the important people. One of the more disgruntled and vociferous mess members was whining about it at scoff one evening when our sergeant major, an old-school Parachute Regiment hard-nut called Wags was sitting nearby.

"If any of those PF boys start taking the piss, I'll be the first one to go round there and give them a slap!" he boasted, unaware of Wags' proximity.

There was no way in hell Wags was letting that go unanswered. "Gents!" he called out as he stood up, getting the attention of everyone in the dining area but directing his speech to the outspoken soldier. "My blokes have been keeping their heads down and staying out of your way, but rest assured, if any of you think you can go into their accommodation and gob off or abuse them without getting your heads smashed in, you can fucking think again. Leave them alone and they'll leave you alone!" Wags didn't muck about.

The following day Wags told us about what he'd said and a few of us chuckled, thinking he was just kidding. "Lads, I'm not joking!" he clarified. "If some idiot comes into the block and starts gobbing off, acting like some kind of tough guy, I want you to smash his fucking head in! Batter the bastard! Just let me know straight away so I can sort it out!" Wags was a brilliant sergeant major who was one of the original men that made up the pathfinder platoon when it re-formed in 1985. He loved the PF, the Parachute Regiment, and all things airborne, and best of all, you knew he had your back if you ever needed him.

A few weeks after moving to Wattisham Airfield I was sent to R.A.F Brize Norton to start the Military Freefall Course. Traditionally, whoever was awarded "Top Student" on the selection cadre was rewarded with a place on the next MFF course, and fortunately for me I'd been given that honour. After a short period in Brize Norton where we received a few theory lessons on freefall, got suspended from the ceiling in a skydiving harness a couple of times, and spun around like children on some odd-shaped skateboards, we flew out to the USA to begin the fun part. As far as military courses go, that is probably the most wished-for, or desired one in the British army, but it's only available to soldiers from the special forces and the PF because of the niche capability it caters for, plus the substantial costs and resources required to run it. Our course was conducted in Yuma, Arizona, and for the duration we were accommodated in a hotel in the middle of town, opposite a McDonalds restaurant on one side, and a pawn shop on the other. For me this kind of treatment was difficult to get my head around. If the army were organising the course we'd have been out in the middle of the desert, sleeping on the floor under a poncho, or tent if we were lucky. But here I was with my new friend Mick, sharing a big, air-conditioned room with two double beds, en-suite shower room, cable T.V, and a fridge. It was like being on holiday, except I couldn't have afforded a holiday like that.

The course itself was great, we got up at about 0430hrs for breakfast, drove to the nearby base, and jumped until around lunchtime. In the afternoon the desert winds would reliably pick up to a speed beyond our safety limits and we'd have to stop, giving us the rest of the day for ourselves, so along with all the other PF guys I joined a local gym where we trained every day. We also made the most of any days off we had too, visiting San Diego, Las Vegas, and Mexico on different weekends. The drop zone at Yuma was a massive clear area of soft, freshly ploughed desert sand, measuring 1km x 1km squared with large purpose-built shelters in the corners for parachute packing. My accuracy under canopy was initially so bad, I actually landed closer to a shed at the other end of the drop zone to our one, which meant a walk of over 500m to our packing area. Carrying my fifty-pound parachute across the soft, ploughed sand in the searing desert heat taught me to never do that again. The jump programme was run by RAF Parachute Jump Instructors who were very experienced parachutists, and all of our descents were made from an RAF C130 Hercules, mostly off the tailgate but sometimes out of the side doors too. By the end of the course we'd completed

63 jumps and qualified as military parachutists in both high altitude low opening (HALO) and high altitude high opening (HAHO) parachute techniques.

While in Yuma I learned that I'd been selected to attend a month-long arctic warfare long range reconnaissance patrol course in Sweden. Ran by the Swedish special forces at their Army Ranger School in Karlsborg, the course was designed for a UK special forces reservist squadron, who kindly offered places to the PF as a favour. Our platoon sergeant, Steve Heaney picked four men to accompany him, and because of our Arctic experience in Norway with 3 PARA, Bryan Budd and I were chosen, along with Tricky from the Airborne Signals Squadron, and Will from 1 PARA. The Fallskärmsjägarskolan (FJS) soldiers were excellent instructors and led by an eccentric, if not slightly crazy officer called Major Greus. One of the first things they had to do was teach everyone how to ski, so for a couple of hours we went round and round a circuit they'd made in some deep snow. I was already a military ski instructor after completing a four-week course in Norway with 3 PARA, and Bry was a good skier too, so for us it was a bit of fun. For the majority of the others on the course it served merely as a confirmation that they couldn't ski, so they basically learned how to walk on skis instead, which wasn't ideal because there was a fifty kilometre cross-country ski-march to be completed at the end of the course. Over the four weeks we slept mostly outdoors in tents and improvised shelters, learned survival techniques, conducted ice-breaking drills in freezing cold water, parachuted onto a snow-covered frozen lake, and skied all over the beautiful Swedish countryside practicing arctic warfare tactics. It was a fantastic trip, and I formed some strong friendships with people I didn't really know beforehand.

As a young, single man in Pathfinders I didn't keep on top of current affairs like I do now, and like everyone else living in the block my television was either playing VHS porn videos, war films, or porn videos, certainly not boring current affairs, or political programmes. So when we were unexpectedly recalled to the PF compound on the afternoon of May the 5th and warned that we might be deploying to a small West African country called Sierra Leone, I was quite surprised. On Sunday the 7th of May I was supposed to be starting the sniper course in Pirbright, something I'd always wanted to do, and I'd just finished making a camouflage ghillie suit that had taken me many hours to prepare. Instead, less than 48hrs later we were landing by airplane in Sierra Leone on Operation PALLISER with the 1 PARA battle group. It hadn't taken us long to get everything ready because we were permanently at high-readiness, and most of our kit was already packed. We loaded it on to the vehicles that afternoon and while we waited for the call to deploy we learned what we could about the situation in Sierra Leone. The next day we left Wattisham Airfield and drove down to the Air Mounting Centre at South Cerney, where we grabbed a shed-load of ammunition for our rifles and machine guns, along with some hand grenades, 51mm mortar bombs, 94mm light ant-tank rockets, and PE4 plastic explosives. While our kit was weighed and flight manifests were drafted we received a couple of short impromptu pre-deployment lectures from people, who haphazardly tried their best to get our attention and herd us into a quiet space where they could be heard. A medic issued us some anti-malaria tablets to be taken immediately, said something about the signs and symptoms of heat exhaustion and drinking lots of water, then warned us of the high risk of contracting AIDS from African prostitutes, before offering some free condoms. Another bloke said something about the Red Cross, and what we should or shouldn't say if we were taken hostage or prisoner. However, the primary focus of his brief seemed to be to warn us all that we might get raped, and if we did get raped, not to feel guilty or ashamed about it, especially if it was in front of our mates. He even went out of his way to explain that some men might ejaculate while being raped because of the stimulation of their prostate but assured us that that didn't mean they liked it, and if it did happen we should all support each other. He was very thorough about that particular detail, but it was a bit weird, and ended up being the only part anyone actually remembered. Once the admin was completed we headed over to R.A.F Brize Norton to catch our flight.

We boarded the RAF passenger plane with our weapons and ammunition, placing them on the overhead shelf and took our seats before receiving the usual flight safety briefs. Usually we'd go through tedious checks and equipment searches by the dreaded RAF Police prior to boarding these type of aircraft, and the blokes would often have knives, machetes, and cooking gas confiscated as prohibited items of "dangerous air cargo". This was more like it, the RAF and army actually working as a team to get us deployed, instead of jobsworths making things difficult. Above my head, in my personal kit alone was four-hundred-and-eighty rounds of rifle ammunition, a belt of two-hundred machine gun rounds, and two high-explosive hand grenades.

Our flight landed in the neighbouring country of Senegal where we transferred onto C130 Hercules transport planes, then flew to Lungi International Airport in Sierra Leone. 1 PARA, with support from 2 PARA quickly secured the airfield and we were given orders to deploy patrols into a nearby forest that night. Our first job was to observe likely approach routes that the enemy might use to mount an attack on the airport, and after being dropped off by a 1 PARA vehicle patrol under the cover of darkness, we quietly patrolled into some woodland to overwatch a jungle track. Nothing happened that night apart from us scaring the living daylights out of a couple of cyclists who we stopped as they rode in the dark. Stepping out of the shadows with camouflage cream on our faces and rifles in hand we probably looked quite intimidating to the unsuspecting civilians. The next day we patrolled back to the airfield via a 2 PARA sentry position and got a few sideways looks from people wondering why we were the only soldiers in the entire battle group wearing camouflage cream. We rendezvoused with the rest of the PF in an old hangar close to the passenger terminal and were told of our new mission.

Military intelligence had learned that a large group of rebels from the Revolutionary United Front were advancing towards the capital city of Freetown and the strategically important Lungi Airport . They numbered anywhere between six hundred and two thousand, and because of the limited roads and infrastructure in the region their only viable route was via the Port Loko Road. On that road, about twenty kilometres north-east of Freetown was a small village called Lungi Lol, and it was determined that the RUF would have to pass through Lungi Lol on their advance to the capital. Our task, along with a platoon of Nigerian, United Nations soldiers, was to act as a trigger, and alert Battle Group Headquarters of any advancing enemy forces heading their way. We were thirty-men strong, the Nigerians about the same, and the much larger force of enemy rebels was closing in on Lungi Lol fast. "Dead or alive, nobody gets left behind!" was part of the orders we received. Apparently, on previous village assaults the RUF had started with a probing attack, and if repelled they'd surrounded the target and attacked from all directions simultaneously. High on drugs and convinced they were bullet proof, they were reckless and brutal in their methods, savagely hacking at villagers with machetes, and firing weapons indiscriminately from the hip. Outnumbered by at least ten to one, we were briefed to hold our position for as long as possible then withdraw through the jungle if overrun. Casualties would be loaded onto the single Pinzgauer 4x4 vehicle we had and driven down the track to the nearest friendly forces, while the remainder covered their withdrawal then escaped into the jungle on foot.

Flying towards that village was the first time I truly felt

like I was going into a situation where people were going to be killed, and I couldn't help looking around at the others on board, wondering which of us it would be. I thought about who would be affected by my death. I was young, single, and had no children, my brother and dad would be upset for sure, but my mum would be the one worst hit. She never wanted me to join the army in the first place, she wanted me to be a plumber, reluctantly signing the parental consent form when I applied because I was under eighteen years old. On that helicopter were men with wives and children, and I quickly came to the conclusion that I was the most expendable. I didn't want any of us to be killed, but I wasn't afraid of dying, and genuinely thought it should be me before anyone with a wife or kids.

The village was centred on a red dirt-track T-junction, where the Port Loko Road ran east to west, and another road headed south to a coastal village called Pepel. It was determined that the large RUF force we were expecting would have to select one of these roads as their route to Freetown. Lungi Lol was a small village mostly made up of traditional mud huts with grass roofs, and the odd corrugated steel shed. The people were friendly to us, but very cautious, understandably anxious about what was coming their way. A platoon of Nigerian United Nations soldiers were already at the village when we arrived, and they weren't particularly liked by many of the locals, who saw them as an occupying force rather than protectors. To be fair, the Nigerians were brutal, adopting a zero tolerance policy towards the Sierra Leonians, and meting out rough justice to anyone who broke their unwritten rules or standards of acceptable behaviour. In their defence, they'd been in the country for a long time as peacekeepers and were loathed by the rebels who saw them as evil demons. One explained to me how the rebels would kill the Nigerians twice if they ever captured one of them.

"How can you kill someone twice?" was my obvious question.

"They will shoot us, then they will take our dead body and put a long nail through our eyes and into our brains!" he told me, using his two index fingers to demonstrate the length of the nail required. He was very intense. "If they do not do this, they are scared we will come back to life and kill them!"

It all seemed to make perfect sense to him, so who was I to question it? "Fair enough mate." I said. "Don't let them catch you then."

Acts of disrespectful behaviour that boiled the blood of the Nigerians were usually insignificant, innocent actions that the average person wouldn't even notice. I saw them beat people with sticks just because they'd cycled past them, or because they'd walked past them while wearing a cap. Apparently that was outrageous behaviour, and fully deserving of a hiding, because they should always dismount from bikes and walk past the soldiers and remove any hats as they passed them too.

One day I woke to the sound of screaming from the direction of the Nigerians and went to investigate. A group of male children were face-down on the jungle floor, balancing only on their foreheads and tip-toes with their asses in the air and hands behind their backs. As their bodies trembled from the stress of the position a Nigerian soldier walked amongst them, randomly whipping their backs and legs with a long, thin stick. He was shouting aggressively at them, and they were whimpering and crying in response, all of it incoherent to me.

"What have they done wrong?" I asked one of the Nigerians I recognised called Sunday.

"They are rebels!" he stated agitatedly.

"How can you tell? They look like normal kids to me." I responded. "How do you know they're rebels?"

Sunday pointed towards the village, and with a sweeping motion of his hand he angrily told me "All of them are rebels!"

For all I knew he was right, but to me it just looked like

bullying.

Military intelligence predicted an attack on our position was imminent, with the large RUF force apparently moving closer each day on their murderous advance from the east. In their wake they left a devasting trail of destruction as they raped, murdered, and mutilated the occupants of the villages on their axis of advance. Rebel fighters made sickening bets on the gender of unborn babies before cutting open pregnant women and pulling out the foetus, mercilessly tossing it away like a piece of rubbish once the winner was established. Arms and legs were savagely hacked off with filthy machetes, and children were forced to kill their own parents then join the ranks of the RUF. Wags, our sergeant major, ordered us to prepare defensive positions in preparation, and with the help of a local workforce we got to work. Using metal H83 ammunition containers each patrol made improvised Claymore mines that were placed around the village perimeter and overwatched by sentry positions. We'd been unable to get hold of the manufactured M18 Claymore anti-personnel mines at such short notice, but we did have plenty of PE4 plastic explosives to make our own. Inside the ammo tins, instead of the 700 steel ball bearings found in the issued version, we placed nuts, bolts, nails, screws, and any other pieces of metal we could get our hands on, which on detonation would become lethal projectiles blasted towards the enemy. Local men used picks and shovels to dig fighting trenches all the way around the village too, with some even getting roofs made from cut branches, leaves, and dead grass to protect us from the scorching Sun. On the main axis, where the enemy were most likely to approach from, additional rudimentary defences were prepared by the blokes. Long, straight branches were cut, then sharpened into spears that were driven into the ground, with their sharp points tilted towards the enemy like some sort of post-apocalyptic fortress. More of an obstacle than a weapon, they would hopefully slow down an attacking force and channel them into a killing area covered by machine-gun fire.

Once word got out that British soldiers were based in the village hundreds of people started migrating towards it, seeking refuge from the advancing RUF. Some stayed, erecting temporary shelters, or sleeping rough on the floor, but most continued on their exodus towards the airport or the capital. Lorries, minibuses, pick-up trucks, and cars would approach our checkpoint slowly, with their wheel arches almost touching the tyres as they strained under the weight of their load. To ensure no rebels or weapons were being smuggled through we'd halt the vehicles and get the passengers to de-bus so we could conduct basic searches and ask some questions. Sometimes it was hard to believe how many people got off of those wagons, there could be forty people on a minibus or twenty in a Toyota Hilux, but somehow they always managed to get back in, and on their way, usually after bump-starting the engine back to life, then cramming themselves inside like sardines. Several would sit on the roofs or stand on the bumpers and continue on without complaint, it was still better than walking. Of course we had no way of telling who the people were that came through, and unless they were carrying AK47's, chewing on a human heart, and wildly swinging a machete at us, it was impossible to differentiate friend from foe. Some showed us passports, driving licences, or other forms of identification, and some were even dressed in police or military uniforms, but we had no way of actually verifying anything. We had no idea what those documents should look like, and for all we knew any one of those people could have been a member of the RUF, scoping out our position with murderous intentions.

One day our location was visited by some soldiers from the UK special forces who were transiting through with some local soldiers. Like us they had also been deployed at short notice. However some of them were literally deployed with zero notice, when they were ripped from a snow-covered mountainside during an extreme cold weather exercise and sent straight to Sierra Leone, without even a chance to re-pack their kit for the hot and humid jungle environment. Among the men in that team was a friend of mine from 3 PARA called Matt. We'd done the Pathfinder's escape and evasion, and the military ski instructor courses together before he passed SF selection and left battalion in 1998. Everyone in 3 PARA knew Matt, he was a paratroopers paratrooper, hard as nails, but humble, and very funny. Among us in PF there were several blokes who'd served in 3 PARA, so when Matt told us that he was sweltering in his arctic socks, winter boots, and windproof trousers, everyone dug out any spare clothes they had to help him and his team out. The location Matt was working from had been involved in some vicious fighting with the RUF, successfully repelling multiple attacks by the rebels, and in an effort to deter further attacks, some of the Sierra Leonian soldiers had cut off the heads of their slain enemy and posted them on big sticks along the routes to their base. To most people this probably sounds like some kind of historical, brutal savagery from a bygone era, but this type of behaviour can still be found in many parts of the world where life is cheap, and the rule of law is nothing more than survival of the fittest.

Another time we were visited by a foreign journalist who was intending to head further east, to report on the advance of the RUF. The PF soldiers he spoke to strongly advised him not to venture any further, because once he passed us, he would be entering unknown territory, no-man's land. He was travelling in a Toyota Hilux pick-up truck with some locally hired security guards. The driver was armed with an AK47 that was laid in the middle of the front seat and in the rear another man stood with a 12.7mm DShK heavy machine gun, a potent weapon which is the Soviet era equivalent of the Browning .50cal used by the British Army. However, its potency and effectiveness is very much dependent on the quality of its user and mounting system. This particular example was being handled by a young man who looked like he didn't know which end was the dangerous one and lacked the muscle mass required to cock his own leg, let alone the gun. Weighing about seventy-five pounds, it was also seriously in need of a stable firing platform, because a weapon of that size is far too cumbersome for a man to manoeuvre quickly. Instead it was just resting precariously on the roof of the front cab, rendering it pretty much unemployable and useless.

"I've got my own security, but you guys will come and help me if I get into trouble right?" the journalist asked expectantly.

The blokes were bluntly honest with their reply in an effort to deter him. "No. We can protect you here, but if you go down that track you're on your own, we can't help you." they warned.

He chose to ignore the advice, and not long after that we heard that he'd been captured and murdered by the RUF who'd brutally beheaded him. His guards had apparently offered no resistance and abandoned him without a single shot being fired.

On a separate occasion some British journalists came to see us, but they stayed within the security of our boundaries. They were from the Daily Telegraph and wanted to take lots of photographs of us patrolling through the village, to capture the atmosphere of the place and the people. None of us wanted our picture taken, we were all very conscious of operational security and didn't trust the media, so in the end Wags, the sergeant major ordered four of us to do it, choosing the newest blokes to the PF within his arcs of view at the time.

"Paul, Steve, Ginge, Nick, you're fucking doing it!" he said. Decision made. Nobody argued with Wags, and we spent the next twenty minutes walking around acting natural and trying not to look at the camera while the photographer snapped away. Twenty-one years later I found out that photographer was a man called Heathcliff O'Malley and reached out to him to see if he still had any of the pictures. He did, and very kindly sent me copies, so in hindsight I'm glad I was picked.

Taking a break after patrolling through the jungle to visit another village. We're drenched because we'd just found a stand-pipe and took the opportunity to soak ourselves in the cold water.

Back row L-R is Ginge L, Ginge W, Loz, Paddy, and me. At the front is our patrol commander Daz.

The mapping we had was quite old and lacking in detail, showing only the big villages, main tracks, and large water courses, and during conversations with the village elders we learned that there were some other small settlements close to our position that weren't shown on our maps. Wags spoke to the village elder and asked for a guide to help us navigate our way through the jungle to pay them a visit, but the locals were reluctant to assist, it turned out they didn't like going off-track, they only stuck to the well-trodden routes and trails that we wanted to avoid in case they were ambushed. Eventually one man was ordered to be our guide and about ten of us headed northwards into the jungle, led by a very nervous and unenthusiastic villager. We'd only covered a few hundred metres when the patrol came to a stop and the message was passed back that our guide had vanished. Ahead of me was my mate Ginge, who turned around to face me.

"Has anyone seen the guide?" he asked quietly.

I shook my head to let him know that I certainly hadn't, before turning around myself to ask Paddy who was behind me. Nobody had seen him, he'd seemingly disappeared into thin air, so after a short wait to see if he'd return we continued on our way, this time using the much more reliable map and compass as our guide. I have no idea what happened to that man, or why he ran off, but he was clearly afraid of something. Maybe it was the thought of bumping into the RUF, maybe he was scared off by a snake, or maybe it was the ten foreign soldiers armed to the teeth and taking him for a nice quiet walk in the jungle, I'll never know. Maybe he's still out there, lost and walking around in circles with a huge beard and bedraggled clothes.

After a short while we started to see evidence of habitation and knew we were getting close. Narrow footpaths that weaved their way through the jungle, and items of discarded litter indicated a recent human presence, so we approached with caution, stopping to look, listen, and smell for any sign of activity. Eventually we entered the small village that comprised of only a handful of small, modest dwellings and discovered it had obviously been deserted. The washing lines were vacant of clothing, and the buildings were empty shells, likely abandoned by their occupants in anticipation of the advancing RUF. What it did have though, was a standpipe that was connected to a natural underground water source, so after we'd all refilled our water bottles we took it in turns to stand underneath it, while someone else pumped the large metal lever and doused us in nice cold water. Patrolling in the heat of day was hot work, and it was a good way to cool down, as well as give our sweaty clothes a bit of a rinsing off too.

On return to Lungi Lol we immediately noticed a drastic change to the local landscape. Dozens of men and boys were hard at work clearing the flora that surrounded the village using machetes, axes, and controlled fires, it was an amazing feat of forest management. In the space of just a few hours they'd flattened acres of trees, bushes, plants, and tall grasses, razing it to the ground, in order to provide us with clear arcs of view, and to deny the enemy a concealed approach from where they could launch an attack. It was astonishing that they'd been able to do it so efficiently and avoid it getting out of control, obviously having mastered it over many generations. We wondered how much further they were going to go, and my patrol commander Daz approached one of the older gentlemen who appeared to be supervising.

"When are they going to stop?" he asked. To us it seemed they'd already gone far enough.

"They will stop when you tell them to stop." he answered.

Daz informed the PF HQ, who then came to inspect the progress.

"Fucking hell!" Wags exclaimed, himself equally surprised at the speed of the clearance operation. "Tell them to stop now, before there's nothing left!" he instructed.

One day we received intelligence that we were going to be attacked that night. Intercepted communications suggested that a large force of rebels was assembling close to our position in preparation for a full-on night-time assault. There wasn't much more we could do to get ready. Our trenches were dug, our defences were in place, and our weapons and ammunition were primed. Based on the information, what we did do was raise our alert-state. Working in pairs we manned all of the trenches, instead of just the sentry positions, and took turns watching and resting, with half of the platoon on sentry duty at all times. In my trench we started with one-hour intervals, but during the night we ended up reducing it to twenty minutes because we were both struggling to stay awake. At one point I was so tired I was hallucinating again. This time I could see what looked like a man in uniform kneeling down. It was very dark, so I was using a night-sight to scan the ground to my front, and I couldn't work out if he was really close and kneeling next to some small saplings, or far away, and kneeling next to some big trees. When I first saw it I stared at the image for a long time. It looked like a British soldier from World War Two, wearing old battle-dress clothing and a round, metal helmet with a brim. His head was dropped forwards like he was praying, and he held a rifle in one hand, with the butt resting on the floor and the barrel pointing upwards. I lowered my weapon, shook my head, and took another look, expecting him to disappear, but I could still see him. It was a bit unnerving, but I knew my mind was playing tricks on me, it made no sense. That night passed very slowly, but without incident, and in the morning light I was able to identify the figure as a small stump of wood that had been the base of a tree before the locals had cut it down for us. It was just a few metres from the trench.

The night we eventually were attacked, we were less prepared. Moments before it kicked off I was fast asleep on the floor when my friend Loz woke me up with the words every sleeping soldier dreads to hear.

"You're on stag mate." He said quietly, giving me a gentle shake.

I sat up on my small piece of cut-down roll-mat that I'd had for years and was held together with bits of green, sniper tape. "Okay mate. Cheers." I responded. We slept fully clothed, and the sentry position was only about ten metres from where I was lying, so I was in the trench manning the machine gun almost immediately, and Loz walked off to go and get his head down for a few hours. Suddenly I heard some rapid footsteps approaching from behind me and turned just in time to see a Nigerian soldier called Sunday skidding to a halt beside the trench.

Pointing down the track to my front he whispered, "They are here, get ready!" before turning to leave again.

"Who's here?" I said, quickly scanning the open ground to the south with a night sight.

Sunday replied with a sense of urgency. "The rebels!"

Back then there weren't any brackets to affix the night-sights to the machine guns, so we used them like a telescope instead. My heart-rate increased, and I felt a buzz of excitement at the prospect of imminent action, but there was nobody there. The dirt track was clear, and the deforested clearing remained an empty wasteland.

"Well I can't see anyone." I told him dismissively.

Sunday spoke once more before running back to his position. "They are here!"

As he disappeared into the darkness the radio kicked into life. "All callsigns this is Zero, Maximise, Maximise, over."

I'd never heard the word "maximise" used on the radio before but took an educated guess what it meant and called out to Loz, who was sorting his kit out before getting his head back down.

"Loz!" I huffed, in a loud whisper.

"What?" he replied.

"They've just called maximise on the radio, I guess that means stand-to." I said.

Loz confirmed that it did, and quickly woke up the rest of the blokes in our team, who immediately grabbed their weapons and ammunition before sprinting into the trenches and adopting firing positions. My patrol commander Daz landed with a thud next to me within seconds and I told him what had happened. I could tell he was as excited as me, grinning broadly. I was chuffed to be on the GPMG, a firm favourite of the British paras, with its belt-fed 7.62mm stopping power. I felt confident I could do some real damage with that beast. Daz had only been in the trench for a few seconds when it all kicked off and bullets started flying in both directions, with rounds cutting through the village and tracer zipping overhead. From my position I could tell where the enemy were firing from but couldn't actually see them because they were attacking from the east, and my arcs were to the south. Between us were huts and other PF trenches, I'd have to wait my turn.

Not being able to fire was frustrating, the attackers were so close, and some of the blokes were seriously getting some rounds down, so I was really envious and wanted a piece of the action. In those situations you worry about your mates because you don't know if they're taking accurate fire, and it's tempting to run over to support them, but you can't. They have their arcs, you have yours, and everyone has to defend their own piece of ground while trusting their mates to do the same. The firefight went on for a while then stopped, the gunfire replaced by the sounds of people screaming and crying. I was bouncing with nervous energy, the RUF's usual tactic was to encircle a village and attack from all sides, so I was expecting them any minute. They chose not to this time though, the blokes had convinced them to abandon their attack completely, and the rebels scarpered into the jungle, leaving their dead behind. We were all gutted when they didn't try again, but the firepower that greeted them the first time had been overwhelming, it was a wise decision. Luckily none of our blokes were hit in the violent exchange, the trenches served us well, but there was one casualty in the village. A girl was hit by a stray AK47 round, but the blokes patched her up and got her evacuated to a hospital promptly, so she was okay.

The RUF were on the back foot and our HQ wanted to mount a follow-up patrol as soon as possible, so 1 PARA deployed their QRF by Chinook helicopter, and their blokes took over our positions so we could get after them. While we prepared to go the Nigerians loaded onto a truck and drove out of the village in the direction of the fleeting enemy. They negotiated the checkpoint barriers slowly, then swerved around the bodies laid on the track before disappearing around a bend. About a minute after they left several shots of rifle fire rang out, then it was quiet again, and after a short wait the truck reappeared in the distance heading back towards us. Draped across the bonnet was the lifeless body of a young man with blood trails running from underneath him and down the front-left wing of the vehicle. Our guess was that he'd been badly wounded in the original firefight and opened fire on the Nigerians with the last bit of energy he had when they drove past. In return three of them had nailed him at close range, finally putting him out of his misery.

Despite the fighting, refugees kept on coming as the day began, and with them came information that the rebels had taken over a small village a couple of kilometres to our east, where they were tending to the wounded.

We left Lungi Lol and headed east through the jungle in pursuit of them, with half of us on the north side and half on the south side of the track. Weapons, spent ammunition cases, items of clothing, and blood trails littered the ground where the RUF had hastily retreated, confirming we were heading in the right direction, and before long we reached the outskirts of the neighbouring village. Stopping short we observed the small settlement and watched for any sign of movement. The buildings were mostly small, circular dwellings, made from locally cut-down foliage, with grass roofs and mud floors. Grey smoke rose from a couple of them suggesting someone was inside, so after the machine guns were set up in fire-support positions we began the assault. Silently, using hand signals, we were split into pairs and despatched to clear the buildings one at a time by our platoon sergeant Steve Heaney. I was partnered with my mate Ginge who I'd done the cadre with, and on command we sprinted across the open space from our position of concealment to the first hut. My safety catch was off when I booted that door open, and we burst inside. Three pole-beds made of natural materials formed a hollow square in the small space, but they were all empty. There weren't many places to hide in that hut, so after we'd checked under the beds it was pretty clear the place was unoccupied. However there was evidence of recent residency and a hasty exit. Bedding and clothing were scattered across the floor, and a half-finished drink sat on a small table. Also a Tilley lamp had been lit, but its glass globe and hood hadn't been replaced, lying idly on the table next to it, as if someone had suddenly rushed out mid assembly. We declared the building clear, and another pair of blokes moved quickly onto the next one, systematically taking it in turns to clear every building in the village. It was exciting, but very disappointing when we realised the enemy had once again fled. Our chances of a successful counter-attack were fading with every minute, and we were venturing deeper into unknown territory with every step. I was appointed Lead-Scout and we continued our pursuit into the jungle in the hope of catching them as they retreated. Eyes wide open, my senses were on high-alert as I patrolled through the undergrowth with my weapon in the shoulder and safety catch off. I even switched my rifle to automatic fire, so if I did bump into the enemy I could get maximum firepower down on them in the initial engagement. The trees were close together and visibility was down to about twenty metres, so any engagement would be at close quarters, and I was determined to win the firefight. To our utter frustration, after a while we were forced to abandon the patrol. It was too risky to keep going deeper into the jungle. We didn't know what size force we were chasing, and we didn't know where or when enemy reinforcements might arrive. We returned to our positions in Lungi Lol and stayed there for several more days without further incident, seemingly the rebels had been deterred from trying again.

When the evacuation operation was complete the order came to extract back to the airport. We kept it low-key that we were going. The Nigerians and the villagers liked us being there, it made them feel safe, and they wouldn't be happy with us abandoning them, especially after we'd just smashed up a load of rebels. We had minimal kit, so packing away our things discretely was easy, but we couldn't leave the improvised Claymore mines behind, so we detonated them in a safe area then left with minimum fuss.

The RUF never returned to Lungi Lol. I think the PF's ferocity in defence, and eagerness to get after them had exceeded their expectations and ruined their enthusiasm. We were only a small group of men, but we were well-trained, well-armed, and well-up for a scrap. It was reported shortly after we left that the bodies of several more rebels were discovered in hastily dug graves in the neighbouring village, meaning the RUF had suffered a total of thirteen dead in the firefights with PF.

Prior to Sierra Leone the only anti-malarial prophylaxis I'd ever been issued were tablets called Paludrine and Chloroquine. We'd all taken plenty of those on numerous overseas exercises to places like Belize, Brunei, Kenya, Botswana etc. However, for that medication to be effective it needed to be taken every day for two weeks prior to a deployment, throughout the deployment itself, and then for four weeks after returning to the UK. Because Op PALLISER happened so fast, it was determined that we'd be issued with a different medication, one we'd never seen before, a branded version of a drug called mefloquine, and we started taking it on the same day that we flew out. It was much less hassle than the old stuff, only requiring us to take it once a week, but for a lot of people that anti-malarial caused significant side effects that presented within a couple of days of taking the first dose. Of course nobody had bothered to read the information sheet inside the box, it was either take the tablets or risk contracting malaria, not a difficult choice at the time. However, after a few days it became apparent that a high percentage of the blokes were experiencing symptoms such as vivid nightmares, insomnia, and nausea, so we decided to take a look at the leaflet. Sure enough all those things were listed as possible side effects, alongside diarrhoea, vomiting, dizziness, confusion, paranoia, suicidal thoughts, and psychotic behaviour. You could definitely make the argument that it wasn't the optimal drug to be issued to hundreds of aggressive young men with loaded weapons, hand grenades and a tendency for violence.

In the army you get used to taking medications you've never heard of. For some reason Ibuprofen was called "Brufen" and also known as "Smarties", because of the way it was handed out so readily by the doctors, and the common joke amongst the blokes was that any ailment or injury could be fixed with a bit of Brufen and some Tubigrip. I reckon I tried just about every pain relief option the medical centre had to offer during my time; Brufen, Codeine, Diclofenac, Co-Codamol, Voltarol, Naproxen, Cortisol injection, Shockwave therapy, TENS therapy, physiotherapy, heat, infra-red heat, ice, Tubigrip, neck brace, splints, and plaster cast. I even sought alternative treatments that the army didn't offer as well, like acupuncture, cupping, chiropractic manipulation, and sports massage. You also get used to being routinely vaccinated or inoculated against all kinds of obscure diseases as a soldier too, including hepatitis, diphtheria, tetanus, typhoid, yellow fever, anthrax, rabies, and Japanese encephalitis to name a few. You could walk into the med centre for a basic health check feeling fit as a fiddle and limp out five minutes later after being given five booster-shots, a week's supply of Brufen, a prognosis of imminent arthritis, and a vasectomy appointment.

After returning to the UK from Sierra Leone, a soldier from 1 PARA was admitted to hospital for a non-related ailment when a doctor asked him if he'd been taking any medication.

"Yes, I've just got back from Africa and was taking anti-malarials for a few weeks." he replied.

"Do you know what they were called?" the doc enquired.

The soldier told him it was Larium, but the doctor was immediately dismissive. "It wouldn't have been Larium." he said. "It would have been something else. We don't really issue Larium in this country." Apparently he took some convincing but was surprised and concerned that the MOD had issued it to its servicepeople. That was the first time I witnessed multiple people suffer an adverse reaction to a medication, with the most common symptom being nightmares. Every day and night in Lungi Lol someone would wake up screaming or severely panicked from their dreams, not the best atmospheric when you're anticipating an imminent attack.

Ginge, Paul with his GPMG, and Nick at the rear posing for photos with the Daily Telegraph in Lungi Lol village

In June 2000 I was part of a five-man team that went to Germany to compete in an international military parachuting competition in the historic Bavarian city of Regensburg. Team GB as we were called, was made up of three of us that came from 3 PARA, and two brilliant blokes that were originally from 216 Parachute Signals Squadron. At the time I had only completed about one hundred jumps, with around sixty of them being freefall descents, and was one of the least experienced skydivers there. However the contest also included fitness and marksmanship events which I was more confident in, so I was pleased to be on the team. Before it started we didn't have much time for any team preparation, but we did manage to get three practice jumps in at Weston-on-the-Green drop zone and went for a couple of runs together before the competition kicked-off on the 26th of June. On the 25th of June, en-route to the competition we were involved in a crash on a German motorway. Our team captain John had insisted on driving our rented minibus the entire way from Ipswich to Regensburg and refused to let anyone else take the wheel. I don't know what caused it, you could probably argue that his tiredness was an attributing factor, but all of a sudden there was a loud bang, followed by John shouting "Stand-by lads! Stand-by!" and the wheels screeched as we spun through a 540° turn at 60mph. We came to a halt facing the wrong direction on the carriageway, and John immediately drove onto the hard shoulder, with steam and smoke billowing from the engine. The vehicle was written off, we'd hit something, and the front end was smashed in. Luckily we were all ok and had a good laugh about it, and the hire company provided us a new vehicle within a couple of hours.

The airframe used for the parachuting was a German Air Force CH-53 Sea Stallion, a huge helicopter that could carry five or six teams at a time to the seven thousand feet jump height. Jumping from a helicopter was something I'd never done before, and it was exciting. I'd jumped from a tethered balloon, where you plumet vertically in still air, and I'd jumped from a couple of different planes where you exit into a violent slipstream, but never a helicopter that was moving forwards, albeit at a much slower speed than an airplane. To score points on the competition we had to jump from the rear ramp of the helicopter, come together in a 4-way speed star, then move into a 5-way formation as chosen by the adjudicators. Not allowed to leave the ramp holding on to each other, there were lines marked out on the floor of the helicopter that we each had to stand behind before the jump signal was given, then we'd sprint out as fast as possible and try to get together quickly in freefall. The jumps were watched through binoculars by judges on the ground and scored based on execution and speed. More points were available for landing accuracy and there was a small circular sandpit with a tiny pad in the centre for maximum points. The skydiving was great fun, and that was the only reason most people were there really, the other events were just token efforts to make it look like a bona-fide military skills contest. We got to do ten jumps over four days, had a go at formation skydiving, and enjoyed the obligatory hog-roast party organised by our fantastic German hosts.

In addition to the skydiving there was a running race, a shooting contest, and the first event, which was a swim. Stood beside the Olympic-size outdoor swimming pool wearing our normal green camouflaged clothing, we couldn't help noticing that most of the other teams appeared to be dressed in clothes that were several sizes too small. Skin-tight ¾ length trousers and shirt sleeves that barely passed the elbow suddenly seemed to be the latest fashion. Ours were the usual unflattering British fatigues, with extra-long legs and baggy shirts, and the penny didn't drop for me until the event began. The race was a freestyle relay with each member of the team swimming 100 metres before handing over to the next. Two lengths of the pool sounded easy enough, just a couple of minutes hard work, and after looking around at the competition I thought our team looked pretty good. My good friend Ginge, who I'd known for many years, and trained with hundreds of times, volunteered to go first. He was a very good runner and excellent tabber, so I assumed his swimming would be pretty good too. On the whistle blast he executed a nice shallow dive and resurfaced quickly, immediately taking the lead as his arms rapidly powered through the water like propellers. It was so fast and frantic compared to everyone else's smooth, controlled action, I wondered if it was sustainable. I turned to Bobby, another member of our team.

"He's either outrageously fit, or he's going to gas any second!" I said, suspecting it would be the latter.

Bobby was grinning broadly, obviously thinking the same as me. "Yep!" he nodded.

Half way into the first length Ginge abruptly stopped, and his head popped up as he trod water for a few seconds to get some oxygen into his lungs. I don't think he'd taken a single breath up to that point, working anaerobically, and was now sucking in oxygen from Timbuktu. After a few hasty breaths he continued swimming at a distinctly reduced pace, and slowly but surely all the other swimmers overtook him as he stopped a few more times to breathe, dropping him from first-place to dead last. It was becoming obvious that we were ill-prepared for the swim and were going to lose badly, but we couldn't help but laugh at Ginge, he was in tatters, and when he finally dragged himself out of the pool he promptly vomited water all over the floor. Even he was laughing, probably because he knew that we were all about to suffer the same fate. Swimming in those baggy clothes was like swimming in a heavy suit of armour, it was hideous, and by the time our last man entered the pool everyone else had already finished. We were crappy swimmers, but we did well in the running and shooting events, achieving the top two times and some of the best scores, which was far more important to us anyway.

In July 2000, shortly after returning to the UK, we deployed on an annual brigade exercise called "Eagles Strike". This was a well-established exercise that many of the blokes had done several times before, but for me, as a new member of the PF it was a first. As the brigade's advance force, we were to insert a few days ahead of the main battle group and gather vital intelligence on the ground and the enemy, before hundreds of paratroopers were committed to an assault. To insert covertly we were conducting a HALO jump from eighteen thousand feet, at night, with full equipment, where we'd freefall to about four thousand feet, before activating our parachutes, then steer them silently onto a designated area on a drop zone called Braid Fell DZ. At least that was the plan. In total I'd completed seventy-three freefall descents before that exercise, with only three of those at night, and this was my first time jumping into an exercise with a bergan fully laden with all my operational equipment, weighing well in excess of a hundred pounds. It also turned out to be my first experience of an involuntary turn during freefall. My exit had gone well, flopping forwards off the tailgate weighed down with the crushing weight of the GQ360 parachute, oxygen system, weapon, and bergan, but as I settled down into a belly-to-earth position, I quickly realised I was unstable. The left-hand rotation started slowly, but as I tried to counter it, I felt it pick up pace at a frightening speed. Like we'd been taught, I arched as hard as I could which slowed the turn down. I could feel my bergan was sitting off-centre on the back of my legs, so reaching behind me with both hands I grabbed hold of it and pulled it up as high as I could, but as soon as I let go the spin started again, winding up like a spring-loaded propeller. Moving my arms and legs into different poses I managed to find a stable flying position with both legs out straight, one arm out to the side at 90 degrees, and the other arm straight out above my head like I was hailing a taxi. Somehow, contrary to the laws of physics, that worked, and when I got to pull height I yanked on the main canopy handle as fast as I could, before I could start spinning again. My parachute opened nicely, which is always a relief, but when I looked down I couldn't see the drop zone. It was supposed to be marked by three white lights, but as I steered through a full 360° turn I could see nothing that resembled what I was looking for. There were lights all over the place, but they were mostly in the distance, and I guessed they were probably farmhouses or vehicles. By the time I'd descended to about a thousand feet I gave up looking, and instead assessed the wind direction, turned in to face it, and landed safely on some soft, sodden grass. About three-hundred metres away from where I landed was a large barn with some lights on inside, so once I sorted my kit out I grabbed everything and headed towards it, hoping I'd be able to orientate myself to where I was from there. Fortunately there were some RAF engineers in the barn who were there to collect our parachutes and take them away for re-packing, so I dumped mine off with them and headed to where they told me the actual DZ was. The rest of my patrol were waiting for me patiently at the DZ and gave me a good slagging as soon as I got there. They'd all managed to identify the lights and land in the right place together, so there was no doubt the fault was mine. My freefall position had definitely caused me to drift a long way off-track, but there was no way the lights weren't within my arcs of view while I was thousands of feet above the ground. I just couldn't see it for looking. The others had already done a map check while waiting for me, so within a couple of minutes we set off into the darkness on the long march to our target area. We'd only been going for a few minutes when we came across a stream, the first of many obstacles that weren't shown on the map. It looked narrow enough to jump, so we decided to remove our heavy bergans, throw them over first, and then make the leap with just our weapons and belt-kit. Tommo, the patrol commander went first, athletically clearing the water and landing safely on the other side, so I made a mental note of where he'd launched from and used the exact same spot. However, Tommo was a lot skinnier than me, and my extra weight proved enough to dislodge the hard mud of the take-off point, and I went feet first into the cold water, right up to my chest, momentarily taking my breath away. Whenever you go on exercise, you accept the inevitability that you will be getting cold and wet, but that was about as bad as it could have got for my first exercise with the PF. It was good for everyone else's morale though, they had a right laugh at my expense.

Military freefall is a niche capability in the British army that only the pathfinders and special forces are trained to conduct. So when one of the SF squadrons found themselves under-manned before an exercise to Kenya and invited PF to support them in August 2000, the offer was gladly accepted. Me, Bry Budd, Bob from the Household Cavalry, and another good mate from 3 PARA called Leo were picked to go, and after a couple of weeks training with the squadron in the UK we found ourselves in a tented camp in the Archers Post training area of Kenya. Our hosts were great blokes, who treated us as one of their own for the duration of the exercise and we had a good time working alongside them, practicing patrol skills, live-firing, and parachuting. Sadly though, two men from the squadron were killed in a road-traffic accident, and shortly afterwards the exercise ended prematurely, when the squadron were tasked with a hostage rescue mission and flown back to the UK at short notice. To highlight the mortality of the British soldier, and the inherent dangers of their work, another four men from that exercise were killed in the line of duty over the next six years. One in Sierra Leone, two in Iraq, and one in Afghanistan.

As a British infantryman I was used to spending a lot of time in Sennybridge, but as a pathfinder we'd often spend at least 12 weeks per year there, because that was where we conducted our selection cadre every February and October. By October 2000, a year after my own PF cadre I was helping to take a new batch of hopefuls through theirs as an instructor. It had been a whirlwind twelve months of courses, exercises, and an operational deployment for me, so I was having a brilliant time, and keen to encourage others to join too. As a DS I was demanding, but fair, and I treated everyone with respect. I didn't want anyone to feel the frustration I'd felt towards some of my DS, so I made it clear from the outset what I expected from them, and what they could expect from me. I saw no benefit in treating the candidates badly or with disdain, the course was hard enough without that nonsense. I called the officers "Sir" and everyone else by their first names, and when we were out of camp I asked them to address me by my first name too. In my opinion it worked well being a bit more informal. I was still in charge, but there was a mutual respect between us.

Before the cadre finished I was sent away again, this time as a student on the Section Commanders' Battle Course (SCBC). Passing that three-month course was a pre-requisite for promotion from lance-corporal to corporal, and the first half of it was spent on the phase known as "Skill at Arms". For six weeks we learned how to teach weapon skills on all the various weapons a rifle company would hold, from the very basics to advanced shoots, splitting our time between the classrooms in Brecon and the ranges on Sennybridge. Like most soldiers I didn't enjoy it very much, but I got to hang around with some old friends from the battalions who were also on the course and have a bit of a laugh.

It was during that course that I rekindled my friendship with a girl from school. We'd spoken on the phone a few times in the previous months and arranged for me to go to Aylesbury for a night out. Carmen and I had been friends throughout secondary school, and I still remember the first time I saw her in class. She started at The Grange a few weeks after everyone else because she'd swapped schools, so it was hard to miss the pretty new girl with purple punk-rocker hair when I sat down at the back of the classroom. The boy sitting next to me knew her from middle school and told me her name was Carmen and we became good friends. I'd only seen her once since I'd joined the army, but a mutual friend called Azi had passed her phone number to me when he realised we were both single, and both had a crush on each other. One weekend during the course I made the long drive to Aylesbury, and we went on our first date. We had a great night catching up, and I treated her to a McDonalds, several litres of alcohol, and a performance of the airborne two-step. I spent most weekends in Aylesbury after that, driving there on a Friday afternoon, and back to Wales on Sunday night. Skill at Arms finished, and I spent Christmas leave with Carmen as our relationship flourished.

CHAPTER TEN THE PATHFINDER

My second year at PF would be equally as hectic as the first. Courses, overseas exercises, and another operational deployment meant I spent significant time away again, learning, and practising military skills.

Straight after Christmas leave in January 2001 I was back in Brecon for the second half of SCBC, known as "Tactics" and the next six weeks were spent mostly in the field, traipsing across the unforgiving terrain of Sennybridge, and living in the numerous forestry blocks within its vast boundaries. Despite the horrible weather conditions and sleep deprivation this half of the course was much more enjoyable than the first though, because we were actually soldiering, instead of being stuck in a classroom reciting pamphlets word-for-word. "Tactics" was the first time I got to soldier with a broad range of infanteers from other regiments. I'd worked with Guardsmen on my first promotion course, but SCBC threw soldiers from every infantry regiment in the British Army together. There were Light Infantry, Armoured Infantry, Jocks, Micks, Welsh ,Welch, Highlanders, Anglians, Staffords, Kings Own, Princess of Wales's, Duke of Yorks, Duke of Wellingtons, Black Watch, Green Howards, Fusiliers, Gurkhas, Guards, and Paras, all with their proud histories, battle-honours, and traditions. SCBC reinforced my belief that the Parachute Regiment was the best of the best, but it opened my eyes to the fact that there were excellent soldiers in the other regiments too, and the men who performed the best were generally the one's who'd spent their career in the rifle companies instead of moving on to specialist roles. Tactics finished in February, and I was glad to get it over and done with so I could return to PF and crack on. I met many good soldiers from the wider army on SCBC and made new friends in the parachute battalions too. Overall I enjoyed it, and despite the best efforts of a few power-pissed instructors, who spent their entire time shouting and screaming at us instead of teaching us anything of use, it was a good course.

In March 2001 an international military competition called "Airborne Africa" was held in the South African city of Bloemfontein, home of the South African Parachute Regiment and parachute training school. I was lucky enough to be part of the five-man team that PF sent, and on arrival at Tempe Military Base, along with paratroopers from all over the world we were briefed on the competition's rules and schedule of events. It was basically a "march and shoot" contest, and every day there would be a loaded march of about twenty-five kilometres followed by a shooting competition. A kit-list was produced so that everyone had the correct safety equipment and to ensure we all carried the same weight, and the different types of shoot were also explained so that we could choose who would represent the team each day. There was a rifle range, a pistol range, a 60mm mortar range, and we'd also be conducting an escape & evasion exercise, and parachute jump. It sounded great. On the first day the morning parachute descent was delayed while the hosts cleared a pride of lions from the drop zone, but once they'd done that we all jumped in safely, using their parachute system, and earning our South African wings. The first march was only twenty kilometres long, so as a team we agreed to do it at a fast pace, hoping to take an early lead in the event. We were all fit blokes, and figured we'd be hard to beat, but when the jump was delayed we should have amended our plan, because instead of tabbing in the relative coolness of the early morning, we ended up doing it in the intense heat of late morning. In the first hour we overtook several teams that had set off before us, running past them as they walked along the dirt tracks of the training area. Most offered well-meaning words of advice as we went past like "Slow down", or "Take it easy guys", reminding us that it was hot, but we felt strong, so carried on. Along the route we also saw two teams that had already decided to quit. The Jordanians had completely sacked it. They were sitting on top of their bergans at the side of the track, complaining that the route was too far, and they were not walking any further, and a team from the US had also halted because they'd run out of water, and said it was too dangerous to continue. Not long after that we also halted unexpectedly when Taff, a big PF bloke from the Welsh Guards suddenly collapsed from heat exhaustion without warning. We got him in the shade quickly, and one of our blokes Dolly had him canulated and on an intravenous saline solution in seconds. Using the radio we'd been given we called for medical support and waited for it to arrive, while keeping Taff cool and hydrated. A few of the teams we'd previously overtaken filed past while we waited there, no doubt itching to say, "Told you so", but refraining, and after a long wait an ambulance arrived and took Taff away to the medical centre. It turned out he wasn't the only one who'd succumbed to the heat, there had been several others too, hence the long wait for assistance. When we eventually got going again, now as a team of four, we took it easy. Any lead we might have had was long gone, and when we passed a South African team that was dealing with one of their soldiers who was in convulsions, it became clear that the heat was a real threat to all of us.

At the end of the first day several teams withdrew from the competition completely. It wasn't just the heat, it was the organisation. There was insufficient water, the radios were unreliable, and the response time of the medical cover was painfully slow. The organisers amended the programme in an attempt to change their minds, reducing the daily distances and adjusting the timings, but for some the damage was done. We continued without further incident, and overall it was a good experience.

In April I went to Jordan on Exercise Sandhawk, where we were to run some training for a Jordanian special forces unit and conduct our own tactics, live-firing, and parachute practices. We stayed in a Jordanian army camp in the capital, Amman, but true to form the RAF detachment there to support us stayed in a posh hotel in the tourist district of the city. The first night in camp we were all getting changed out of our uniforms into some P.T kit when someone noticed we were being watched. The accommodation block was a ground floor dormitory with about twenty single bedspaces in it, each with their own bed, locker and window without curtains, and those windows quickly became full of excited Jordanian soldiers, jostling for position and staring at us as we got undressed and dressed. It was very strange. We spent a couple of weeks training in the desert, conducting military freefall from a C130 airplane and a Super Puma helicopter, teaching some patrol skills, and even got to visit one of the Seven Wonders of the World, the ancient city of Petra.

At the end of the training period our hosts organised a special meal for us all to enjoy together where I took a crash course in middle-eastern etiquette. We started in a large room with a long coffee table and two rows of opposing seats either side of it. On one side were the Jordanians who were already seated when we arrived and motioned for us to sit down too.

"Don't sit like that!" I was told as I got comfy in my chair.

"Like what?" I replied, completely oblivious to the unwritten rules.

"You can't show them the soles of your feet. It's offensive over here." my mate told me.

I sat up straight and put my feet flat on the floor so I wouldn't upset anyone, and after a couple of minutes we were called through to the dining area. The main venue was a large marquee with several high, round tables without chairs. On each table was a huge mound of white rice, and on top of that rice was a mound of perfectly cooked, jointed-up meat. The top-table, where the highest ranking officers assembled had an additional, signature piece atop their food pile, to signify their superiority. However, the Lambs head in the middle of their platter didn't look that appealing to me, and I know it didn't whet the appetite of our vegetarian Drop Zone Safety Officer much either. Apparently she wasn't very hungry that night, but as an officer representing the RAF she was compelled to take her place at the table. I was hungry but waited patiently for the cutlery and plates to be brought out so we could start eating, but the Jordanian bloke next to me seemed to be ravenous, picking at the meat with his bare hand and rolling it into a ball with some rice, before devouring it.

I looked across to my mates. "Someone's hungry!" I said sarcastically, then looked on as the others started doing the same. Evidently there were no plates or cutlery. To help me out the bloke beside me created another ball of food and offered it to me, placing it down on my section of the table and gesturing for me to eat it.

"Ah ok, thankyou very much." I said, before digging in to the platter myself.

"Steve you can't do that mate, it's offensive!" I was warned again.

I had no idea what I was doing wrong, everyone else was eating with their hands too.

"What have I done now?" I snapped. Nobody had told me that eating with your left hand was deemed as rude in the Arab world. The left hand was the dirty one, used for cleaning yourself, the right hand was the clean one, and used for activities like greeting someone, passing things along, and eating food. To be fair our hosts didn't seem bothered, and we had a good night out.

The PF selection cadre in February 2001 was disrupted by the foot and mouth disease that was sweeping across the UK, forcing the closure of public rights of way and military training areas, including Sennybridge. The cadre was almost finished, with just the final exercise remaining when the PF were told to leave, so the boss made the decision to take on the candidates that were expected to pass, on the understanding that they'd be tested on the next big exercise or deployment PF took part in. In July I was tasked with leading a six-man team on the International Long Range Reconnaissance Patrol Course in Belize, and four of them were blokes from the February cadre. A great friend of mine and excellent soldier called Ginge was nominated as my 2i/c, and it was our job to assess the others while we were all assessed by the ILRRP course DS appointed to our patrol. A brilliant bloke from 2 PARA, a Scotsman called Bob McLeod was our instructor, and his teaching style made the course far more enjoyable than Brunei. It was almost five years since my first jungle LRRP course, but I hadn't let myself forget how hard it was and knew it would be a real test for our new members. I also knew it would be a good opportunity for me to test myself as a patrol commander too. We spent a month in Belize alongside soldiers from the Netherlands, U.S.A, and Ukraine, cross-graining through the jungle conducting various patrol tasks like searches, close-target reconnaissance, and camp-attacks. I learned a lot about leading a patrol on that course and built some strong friendships with blokes I barely knew beforehand. When it ended we were nominated as "Best Patrol" and returned to the UK to find out we were deploying on tour to the Balkans.

Operation ESSENTIAL HARVEST in August 2001 was a NATO deployment to the Former Yugoslav Republic of Macedonia, now North Macedonia. When I heard we were going I told my step-dad, but to avoid worrying my mum, I told her I was going on exercise for a few weeks. It worked for a few days, but she soon sussed it out because of the media coverage, and she interrogated Dave until he told her the truth. The main British contingent was a 2 PARA Battle Group, plus the Pathfinders, and a squadron of UK Special Forces. Because of the size of their task UKSF asked for PF support, and we were temporarily attached to them to bolster their numbers, conducting joint patrols and stand-alone tasks as directed by them. For this tour I was nominated as the patrol 2i/c, and Gareth, who I'd passed the cadre with was the patrol commander. One of our first tasks was to overwatch the Tetovo Valley from a military base to the east of the city called Eribino Barracks. Fierce fighting between the ethnic Albanian and ethnic Macedonian communities had taken place there and was still going on, despite a ceasefire. Several rural villages could be seen from our high vantage point, including Ratae, Zhilche, Shemshevo, and Leshok, some of which were on opposing sides of the conflict, but in very close proximity to each other. Our first night highlighted the level of tension and hostility there when we observed a vehicle being engaged by multiple machine-guns as it drove along a road in the dark. The headlights drew a large amount of fire and we saw the red tracer rounds zipping across the countryside before the sound of firing made its way to our position. The vehicle stopped, turned around and sped back the way it came, with the driver eventually realising the lights were acting like a homing beacon to the bullets and turning them off. There was no apparent crash, so we assumed they'd got away, but never found out. I was on duty with my good friend Bob, a soldier from the Household Cavalry Regiment who held the unusual rank of Corporal of the Horse and loved playing up to the stereo types of the upper class Guards Division and mindless thugs of the Paras.

"Did you see the state of that crappy old car?" Bob asked me, continuing before I could answer. "The people here must be so poor and desperate to drive in an old banger like that! I feel sorry for them, it must be humiliating."

I had a good idea where this was going. Bob had one of the driest, most sarcastic sense of humours I knew, and I loved it. Neither of us could have identified the car from where we were, even with our night-vision equipment it was too far away, and the lights flared-out the optics.

"No mate, what was it?" I replied.

Bob went on to describe *my* car that I nicknamed The Red Bomb. "I think it was a shitty, old, red Vauxhall Cavalier." he said. "Like the one's taxi drivers used to drive twenty years ago."

"You know my car is a red Cavalier don't you?" I said, feigning offense.

Bob carried on. "Is it? You're joking! Well it can't be yours mate, that one was a K-reg, yours must be brand new with the wages you're on."

"Mine's a K-reg, but I'm pretty sure I locked it before we left." I said. "As long as the number plate didn't end in CVS we're alright."

"Bastards! They've got your car!" Bob snapped angrily. "Don't worry mate, we'll find them, we'll get your crappy little old taxi, I mean your pride and joy back."

That little joke kept us entertained for weeks. Every time we were together, and a vehicle got shot at, or we came across a burnt out wreck we'd get excited that we'd found the Red Bomb. Small things amuse small minds.

Neither side of the conflict took kindly to us being there, and that became clear early on in the tour when a British soldier was killed on the 27th of August. Sapper Ian Collins from 9 Parachute Squadron, Royal Engineers died after a lump of concrete was thrown through the windscreen of his Land Rover and struck his head, causing catastrophic injuries. He was only 22 years old. Ethnic Albanians made up the majority of the population in the Tetovo Valley, but ethnic Macedonians were the majority in the country by quite a margin, and both felt that our presence was hindering them and helping the other side. Ethnic Macedonians were being forced out of their homes and villages and couldn't understand why we weren't defending them, while ethnic Albanians saw themselves as an oppressed minority who's plight was being ignored. It was way above my pay-scale, every person I spoke to had an equally convincing argument as to why they were the good guys, and the others were evil. All I knew was we had to remain impartial.

One day in a village we'd visited several times before, I found myself separated from the rest of my team and surrounded by a hostile crowd. Armed Macedonian soldiers looked on apathetically as my Land Rover was rocked violently and pounded on with angry fists by the locals, who'd been hiding inside nearby buildings before the pre-planned ambush. The civilians weren't armed, but they were very angry, and I thought it likely they'd get the door open or smash the window and drag me out eventually. I told Chris who was driving to get us out of there, but we could only move slowly because there were men, women, and children in front of the vehicle. I'd already decided that I was going to start shooting the second the door opened, or glass was broken, and told Chris my intentions. The killings in 1988 of Corporals Derek Wood and David Howes by the IRA was at the forefront of my mind. They'd been dragged from their vehicle in Belfast and brutally murdered when I was a teenager and the images of their lifeless, battered bodies had been published on the front pages of every newspaper in England. There was no way I was getting beaten or mauled to death by an angry mob without taking some of them with me. I wasn't scared, I was just conscious that it was a very dangerous situation that could quickly escalate out of control. I remember staring into the face of a man who was banging on my window, screaming hysterically.

I was completely unemotional as I sat there with my rifle resting across my legs, pointing straight at his mid-section on the other side of the door. My safety catch was already off, and I found it annoying that he thought he could intimidate me. He was the one who was going to die first, he should have been worried, not me. The melee only lasted a few minutes before we were able to move away from the crowd and reunite with the rest of the patrol, but it was a stark reminder of how vulnerable we were to attack and how much our presence was unwanted.

During a patrol one afternoon we were informed of an incident where a man had apparently been shot in the head in a remote area. With no proper roads in the forest it was impossible for an ambulance to navigate to the scene, so because of our off-road capability we were tasked. Conscious that it could have been a trap, we made our way quickly but vigilantly along some eroded dirt-tracks and into the forest, arriving at the site within about fifteen minutes to discover a man on the floor with a nasty head wound. Standing next to him was a very frightened young boy who turned out to be his son, and who also turned out to be the person that had accidentally shot him while they were out hunting. One of our blokes, Rob, took control of the casualty, quickly securing his airway, attending his wounds, and canulating him to administer intravenous fluids, while another got on the radio to call for helicopter support to extract the casualty. Within a few minutes an Army Air Corps Lynx helicopter was inbound, and we used a smoke grenade to mark our location on the side of a big hill at the edge of the forest. The only clearing we could find nearby was very small and well under the normal, permitted dimensions of a landing site, so I was expecting a helicopter with a winch to come. However, there was no winch, and that pilot carefully backed his machine into the tight space, under the direction of his crewmen, in the most impressive demonstration of flying skill that I have ever seen in my life, with his main and tail rotors missing the trees by mere inches. The casualty and his kid were loaded onto the Lynx quickly, and the pilot expertly navigated his way back out of the forest and towards the hospital, where the doctors and nurses took over his treatment. A couple of weeks later I met the crew of that helicopter and told them how impressed I was by their bravery and skill during the incident. The pilot's response was humble, but very reassuring. "We thought it was one of you guys that had been shot." he said. Had they known it was a civilian it was unlikely they'd have taken the risk. It's great to know that your supporting assets are prepared to go the extra mile for you if you need them, and that they are actually as motivated and passionate as you are about achieving the mission.

Our area of responsibility housed a few ethnic Albanians who ranked high on the Macedonian Army's "Most Wanted" list, with the most prominent one being a man known as Sascha. One day we were tasked with smuggling him out of the village he was hiding in and transporting him to a secret meeting with government officials. I immediately took a dislike to him when he got into the back of our vehicle and pointed demandingly to a camouflage smock that was folded up on one of the seats. He wanted to wear it, so he'd blend in with the rest of us, and I handed it to him reluctantly. Being impolite was the least of his worries really, because if he got caught in our wagon we'd all have a lot of explaining to do, and he'd be in for a rough time if he was dragged out. We drove through a couple of Macedonian police and army checkpoints, with Sascha nervously keeping his head down, and delivered him to the pre-arranged rendezvous point without incident.

"Thankyou! You're welcome. Don't mention it you prick!" I said sarcastically as he jumped out the back of the vehicle without saying a word, leaving a hastily screwed-up smock behind him.

On the 11th of September I was standing in a cookhouse

queue waiting to get some food, when I saw footage of a passenger plane crashing into a New York skyscraper. There were probably in excess of a hundred people in that room, all talking, joking, and complaining about the scoff, but it was suddenly very quiet. My mum says that everyone her age remembers the moment they heard about the assassination of JFK but the two times in my life that I remember like that are the death of Diana, Princess of Wales in 1997, and that attack on the World Trade Centre on 9/11 2001. I watched that video clip over and over again as the news channel repeatedly played it, reading the scrolling headlines at the bottom of the screen that described what was happening. I was transfixed by the surreal sight of that huge aircraft ploughing into the building and disappearing in a ball of flames. The next day a senior officer from the UK came to visit us and gave a briefing in that very same cookhouse about what to expect as a consequence of the attack.

"Gentlemen." he said. "Yesterdays events will change the future of military operations. I know they will change your life, and they will certainly change mine. Be prepared to be busy on operations for the foreseeable future." Little did we know how right he was.

We returned from Macedonia after a successful deployment, and it wasn't long before I was off again on another course.

My team in Macedonia 2001. Rob, Steve, Gareth, Bob, Ash, and me.

In the PF every patrol had at least one Forward Air Controller, which is someone trained to guide a pilot and the munitions they are carrying onto a specific target. This can be done verbally or electronically, including the use of lasers, and is a priceless asset to have on operations. Along with my good friend Paul, who I'd done the cadre with, I was fortunate to get a place on the course in October 2001. We drove to RAF Leeming in North Yorkshire, and spent the first few days conducting theory lessons, before travelling to Aalborg in Denmark via ferry for the practical phase. Part of my course was a passenger experience in the back seat of a Hawk fighter jet. The aim of the exercise was to show us how difficult it was for a pilot to visually acquire a target on the ground from a verbal description received over a radio. All this while navigating and manoeuvring a plane at 600mph. The pilots that flew the Hawks for the course were a pair of old-school RAF officers, probably only in their fifties, but seemingly ancient to me at the time. Their names were "Sinks" and "Wilkie", and they were grumpy old buggers that had obviously exhausted their tolerance for stupid soldiers long before my course ever started. Over the radio they quickly became impatient and snappy with us as they got bored of simulating attacks on the same targets over and over again. It wasn't our fault, there were only so many buildings, bridges, or parked vehicles in the area we were using, but for these super intelligent, highly skilled aviators it was mundane and didn't test their ample abilities. To make it more difficult for us, and more interesting for them, they starting to make landmarks "disappear."

"No more using the wind turbines as reference points! They've been destroyed!" They'd inform us.

"Red roofed houses are no longer in play!"

"The crossroads are obscured by smoke and not visible anymore!"

The course was in rural Denmark where the farm land was very flat and populated with dozens of white walled, red roofed houses. The only other structures were wind turbines, so that really narrowed our options. During my flight in the Hawk I quickly understood their frustrations when the first student came on the radio and stated that the target was a red roofed building.

Sinks spoke to me on the intercom. "Right, look to your front and tell me how many bloody red roofed buildings you can see!"

We weren't very high, only flying a few thousand feet above ground level, but our arcs of view across the flat Danish landscape were massive, and his point was obvious, almost every building to our front fit that description, it wasn't particularly helpful information. Before Sinks wrote on his leg and worked out his attack run he gave me instructions on where to head for, then handed over control of the plane to me.

"You have control." he said.

I replied with the terminology he'd briefed me to use before take-off. "I have control" I acknowledged apprehensively. I'm glad I got the chance, and grateful for it, but I didn't enjoy flying that plane at all, and I only had the gyroscope, Sinks did the rest. At one point during a turn he'd told me to make he suddenly re-took control.

"I have control!" he snapped sharply.

I quickly let go of the gyroscope. "You have control." I replied, as we immediately straightened out.

He seemed pretty pissed off. "If you'd continued like that we would have spiralled all the way into the ground!" he said despairingly.

I wasn't cut out for that flying lark. Far too much coordination was required for my little brain to deal with, and I was letting the nose drop every time I did a turn. I was a bit disappointed with my performance, but it's not like I ever claimed to be a pilot, well maybe once or twice after a few pints while trying to impress the girls. As well as his ability to muti-task, Sinks also impressed me with his ability to withstand G-force. On several occasions he executed turns that made me feel like my body was being crushed into the seat. The anti-G suit I wore would automatically initiate to stop my blood pooling in my legs and I could hardly talk, pathetically trying to perform the breathing techniques we'd been shown, similar to those a woman does during childbirth. Sinks seemed completely unaffected, chatting away continuously as we hurtled across the sky, but I was in bits. Other students on the course had fared much better than me, taking the controls for far longer, and enjoying the experience. One bloke even claimed he'd landed the plane too, but I don't know if that was true. I definitely would have killed us if I'd tried that.

New year's eve 2001 was one of the few where I watched a fireworks display, and the only time I've watched one with a bunch of other soldiers. However it was from quite a distance because I was once again at the Air Mounting Centre in South Cerney, Gloucestershire, this time on my way to Afghanistan, and the displays were happening in gardens, villages, and towns in the surrounding Cotswold countryside. The two-hundred mile drive there from our base in Wattisham Airfield had been a feat of endurance for me and my good friend Bryan Budd. Soon after leaving camp when we reached about 40mph we realised the roof was improperly affixed to the windscreen and was lifting up, allowing a jet of cold winter air to blast through the small gap into the vehicle. After a quick discussion we decided to continue driving, because fixing it would probably mean stripping the entire roof off and starting again, and it wasn't that bad after all. However, we regretted that decision once we hit the motorway, reached 70mph, and watched helplessly as the canopy lifted even more, until the gaping hole was about a foot wide. It was absolutely freezing, and the noise made it impossible to have a conversation. Instead we just exchanged glances every now and then to laugh at each other, as we shivered violently. We'd missed the opportunity to stop and fix it at the start, and now we were part of a big convoy heading southbound on the A12.

In response to the terrorist attack of 9/11 the U.S military had just launched Operation Enduring Freedom to remove the Taliban from power, and now a multi-national force was required to help stabilise the country while a new government was formed. On January 1st, 2002, we arrived in Afghanistan, landing at Bagram Airfield, a large military base situated about forty miles north of Kabul, before making the drive down to the city. For that tour our trusted Land Rover WMIK's were only fitted with a single machine-gun in the rear. The extreme cold weather of the Afghan winter, the relatively low threat, and the intent to portray a non-aggressive posture meant our usual front-mounted guns were left on the shelves. It was a merciful decision that meant we kept the windscreen and canopy on, with only the rooftop rolled forward to expose the rear turret. At almost 6000ft above sea-level and surrounded by snow-topped mountains, Kabul in January is very cold, reaching as low as -27°C during our time there.

Kabul had a very distinct smell to it, especially in the early morning when people started to wake up and light their fires. As the sun crested the horizon a blanket of smog would become visible about a hundred feet above the city's roof tops, lingering like a sheet of putrid toxic waste. I've only ever smelled that scent a handful of times since being in Kabul, but when I have it's taken me back there instantly. I can't explain what it smells of but would recognise it in a heartbeat. To me it's like a mixture of burning wood, raw sewage, and oil, not something I miss.

Despite the fact that the majority of the population were reportedly illiterate, we were given thousands of leaflets to dish out to the people of Kabul that detailed who we were, and what we were doing there. Basically they explained that we were the International Security Assistance Force, were invited guests of the Afghan government, and were there to help. The massive wad that I'd been given was stowed away safely in one of the vehicle side-bins, where I assumed it would probably stay, but during one drive through the city someone in the lead vehicle decided to hand some out to a small group of people on the roadside.

"What the fuck are they doing?" I said to my driver, anticipating a negative reaction.

Instantly all eyes were on us, as people started to wonder what was being given away, and inquisitively make their way towards our stationary Land Rovers to find out. Within a matter of seconds that trickle of people turned into a torrent, and bodies appeared from all directions in what had been a quiet street moments before. Thinking that something of value was being handed out, and worried they might not get some of it, people swarmed the front wagon, holding out their hands, shouting loudly, and pushing each other out of the way to get to the front. A short bound behind them, my vehicle only attracted a few people, who quickly moved on when they realised I had nothing for them. We sat and watched as people walked away with faces of utter contempt, when they realised it was just a worthless piece of paper they'd been fighting over, and not something useful like a handful of US dollars or some food stamps. After a couple of minutes the crowd had dispersed again, leaving a mass of angrily discarded leaflets scattered all over the ground. No doubt somebody, somewhere, got a massive pat on the back for producing those leaflets, but in reality all they did was get peoples hopes up, and make a mess. Another waste of money. What it highlighted to us was how vulnerable we were to attack. A crowd had amassed in a matter of seconds, and completely surrounded one of our vehicles. If someone had thrown a hand grenade or pulled out a pistol at close range there was no way we'd have seen it coming, we'd have been screwed.

Parts of Kabul reminded me of old pictures of London during the Blitz of World War Two. Large areas had been laid to waste from years of fighting, with streets reduced to rubble, and lonely remnants of buildings standing defiantly upright as a reminder of what used to be. Some less-affected areas where the structures had been damaged but not completely destroyed had been reoccupied as homes or shops, despite having no roofs or massive holes in the walls. Craters from mortar and artillery shells peppered the roads and unexploded ordnance (UXO) lurked amongst the carnage. One day we came across a 120mm mortar bomb sticking out of the road where some children were playing. The round was partially embedded in the ground with the tail-fins pointing upwards. I asked my interpreter to tell the kids to keep clear of it because it was dangerous, but they were having none of it. He exchanged words with one of the young boys briefly before translating.

"He says it is not dangerous." he shrugged dismissively, apparently taking their word over mine.

To prove his point, the boy skipped over to the bomb in his little sandals and started kicking it excitedly. My driver instinctively put the wagon in reverse and moved us away from it quickly.

For clarity, bombs *are* dangerous, especially ones that have been fired thousands of metres out of a barrel and slammed into concrete at terminal velocity. If ever you find one, do not kick it! All we could do was record its location and report it, there was UXO all over the place, and we didn't have the time or resources to deal with it.

Our main job on Operation FINGAL was high-level liaison. After the U.S invasion, the collapse of the Taliban left a huge vacuum of power, and the coalition wanted to ensure that vacuum was filled with the correct people. Thousands of armed fighting-age men were in and around the city, and it was only a matter of time before some of them re-grouped, re-organised, and started fighting again. There were Taliban and other Islamic extremist groups, former soldiers and police who remained loyal to the previous government, and several opposing militias. We'd gather intelligence on different groups, working out who was in command and where they were located, then arrange to meet them, often driving many miles into the desert to conduct a shura, or meeting. Initially we operated in small teams of six men, split between two Land Rovers, but this left us extremely isolated and vulnerable, so we preferred to work in twelve or eighteen-man patrols whenever possible. To portray a non-aggressive posture our patrol commanders would normally go into the meetings unarmed, accompanied by one other man who acted as their close protection with a holstered pistol. Also with them would be the interpreter, and the rest of us would remain outside with the vehicles. That meant one man in the driver's seat, ready to move at all times, and one man in the turret, manning the machine gun. Typically the Afghans would have a much larger force on display, with checkpoints on the approach, men on the high ground and rooftops, and plenty more walking around with their weapons slung behind their backs. As a precondition of the meetings, warlords or leaders would be asked to assure our safety while in their territory, and to their credit, they were always good to their word on that, although we remained vigilant. My patrol commander was Gareth, who I'd passed the cadre with in 1999, and I'd always be relieved to see him walk out of those meetings unscathed, although he did express concern a couple of times about what had been put in the coffee.

"I might have to get myself drug tested after this." he told me after one such meeting. His eyes were like saucers, and he was grinning from ear-to-ear. The coffee was always served black and extremely strong in Kabul, and we didn't know if it was just caffeine, or some kind of special ingredient that gave it the extra kick. I never touched it, but a commander turning down the hosts hospitality during a meeting would be deemed very disrespectful. To avoid offending our hosts Gareth had to eat and drink something every time he went into a shura.

From those meetings we were able to gain a lot of information. Outside we'd record any names we heard, what weapons we saw, numbers of men, vehicles, uniforms, fortified positions, and tactics employed. Inside, Gareth would gather details on the hierarchical structure of the group, its claimed areas of control, numbers of fighters under command, and what they wanted from us. Some of the leaders made big claims about their power and influence in a bid to win favour with the coalition. There were so-called generals alleging to have tens of thousands of men at their disposal, but the numbers never quite added up. What became apparent was that loyalty could be bought, and allegiances quickly transferred for the right price. Hopefully our work out there helped at least a little bit in getting the right people into the right positions of power and authority when the regional and national governments were formed.

PF outside the Presidential Palace in Kabul 2002

In August 2002 I returned to the Fallskärmsjägarskolan camp in Karlsborg, Sweden, where I'd attended the winter patrols course two years before. There was no snow this time though, and it was a beautiful summer, perfect weather for the freefall training we were there to conduct. The Swedes were very efficient, enabling us to complete twenty-seven jumps from a Super Otter aircraft at 12,000ft in less than five days, under the supervision of an RAF PJI and parachute engineer. That was a great week away, but a few years later I learned that a good friend had sustained a terrible injury during it. Warren had only been in PF for a few months when we went to Sweden and I didn't know him very well at the time, so when he had a few hard-openings on his Fury parachute I didn't pay that much notice. Everyone has their own particular way of packing their canopy. Some people like them to snap open quickly, while others prefer it to be a bit slower and gentler. I'm not convinced that we could influence the opening speed that much really, considering we were falling at speeds in excess of 120mph, but I always tried to engineer a softer opening by rolling the nose of the canopy up really tight when I packed. I just assumed that Warren's packing wasn't very good, and he'd figure out his own method eventually, like we all did. Little did we know that he actually fractured his neck during that trip, but the injury wasn't detected until several years later, after he'd completed hundreds more descents, passed special forces selection, and been deployed on multiple operations. Once it was discovered, thanks to the diligence of good doctor, he underwent several surgeries to repair it, but the damage was so bad he was eventually medically discharged from the army and still suffers with constant pain to this day.

Parachuting is pretty cool, and some people love it, spending thousands of pounds on their own equipment and doing it in their spare time, but I never really got the bug. I always volunteered for jumps when the opportunity came and had some good fun doing it, but I think I was always aware that it was just a matter of time before an injury, or a malfunction occurred. I've suffered a few injuries from bad landings in my time, and was entangled with another parachutist once too, but friends of mine have fared much worse than me, with injuries including broken legs, backs, necks, ribs, and pelvis's. Some excellent soldiers I know have had promising careers cut abruptly short through the injuries they sustained from parachuting. I've also been on several jumps where people have had to use their reserve canopies, including me, and I've been on a jump where the person in front of me has died. Your luck has to run out sometime.

CHAPTER ELEVEN
THE PATROL
COMMANDER

In 2003 Saddam Hussein remained in power in Iraq, despite his defeat in the Gulf War of 1991. Based on intelligence that would later be debunked as false, a 160,000 strong coalition force was deployed to the Gulf once more, this time to disarm Iraq of "Weapons of Mass Destruction" (WMD's).

Prior to deploying on Op TELIC we were granted some pre-tour leave, and during that leave I called one of my best mates in 3 PARA, Mick O'Farrell, to see what he was up to, assuming he'd be visiting his family in Northampton like he usually did. To my surprise he told me he was in Watford.

"What are you doing there mate?" I asked.

"Fucking knob! What the fuck do you think I'm doing here?" he replied.

I had no idea. "Have you got a new girlfriend or something?" I said. "I thought you'd have gone home for a few days mate."

Mick sounded pretty fed up. "I was going to go home, but instead I'm sitting in a shitty, old, disused school, pretending to be a fucking fireman, like the rest of the blokes in 3 PARA!"

I hadn't realised that the battalion's pre-deployment leave had been cancelled in order to cover the Fire Brigade Union's strike action, and instead of spending quality time with their friends and family the blokes had been sent on Op FRESCO. The firefighter's row was over pay, but the irony was, the vast majority of the soldiers standing in for them were on far less money than they were, and they were about to go to war. That wasn't fair.

The night before we departed for Iraq I had a strange dream where a crazy old witch was looking at me through the glass panel of a door and cackling hysterically. I could only see her head and shoulders in the small square pane as she floated around in an anti-clockwise circle with straggly hair, white eyes, and crooked teeth. I don't know why but that dream really freaked me out, and I woke up in a panic, embarrassingly explaining to my startled girlfriend that I'd been scared by a little old witch. The following day we began our transit to Kuwait, stopping over in a tented camp in Oman for the night en-route. In the evening along with a few others I went to check out the entertainment, which was a large open ended tent with a big television in it, offering tea, coffee and a stash of free books that had been donated by other soldiers passing through. As if by fate, one book in particular caught my eye. "Dreams Explained" was a tatty old paperback book, with a damaged front cover and well-thumbed, yellowing pages. I picked it up and looked through the alphabetical index on the back pages, finding "Witches" near the end. Foolishly I told my friend Sean of my discovery, and he came over to look. I'd already spoken to him about my weird dream, and he'd already taken the mickey out of me about it. I found the page and all it said was:

"Dreaming of witches = Gay social times ahead."

Sean read it at exactly the same time as me, then we both looked at each other before he burst out laughing.

"I fucking knew it!" he said, pointing at me. "I've seen the way you look at me Brown!"

I got a fair bit of stick about that, and it was quite a while before it dawned on me that the word "gay" back when the book was written, was commonly used instead of words like joyful or happy. I think everyone else had worked it out pretty quickly, but they weren't going to miss the opportunity to wind me up.

In Kuwait we were housed in another temporary camp, with huge white canvas tents, surrounded by a high sand embankment. While we waited for the entire battle group to arrive and for plans to be made we conducted refresher training on the equipment we'd be deploying with, especially the communications kit. This was my first operational tour as a patrol commander, and I was looking forward to getting on the ground with my team. My 2i/c was another corporal called Steve, a very capable soldier from 9 Squadron Parachute Engineers who'd passed the selection cadre right after my own. Steve looked like a typical boxer, with a busted nose, square jaw, and broad shoulders, but the old facial injury was actually from a motorbike accident, and he didn't box at all. Initially I was surprised he was appointed as my 2i/c because the other men in my patrol were all exceptional Parachute Regiment soldiers, albeit junior in rank to him as lance corporals and privates, but I assumed one of them would get the job because of their infantry background. Steve was also exceptional though, and an awesome 2i/c from the get-go, using his experience from tours in Sierra Leone, Macedonia, and Afghanistan to do an excellent job. There was absolutely no need to worry about the cap badge he wore, and I couldn't have wished for a better wing-man. Also in my patrol was LCpl Bryan Budd, a good friend of several years and someone I'd served with in 3 PARA and on three previous operational tours with the PF. Lee was the third member of 3 PARA in the team, along with Ash from 2 PARA who I'd worked with in Macedonia, and Jim from 2 PARA, another veteran of three previous tours, all in all a formidable group of men.

One day we were relaxing in our tent when two men wandered in unannounced, then stood in the centre of it looking around curiously. One of them carried a large camera by his side. PF is only small, so everyone knows everyone, and strangers don't go unnoticed. I intercepted them quickly. "Can I help you gents?" I asked the one who'd led the way in. As soon as I'd laid eyes on him I knew that I'd seen him somewhere before, but I couldn't place where.

"It's ok, we've got unescorted access passes." he answered, flashing a laminated photo I.D that was hanging off his neck on a lanyard. "We're just taking a look around."

Strolling into other people's accommodation uninvited is not the done thing in the military, and anyone doing it is sure to arouse suspicion and mistrust. Not only was our military equipment, including weapons, ammunition, and cryptographic material in there, but our personal belongings too. You just don't do that. His card identified him as a member of the "Press" and I recognised him from the news, probably one of the British mainstream channels. Like most soldiers I had serious misgivings about journalists and their questionable motives because stories about us in the British media at the time were seldom positive, normally painting us as violent thugs, brainless idiots, or depraved alcoholics.

"Well you can't come in here mate, you need to leave!" I told him sternly.

He looked at his badge, then back at me with a deliberate expression of confusion before re-explaining himself and his "Access All Areas" authority. "We can go wherever we want. We have clearance." he stated obnoxiously. I'd had enough by then. We had confidential and secret documents in that tent and if that camera started clicking, I was going to smash it to pieces. "I don't give a shit about your passes! You two better fuck off now, before you get launched out!" I snapped. A couple of other PF blokes had stood up to see what was going on by then which helped the journalists get the message and they promptly left.

During the build-up to the invasion there were periods

of inactivity and during one of these lulls we decided to visit a nearby American base. When overseas, if you were lucky, a British camp might have a NAAFI shop, where you could purchase essential items like a celebrity gossip magazine, an overpriced packet of two green bungees, or some zips for your boots in case you were too lazy to tie them up. These shops often resembled a small kiosk, whose shelves were filled with equipment from a nine-year-old cub-scout's Christmas list, then stripped bare by a bunch of drunken, twelve-year-old cadets, during a midnight raid. U.S bases always had their much bigger, and better version of a NAAFI called a Post Exchange (PX) or Base Exchange (BX) and by comparison they resembled a well-stocked supermarket, with food, military clothing, equipment, toiletries, and electronics. As an extra bonus, they were also tax-free, so everything was really cheap compared to UK prices. Blokes would go in there to buy an ice-cream, and walk out with a pair of Oakley sunglasses, a hunting knife, a stereo, and a massive tub of protein powder. For me and the two others in my vehicle that trip to the PX turned out to be extremely hazardous, almost causing the first casualties of the operation. Driving to the PX along a good, metalled road we were stuck behind a military HGV transporting a large portacabin on its trailer. Travelling at about 50mph we were waiting for a good time to overtake it when the aluminium roof of the building started to lift at the front, then peel back under the drag of the headwind. Before we even realised what was happening the entire roof ripped off and flew horizontally towards our wagon, making me and the driver instinctively duck for cover in our seats as it rattled closely over our heads. It happened so fast there was no time to take evasive action or properly warn anyone else, but we managed to shout, "Take cover!" and "Get down!" between us as we both dropped our heads down towards the gear-stick, and for a split second it went dark, as the massive flying debris cast a shadow over us. In the back of our Land Rover was my good friend Sean, who'd been standing up in the rear turret the entire journey, facing backwards. Popping my head back up I looked at the driver to check he was okay before we both shouted "Sean?!" hoping he was alright too. I stood up and turned around to see him rising through the turret looking shocked.

"What the fuck was that?" he said in his strong Glaswegian accent. The roof had missed him by a whisker, almost decapitating him when he dropped to the vehicle floor after hearing us shout. We all started laughing as soon as we knew everyone was ok and saw the roof had landed harmlessly on the side of the road, without causing harm to anyone behind us. That's how the blokes reacted to most near-misses really, whether it was a bullet, a rocket, a bomb, or just a shitty job, we always had a good laugh about it afterwards.

Training continued wherever we were in the PF, and operations were no different. We had a plethora of niche skill-sets to maintain, plus an arsenal of weaponry and technical equipment to master, so there was no excuse for sitting around idle. Cross-training between different skills and disciplines ensured there was no single point-of-failure in any area, we had plenty of specialists, but everybody was trained to a high level in everything. Our best signallers, usually blokes from 216 Parachute Signal Squadron, used their expertise to coach everyone to a high standard in radios and communications. We learned vehicle battle-damage-repair methods from the soldiers whose original trade was R.E.M.E Vehicle Mechanic. Men who came from the Royal Engineers made sure we all understood how to set up explosives and detonate them in various ways. Forward Air Controllers ensured that every single man was capable of effectively directing the bombs and missiles from fixed-wing aircraft and attack helicopters onto enemy positions. Our best medics took lessons on first aid, with the blokes learning how to deal with complicated wounds such as a pneumothorax or haemothorax, and how to carry out a tracheostomy. Our tracking instructors taught us ground-sign awareness, to help us identify disturbance on the ground that could be a sign of enemy presence or an IED. We were always teaching, learning, practicing, developing, and rehearsing in preparation for the real thing.

Nuclear, biological, and chemical (NBC) warfare was a topic loathed by most soldiers for several reasons. It was extremely dull, full of doom and gloom, and loaded with hard-to-remember acronyms, mnemonics, and data. It was also hideous to practice, with instructors always trying to find ways to make it enjoyable or fun by making us play games of football or rugby wearing respirators and NBC suits. Despite their twisted efforts, it was never fun or enjoyable, hence it was the least practiced subject on the calendar that we'd swat-up on once a year, in order to pass the annual assessment.

While still in Kuwait the order came down for us to start taking nerve agent pre-treatment sets, or NAPS tablets, in anticipation that the Iraqis were going to use nerve-agent weapons against us. This was all part of the "Weapons of Mass Destruction" myth that had been used to justify the operation and would be a massive breach of the Geneva Conventions if carried out, but the threat seemed credible to us soldiers on the ground, based on what we'd been told about the Iraqi army's recent history. It was feared that Saddam Hussein might launch chemical or biological attacks by way of a bomb or missile strike. He'd already shown he was capable of doing it during the Iran-Iraq War, killing thousands of Kurdish people in the 1988 Halabja Massacre. The weaponised agents that the Iraqis were thought to be in possession of included the deadly nerve agent Sarin, the horrific chemical Mustard Gas, and Anthrax. We'd already been given the Anthrax inoculation well before arriving in Kuwait. Reluctantly, we began taking the NAPS tablets, with no real idea of what was in them and what they might do to our bodies. Like most people NAPS tablets massively disagreed with me, and after only a few days I ceased taking them. Everyone I knew suffered some kind of illness from those pills, the side-effects were awful, and continued use would have undoubtedly impacted my operational performance and capability. Like many others I decided it was better for everyone if I took my chances without them.

Apart from the anti-malarial medication we were issued in Sierra Leone, the only other time I saw multiple people suffer adverse reactions from inoculations was after receiving anthrax jabs, and after taking NAPS tablets. Anthrax is a rare, naturally occurring disease most commonly found in the soil and animals of Africa and Asia, and it can be contracted through touching, inhaling, or ingesting contaminated spores. The vaccine we were given was a series of three injections, administered over six weeks, followed by another one after six months, then a booster every year. Some of the blokes were in tatters after the first dose with cold sweats, fevers, and rashes on their skin, but luckily for me I was ok, with no side effects at all. The second dose had the same effect, with a different bunch of people getting sick that time including my good mate Tricky. Straight after our injections we'd driven all the way from Ipswich to Otterburn Training Area in North-East England for an exercise, and he was complaining of feeling itchy for the last couple of hours of the journey. When we got to our accommodation he took his top off and I was shocked at his appearance.

"Fucking Hell!" I said loudly. He looked in the mirror and we both started laughing. He was completely covered in an angry, bumpy, red rash, like he'd been rolling around in stinging nettles.

Several times during our stay in Kuwait the Scud Alarm sounded, to warn us of an incoming missile. Scuds were huge, 37ft long Soviet-era ballistic missiles, which were made famous in the first Gulf War in 1991 when the Iraqi Army fired them into Israel and Saudi Arabia, but they were also notoriously inaccurate. Realistically they were more effective as a psychological weapon than a credible threat, like the V2 rockets the Nazis fired into London during World War Two. The alarm would sound, people would take cover, and shortly afterwards we'd hear the missile pass overhead, sounding similar to a jet plane, sometimes we'd even see it.

The Kuwaiti desert is hot, very hot, with few places on Earth much hotter. Therefore, to avoid dehydration and heat illness you stay in the shade whenever possible, because shade = relative coolness. However, there is one place where this rule does not apply, and in fact despite providing shade, it actually intensifies the heat, acting like a combination of an oven, and a sauna. That place is called a portaloo, and in there you can lose 10% of your bodyweight through sweat within the time it takes to have a pee. As a soldier you get used to taking a crap in front of, or right next to someone else, sometimes it's into a deep trench, where four or five of you sit side-by-side, with dozens of flies buzzing around. Other times it's into a black-plastic bag in the centre of a company harbour area, or a small hole in the ground you dug out with your heel. In many countries, you'll have to check for snakes, scorpions, or spiders before taking a squat. In cold, wet conditions the portaloo is a small sanctuary where you can get yourself out of the elements for a few minutes, but in the desert it's like a form of claustrophobic solitary confinement that you inflict on yourself for the shortest time possible.

For many people, including myself, an unfortunate side-effect of the NAPS tablets was terrible diarrhoea, which meant regular visits to the portaloos, and it was during one of these visits that I heard the scud alarm going off again. I pushed the door open to see people running for cover in all directions while putting their respirators on and shouting "Gas! Gas! Gas!" Some people dived underneath vehicles, while others ran to the shallow trenches they'd previously dug in preparation. I just let the door swing closed, reluctantly put my respirator on, and finished what I was doing. Now, if there's one thing worse than being in a portaloo in the blazing desert heat, it's being in there with an airtight, rubber gas-mask stuck to your face, inhibiting your breathing, and slowly filling up with sweat. Eventually the Scud passed harmlessly overhead, and everyone carried on with what they were doing.

Any soldier that says they've never fallen asleep on duty is either lying, or they've never been beasted properly. Whether it's nodding off at the wheel during a ridiculously long convoy move or dozing while lying completely still and staring into darkness during an all-night ambush, we've all done it. It could be for a second, it could be for ten minutes, all you know is that despite your best efforts, your eyes shut for longer than it takes to blink. It's not unprofessional or lazy, it's just biology, the human body can only take so much sleep deprivation. I've seen people sleep in all sorts of contorted positions, in the freezing cold, the pouring rain, and the scorching desert. I've even seen people fall asleep while walking through the night, carrying heavy equipment, and I myself managed to fall asleep during a rehearsal of the Iraq invasion. We'd driven across the Kuwaiti desert in a huge convoy throughout the night and into the next day when we came to a halt on a long, straight, metalled road. The whole battle group was involved in the rehearsal, with hundreds of vehicles moving from checkpoint to checkpoint, Land Rovers, motorbikes, trucks, artillery guns, and armoured vehicles. It was mind-numbingly boring, just following the vehicle in front, and the lack of stimulation mixed with fatigue put me into a short nap. Snapping awake with a guilty conscience I lifted my head, looked to my front, and to my absolute horror found myself staring at a vast expanse of empty desert. Everyone in front of me had disappeared, hundreds of people had vanished into thin air. I looked to my right to see my driver Ash was also catching forty winks, then quickly stood up and turned around to see Jim sleeping in the back, and a long line of military transport stretched out behind me as far as I could see. I was now the lead vehicle. I tapped Ash on the shoulder and watched him mirror my own reaction, as his eyes opened wide in confusion.

"I'm guessing you never saw where the rest of the brigade went either?" I said. It was obvious we were as guilty as each other and we both laughed nervously.

"Where's everyone gone?" he asked. It was hard to believe that such a massive tonnage of hardware could have moved without waking us up.

I pointed straight ahead. "My bet is that way, but I'll check with the wagon behind us."

Behind me was a hard-top Land Rover with two soldiers from the Royal Artillery in it, and they were tired teddies too, waking up with a start when I tapped on the passenger window.

"I don't suppose there's any chance you saw where that massive convoy went?" I asked sarcastically.

The vehicle commander rubbed his eyes roughly. "What the fuck!? Sorry mate, we must have nodded off.

"Me too mate." I admitted. "No worries, I'll ask the next wagon." To my surprise the blokes behind him were also asleep, so I turned around, went back to my Land Rover, and got my map and compass out. It didn't take long to work out where to go, so within a couple of minutes the second half of the battle group were following on behind me as I navigated us to the next rendezvous point, where we were directed by a series of military policeman into a holding area. That was a long, boring day, but well worth the effort, because the invasion itself went like clockwork.

Entering Iraq on 20th March 2003 was an eerie experience that reminded me of the news footage I'd watched as a teenager of the 1991 Gulf War. The Iraqi army had set fire to several oil-wells as they retreated, in an attempt to hinder the effectiveness of our air-support, and the huge flames illuminated the dark night, while also creating a layer of thick, black smoke. We'd barely crossed the border when we were ordered to don our NBC suits in preparation for a chemical attack, which wasn't particularly good for morale, but to be honest the Iraqis had already demonstrated their lack of accuracy on previous attacks, so we weren't all that worried. It's frustrating when you are bound by a set of rules and conventions that your enemy has absolutely no regard for. To say, "It's not fair!" sounds childish, but it's true, and was a recurring theme on every operational deployment I was involved in. No matter how Machiavellian or treacherous our adversaries acted, we were always restrained by the rules of engagement, and our own moral responsibility to behave professionally. Launching indiscriminate chemical attacks was not an option afforded to us, but seemingly it was to them. Fortunately there was no such attack that night or throughout the tour for that matter, and history would eventually teach us that the whole "Weapons of Mass Destruction" narrative that the campaign was based upon was a lie.

PF temporarily came under operational control of the U.S Marine Expeditionary Force in Iraq, and we were tasked with pushing ahead of the British battle group to conduct reconnaissance on their behalf. The Americans were moving so fast that they were leaving their flanks vulnerable to counter-attack and wanted early warning if Iraqi forces started moving towards them. I was tasked with overwatching some main-supply-routes to the east of the U.S advance, including roads and rivers, and moved into "no-mans-land" with a team of twelve men, in four Land Rovers. Patrolling in vehicles affords several advantages, the main one's being the amount of firepower you can take to deal with any enemy encounters, and the stores you can carry to organically sustain yourselves for extended periods. Generally, distances covered, and speed of movement are massively improved too, but depending on the terrain and enemy threat, that's not always the case. In Iraq we were patrolling in areas where the enemy threat was unknown because nobody had been there before us, and it was our job to find out. At times the visibility was poor due to the terrain, buildings, or foliage, so we'd progress very slowly, sometimes not even getting out of second gear for hours. We'd trundle forwards for a hundred metres or so, stop, scan the area with our night-vision and thermal imagers, then repeat, investigating every heat source or movement on the way. The thermal imagers we used, called SOPHIE sights were brand new at the time, and a fantastic piece of kit. We were able to pick out heat signatures from well over a kilometre away, with a fairly crisp black and white sight picture that could be zoomed in and out or changed to show white as hot and black as cold, or vice-versa.

Within 24 hours of the patrol we'd identified a couple of Iraqi army defensive positions and established an observation post from where we could monitor a major road and river. Hiding four vehicles in the open desert is not an easy task, and we learned during that tour that it's only a matter of time before your position is compromised by the local population. Whether it's a goat-herder, taxi driver, barking dog, or wandering child, someone will notice the presence of four, big lumps of metal amongst the bushes or wadis, no matter how hard you try to conceal them. One day a white Toyota Hilux drove past our position, then returned ten minutes later at a much slower speed, almost stopping when it drew parallel to our observation post where two of the blokes were hiding under a camouflage net. It was impossible to tell if they'd spotted the OP or the vehicles, but it seemed pretty likely that they'd seen something, and half an hour later two men appeared on foot, walking directly towards us. Trailing behind them was a teenage boy, who acted very nervous as they approached, and stayed well back as we engaged them in dialogue through the interpreter. They were unarmed and wore civilian clothes, so posed no immediate threat, but despite their best efforts to appear friendly it was clear they didn't like us. Their demeanour was very military, and their questions were all about what capabilities we had, so I assumed they were either police or military, but they denied that and said they were fishermen. I guessed the child was a prop they'd brought along to soften their appearance as he was obviously uncomfortable with the situation, and after a few minutes they left, heading back towards a nearby bridge that we'd seen Iraqi soldiers guarding. Whoever they were it was time to move. We had to assume they'd be passing on whatever information they'd gathered about us to the enemy. We closed down the OP and relocated to another position several kilometres away.

The following night we were driving through an area close to our abandoned position when I noticed something out of place though the SOPHIE sight and told my driver to stop. Something wasn't quite right. I stared at a large mound of earth near to where we'd been hiding the day before. A slight variation in thermal signature didn't make sense, and I watched it intently for a long time before I saw movement. I whispered quietly to Ash. "I think there's someone hiding up ahead." Without taking my eyes off the mound I quietly spoke into my radio to alert the others and was quickly joined by my mate Steve from the vehicle behind. My heart rate had increased, my breathing had quickened, and my senses were all extremely heightened. In a whisper I explained to him what I thought I could see.

"I think there's people up ahead hiding in the bushes." My throat was dry, and my voice trembled slightly with excitement as I spoke.

Using his own SOPHIE Steve also observed the area. "I can't see anything mate." he said, before taking another look.

Thermal imagers and other image intensifiers don't work as well for some people as they do for others. The binary colours of black and white, black and green, or black and red, don't compute with some people's brains, and the grainy picture can lack detail. I was confident that someone was there, and as we watched I was confirmed correct, when the white-hot image of a man's face appeared and momentarily looked in our direction.

"Seen?" I asked Steve.

"Yes mate, seen." he replied.

A few seconds later another man appeared next to the first, slowly revealing himself from some kind of sheet or blanket that he lay hidden beneath. They were acting like they'd heard something, nervously scanning the area behind them, and I thought they must have heard the engines of our four Land Rovers. There was no wind or other noise, and despite the blokes' best efforts it was impossible to drive in total silence. The suspension creaked, the brakes squeaked, and stones crunched under the weight of the wheels. The first guy knelt up high on one knee and swivelled around through 360°, but without night-vision equipment he was unable to see us, as we sat motionless, engines idling quietly, watching his every move. His pirouette had been more useful to us than it was to him because he'd voluntarily showed us that he was carrying a rifle and wearing an assault vest with extra ammunition. The two men appeared to exchange words briefly before returning to the prone position and covering themselves over again, facing towards where our OP had been the day before.

I briefed the patrol that we had a possible enemy position ahead, and after a quick set of orders we quietly lined the vehicles up so the machine guns could fire onto the target if needed. Covered by two heavy machine guns and four GPMG's I took three blokes and conducted a silent left-flanking approach towards the position, halting in an extended line once we were close enough to get a clear view of the target. Once settled, one of the blokes, who'd moved into some dead ground, fired a flare into the sky to illuminate the ground, and also see how the unidentified men reacted. If they were some kind of extreme crazy-camping club, we'd ask a few questions and continue on our way, but if they were enemy soldiers we'd hopefully be able to take them prisoner and process them for questioning. The flare rocketed into the air, ignited, then descended slowly under its small parachute, hissing as it spiralled down. In its dying seconds, just as it started to fade, automatic gunfire rattled towards our vehicles as our would-be ambushers initiated their attack. I was kneeling down, looking through my night-scope as the first man leapt up and fired from the hip. I saw the muzzle flash and heard the bang of his AK47 firing, and my first bullet left the barrel immediately after his. The message I'd given to the blokes was "If the shooting starts, start shooting", because I wanted to win any firefight with overwhelming force. They obliged perfectly, and the hill was instantly hammered with 5.56mm, 7.62mm, and .50cal rounds. Shortly afterwards I gave the order to stop firing and we all watched in silence for any further movement. The four of us on foot closed in on the enemy quickly, moving in pairs until we were right next to their position, halting once more to watch and listen for movement. A few more shots were exchanged, a couple of hand-grenades were thrown, and then it was silent. We approached the position cautiously after another short wait and discovered a group of enemy soldiers, all of which had been hit several times and killed. I recognised one of them from the day before, except he was now wearing the uniform of a soldier instead of pretending to be a fisherman. We stripped them of their weapons, ammunition, maps, and documents, then hurriedly made our way back to the vehicles before reinforcements arrived. If it hadn't been for our thermal imagers we'd have driven right across their frontage and been extremely vulnerable, and although our firepower was greater than theirs, we'd no doubt have taken casualties. It was a lousy ambush on their part, or at least a poorly executed reconnaissance mission, and as we extracted out of the area the sky behind us began to light up with vehicle headlights and torches, as the Iraqi army scrambled additional troops to the scene. We were in enemy territory and at risk of counter-attack, so we needed to move with some urgency, but we extracted with caution, sticking to the tactics that had served us so well up to that point, conscious there could be more enemy patrols lying in wait. That task continued for several more days before we received orders to move to a new location.

Crossing the Kuwait / Iraq border on the night of the invasion

There's not a lot that will excite airborne soldiers more than the thought of an operational parachute descent, and word quickly spread around 16 Air Assault Brigade when the RAF flew some parachute jump instructors and hundreds of low-level parachutes into theatre. I never saw the parachutes, but I did see some of my PJI mates, and they were cautiously optimistic that they'd be dispatching the blokes in the near future, so it seemed a legitimate possibility. Our platoon sergeant, Nath, was tasked with taking a small team of nine men, in three Land Rovers, to recce an airfield far beyond the front line, with a view to use it as a drop zone for a much larger parachute assault force. At the time the troops that had advanced furthest north were the 2nd Marine Expeditionary Brigade of the US Marine Corps, but they had met fierce resistance at a town called Nasiriyah and were fighting hard when Nath's patrol reached them. To the Americans' surprise and against their advice the PF pushed past the front line, heading towards Qalat Sakur Airfield some 100km to the north, but it wasn't long before they started to question that decision. Intelligence had predicted minimum enemy activity along their route, but the reality proved to be otherwise, and they suddenly found themselves driving past several Iraqi army positions. The sheer brass-neck of the patrol's actions evidently caused enough confusion among the Iraqis to buy them some time, but eventually the enemy soldiers began to realise what was happening and started engaging them with their rifles and machine guns. Acknowledging they were in the middle of enemy territory Nath found somewhere to conceal the patrol and re-assess the situation, and as they observed the road they'd been using, they witnessed a convoy of Iraqi vehicles and soldiers speed past, undoubtedly in pursuit of them. After a quick brainstorming session and failed attempt to get air support the men decided their only option was to turn around and go back the way they'd come, hoping they could pull it off once again. The terrain to the east and west was impassable, and ambushes were likely to be already established to the north, at least they knew what to expect if they retraced their steps. It was the lesser of four evils. With headlights on, so as not to arouse suspicion, they got back on the road and headed south at a normal driving speed. This time however, they weren't so fortunate, and the Iraqis were far less hesitant to open fire. But, by some kind of miracle they managed to make it back to the safety of the US Marines at Nasiriyah, despite fighting through several ambushes on the way. Some good friends of mine were in that patrol, and none of them could believe how lucky they'd been that night. My good mate Cam was one of the drivers, and he described to me how he'd been driving with one hand and firing his pistol with the other as they drove through a hail of bullets and rockets on multiple occasions. My other friend Paul witnessed a rocket-propelled grenade fly between the front and rear axle of another of the wagons as it sped through one ambush. There were bullet holes everywhere; in peoples clothing, their equipment, one of the spare wheels, the seats, the jerry cans. It's amazing nobody was hit. I don't suppose we'll ever know if the Iraqis took any casualties during those exchanges, but the blokes did their best to inflict some, with all six vehicle-mounted machine guns firing, and the three drivers doing their drive-by shootings, gangster-style with their 9mm pistols. In recognition of his leadership and courage during that mission Nath was awarded the Military Cross to add to his MiD from Sierra Leone.

As a rule PF teams don't know the details of each other's missions and tasks. The blokes don't talk about their own, and they don't want to know anyone else's. This is a way of protecting each other in the event that people get captured by the enemy, because you can't give away information you don't have. One morning I overheard one of the other patrol commanders talking to HQ on the radio and was genuinely worried for his safety and that of his blokes. Chris was a good friend and an experienced member of the PF who was unflappable, but the subtle urgency in his voice told me he was in a dire situation.

"Jesus Christ! Listen to this, Chris is well in the shit!" I said to a couple of the blokes nearby.

Chris was explaining that he'd somehow walked into the middle of an Iraqi army tank position during the night, and as daylight broke, it was becoming apparent he was surrounded on three sides by armoured vehicles and tanks.

"Any minute now I am going to be seen by the enemy." he said calmly. "I request an immediate fire mission to cover my withdrawal." He gave instructions for the bombardment, asking for high-explosive and smoke rounds to be used, and after what seemed an eternity, the request was approved. The soldiers of the Royal Artillery did an outstanding job, delivering their munitions with pinpoint accuracy, and Chris watched as the first round made a direct hit on a T55 tank, destroying it completely. As the shells rained down creating thick clouds of dust and smoke, Chris and his blokes were able to escape, and make their way on-foot, back to their vehicles and remainder of his team before getting out of there at speed.

Before leaving Iraq we needed to dispose of any explosives that we'd taken out of its packaging. Not many other people were using it, and those that were didn't want second-hand stuff anyway. To deny them from the enemy if we were captured, some of our vehicles had been rigged with PE4 plastic explosives, and we'd also prepared several shaped-charges for different scenarios. Rather than waste it, we decided to conduct a demolitions day at an abandoned Iraqi army camp we'd stumbled across, in the middle of the desert. We blew up artillery pieces, munitions, armoured vehicles, and buildings that had been damaged during earlier fighting and abandoned by the fleeting enemy. It was good fun, and great practice. My good friend Bryan Budd used the opportunity to practice making an improvised "mousehole charge" in one of the smaller buildings. Using scavenged pallet wood, PE4, detonating cord, and duct tape, he made the charge, fixed it to the wall, and moved a safe distance away to detonate it with a shrike. The purpose of a mousehole charge is to blow a small hole in a wall, so that soldiers can gain entry to a room or building without going through a door. Probably due to a combination of structural instability and over-enthusiasm with the explosives, Bry's charge didn't just make a hole in the wall, it dropped the entire building, by blowing the walls outwards, and collapsing the roof in on itself, which gave us all a good laugh. That was one of the best days of the tour, we were like kids in a sweet shop, doing the kind of stuff you always thought you'd get to do in the army but never got the chance.

In the final days of our tour, while still in Al-Amarah our OC Nick Champion gathered all the patrol commanders together for a brief, and at the end of it asked us if we wanted to nominate anyone for an award. All the unit commanders had been told to submit their nominations to Brigade Headquarters, and he asked us if anyone in our teams had performed especially well, above and beyond what was expected. It was an uncomfortable question to be asked, and the first time I'd ever been asked something like that. Up to that point I'd always used the stories of World War Two or the Falklands War as a benchmark for bravery our courageousness, so the bar was set extremely high.

"Not me." I said. "Everyone in my patrol did a good job, but we didn't do anything special. The blokes in the second world war did much harder things every single day for years."

In turn, every other patrol commander replied with a similar response, with nobody seeking any special recognition for their team's actions. It wasn't a hollow attempt at modesty, or a deliberate effort to disparage anyone's achievements. We were proud of what we'd achieved, but we just felt like we'd done our jobs to the best of our ability, and that was what we were supposed to do. The boss explained that awards were relative to all operations individually, and that if we used the heroics of the soldiers of D-Day or Arnhem as a benchmark, nobody would ever receive anything again. He made a good point, and he was obviously right, but at the time, as young men, we were just happy to be on tour doing what we joined up for. In the end there were a few awards given to the PF for that tour that were published in the London Gazette on 31st October 2003, by order of the Queen. Nathan received his Military Cross, and each patrol commander, including me, received a Mention in

Despatches.

*My six-man patrol in Al-Amarah, Iraq 2003. L-R Ash,
Jim, Me, Bryan Budd V.C, Lee, and Steve*

CHAPTER TWELVE
THE SENIOR NCO

Despite being involved in several accidents and incidents, I think I've only ever been in shock once in my life, and that was during a military exercise on Salisbury Plain in 2004. We were inserting onto an old airfield at night in four Land Rovers, on board two RAF C130 Hercules aircraft, and we sat uncomfortably in our vehicles for about an hour as the pilots flew low-level around the English countryside. C130's tend to be either extremely hot or freezing cold inside. I don't know for sure, because I've never actually asked, but I assume there's some kind of temperature control system onboard, and there are four massive engines hanging off the wings generating a fair amount of heat. That night we were in one of the extremely hot one's and I was drinking a lot of water to replace the sweat I was losing, so when the loadmaster briefed us we were about to land I was chuffed to bits, because I wanted to get off. The wheels touched down and the plane braked hard, coming to a stop promptly, so we could drive out the back and they could get airborne again in quick-fashion. We exited via the tail-gate and immediately made our way to the pre-arranged rendezvous point to link up with the remainder of the team. It was pitch black outside. We were in the middle of the countryside miles away from any light pollution, there was no moon, and thick cloud prevented any ambient light from the stars getting through. We moved slowly and cautiously along the tarmac, because even with NVG's the visibility was poor. I was pressing the buttons of the GPS attached to the dashboard, concentrating on that when there was a loud bang, and I was launched forward into the front-mounted machine-gun. For a second I had absolutely no idea what had happened. Had we hit a wall? Fallen into a ditch? Been blown up? I was completely shocked, and nothing made sense. We were on an airfield runway, there couldn't be obstructions on it.

"Is everyone alright?" I shouted as I straightened myself out and stood up to look around. We'd collided almost head-on with another Land Rover. My driver and rear gunner both declared themselves as ok and the blokes in the other vehicle were all talking too.

"Get some white light out and check each other for injuries." I said. We'd only been driving at about 15mph, but the impact was still enough to wreck the front ends of both vehicles, and I wanted to make sure everyone was alright. I took out my own torch and quickly got around the other five blokes involved so I could see for myself. There's a lot of kit and equipment on those vehicles that could cause injury, but everybody seemed to be ok, apart from a couple of knocks. My good friend Gaz, who was on another wagon approached me.

"Are you alright Steve?" he asked me.

Until then I hadn't thought about that, and when I did, I realised I felt terrible.

"I don't think I am actually mate." I replied. I sat down, leant back against the vehicle, and suddenly became aware of pain in my neck, ribs, and hand, then watched as my legs started shaking uncontrollably. It was very odd, because I felt in complete control, but my legs were telling me otherwise, it was embarrassing.

Coincidentally, Gaz had just returned from a Wilderness Medical Technician course, where alongside civilian doctors and paramedics he'd received intensive training on dealing with casualties in remote areas. Using an aide memoire from that course he went through a checklist of questions and actions then told me his conclusions.

"I'm going to have to immobilise your neck and call you an ambulance." he said.

I was the platoon sergeant and patrol commander. "No chance Gaz!" I told him. "That's not happening. I'm fine, I'll see what it's like after the exercise has finished."

After a short debate about what I needed to do he made a fantastic point. "You send blokes on courses so we can deal with situations just like this, and now, as your medic, I'm telling you that you need to go to hospital to get your neck looked at. If you're not going to take my advice, then what's the point in having a medic?"

He was spot-on, and I couldn't really argue because we'd spent good money advancing his knowledge on the subject, and he knew more about it than me. I had a duty of care to my blokes, but it was only an exercise, and he had a real-time duty of care to me as my medic and friend.

I quit being stubborn. "Okay, do what you need to do." I said, and Gaz immediately laid me down on my back and wedged my head between two daysacs to immobilise my neck. A civilian ambulance was on scene surprisingly quickly, considering where we were, and along with my gunner Leon who'd injured his ribs, I was taken to hospital in Bath. My 2i/c took over command of the patrol and the blokes did a cracking job of getting the vehicles recovered before continuing the task on foot. It turned out I only had whiplash, a broken hand, and bruised rib, and Leon's ribs were busted up too. That was the shortest exercise I ever did.

2004 was the year I attended my third promotion course, the Platoon Sergeants Battle Course (PSBC) in Brecon. I'd already taken over from Nath as the PF Platoon Sergeant and been awarded "acting rank", but just like every other infantry soldier in the British Army I needed to pass that course before it could be made official, which meant another three months on the Sennybridge Training Area. I don't mind admitting PSBC was a steep learning curve for me, because it was classic rifle company stuff that I had relatively little experience in. I'd found my niche in reconnaissance, working in small teams with a good amount of autonomy, and I'd grown accustomed to working in PF with exceptionally motivated soldiers who required minimum supervision. In PF when you gave someone a task it got done, and you didn't need to chase it up or inspect it afterwards, because regardless of rank we were all on the same team, and all striving for excellence. I never had to shout and hardly even raised my voice at PF, but on promotion courses it always seemed essential if you wanted to impress the DS, who viewed it as a sign of taking control, or being a robust commander with a firm grip on his men. Obviously there's a time and place for it, to motivate or inspire your soldiers, or be heard above the noise of the battlefield, but to me the man who shouts unnecessarily has lost control, and his yelling will eventually become insignificant and ultimately ignored. If shouting is your default setting your ability to communicate a greater sense of urgency or intensity becomes limited. In my experience, a commander who is usually calm and collected can drastically change the atmospheric in a group with just a slight change to their tone, or a few choice words. A quote often attributed to former U.S President Theodore Roosevelt sums up the leadership style that I personally think is most effective "*Speak softly and carry a big stick.*"

I naively assumed that all the other aspiring sergeants on PSBC would be of a similar mindset to me and pull together, without the need for constant supervision, but that quickly proved to be an unrealistic fantasy. To be fair there were loads of excellent soldiers on that course from all across the infantry, plenty of whom performed better than I did, but there were also enough bad apples whose laziness or selfishness caused the rest of us a lot of pain and suffering. Once again the soldiers who impressed me the most were the long-serving rifle company men. To this day I think those are the best soldiers in the army, as far as actually winning battles and defeating the enemy goes. The men who stay in the rifle companies, doing the dirty work for years and years are the backbone of the infantry. Marching long distances with heavy loads, before fixing bayonets and attacking enemy defensive positions is their bread and butter, and nobody does it better than the British infantryman. Special forces, pathfinders, recce, and support weapons soldiers are all fantastic in their specialist capabilities, but for me, the most impressive soldiers have always been the ones who've paid their dues in the rifle companies and perfected the basics. In a classic force-on-force fight to the death, they are the one's I'd want by my side.

Driving out of Dering Lines camp in Brecon at the end of PSBC was like dumping a huge weight off my shoulders, because I detested that place. As I drove through the gates I stuck two fingers up at it and shouted, "Fuck you!" as I laughed out loud to myself. In fairness I learnt a lot there from some great instructors, and made good friendships there too, but the negatives far outweighed the positives for me. What ruined it for me more than anything else was the antiquated attitude of some of the DS, who prioritised their own ego over the learning of their students. They'd strut about the place like Lord of the Manor, loudly berating people for every minor infraction instead of offering advice or guidance, and deliberately interrupt their students at inconvenient moments to ask banal questions, in a bid to derail their efforts. On my course there was one in particular that I spent most of my day fantasising about beating to death. In a barrack-block, mess, pub, or street he'd have lasted two minutes talking to people the way he did on PSBC. Many of us were already veterans of multiple operational tours and had carried out the drills he was "teaching" us in the face of a real enemy, but he was devoid of humility and spoke to us like recruits, safely hiding behind his rank and instructor status. Attacking him would have spelled the end of our career and he knew it.

In October 2004 while at our house in Winslow on a weekend off, I got down on one knee and proposed to Carmen. I'd been thinking about it for a while and had even planned to do it when we were in Kos earlier that year, but Carmen fell ill during our holiday on the beautiful Greek island, so my plan to propose at a restaurant in the mountain village of Zia as the sun set was scuppered. After that the perfect, romantic setting seemed to elude me, so I decided to grab the bull by the horns one evening and do it in our cosy, hundred-year-old cottage that we'd bought together. I was surprised how nervous I was as I prepared myself to pop the question, and quickly downed a couple of cheeky whiskey's in the kitchen before entering our living room with the engagement ring in my pocket. True to form, the proposal was short and sweet, but I meant what I said.

"Carmen, here with you is my favourite place in the whole world" I said, kneeling down and taking the ring out. "And you are my favourite person in the whole world. Will you marry me?"

She said yes, and then single-handedly organised the entire wedding, down to the finest detail for six months' time.

Our wedding on the 9th of April 2005 was a fantastic day. Carmen looked absolutely beautiful in a stunning dress that her mum made by hand, and I wore a set of Parachute Regiment No1 Dress. We chose God Save The Queen as one of our hymns which got everyone singing and created a fantastic atmosphere in the 14th century St Laurence Church in Winslow. It was the perfect setting, with big, impressive stained-glass windows, a choir, and a charismatic priest. Father Wally was a nice bloke, who even loaned us his car to get to the reception, a classic 1930's, maroon, Austin 10. Carmen had thought of everything, the bridesmaids, pageboys, venue, food, drink, music, and photographer were all top-notch, and despite hardly seeing each other all night after the first dance we had a brilliant time. I was almost kidnapped by some of the blokes and taken to a nightclub in Milton Keynes, but managed to escape, and ended up the last person to leave the party, stumbling out of there very drunk with my new wife.

Not long after we married Carmen and I moved into a two-bedroomed mid-terraced house on the married quarters in Colchester. It was a far cry from our rural, character cottage in Winslow, and the first time Carmen saw it she actually burst into tears with disappointment. It was quite basic, and overlooked from all sides, but I thought it was ok. It was better than my room in the Sergeants Mess anyway. Carmen kept her job and worked remotely from home, and I was away a lot with the PF, so to keep her company we bought a dog, a Golden Retriever, who we called Barney.

One course that I never really wanted to do was the Military Tandem Masters course, because to me it all looked way too complicated. I used to watch the tandem masters go through their emergency drills before jumping and shake my head in wonder, and when they'd sprint out the back of the plane pushing a massive container like a bobsledder it just looked insane. I was happy sticking with normal high altitude parachuting, there was less to remember doing that, and it was pretty cool too. In 2005 I was asked to nominate two blokes from PF for the tandem course in August, which was taking place in El Centro, California. Checking through the parachute records to see who had the required minimum of two hundred freefall descents I found that we had only two eligible candidates, and I was one of them. Everyone else was either already qualified, away on courses, or didn't have enough jumps, so it was me and my friend Pete I put forward. The course began on 19th August 2005 and as it turned out I really enjoyed learning this new skill under the excellent tuition of the PJI's. By the 24th of August I'd completed eleven jumps with the MTVPS tandem canopy, six of those carrying a passenger, and was about to conduct the second jump of the day. The aim of that particular descent was to practice operating the main canopy by using the secondary handle. The tandem parachute harness had two handles for the main canopy, one on the left, and one on the right, so in the event that you were unable to reach one, you could pull the other, without having to resort to your reserve parachute, which was on another handle. On that jump I exited the plane nicely through the side door, went into freefall, and did a few turns to entertain my passenger Tim as we fell at 120mph towards earth. Approaching pull-height I signalled for Tim to bring his arms across his chest to brace for the opening and I reached for the secondary handle, taking a firm grip, then pulling. It didn't budge. I pulled again, this time harder, but still it didn't move an inch. I was surprised but not panicked, because I knew I still had several options available, so I went back into my neutral freefall position momentarily and started again, pulling with all my strength one last time before abandoning the secondary handle and using the primary like I had every other time before. That worked perfectly, and within a few seconds I had a nice big canopy above my head, and Tim was none the wiser. On the ground I saw Pete and found out he'd had no problem with the secondary handle, but the other two blokes on the course were still in the air so I'd have to wait for their results. As soon as I reached the packing hangar I found an instructor to tell them what happened and could tell they doubted my recollection of the jump. This had never happened before, and it could throw a massive spanner in the works for the course. Fortunately for me, when the other two students landed one of them expressed the same concerns as me, his secondary wouldn't come out either, so they had to take notice and checked out our parachutes. Apparently the handle was supposed to come out with about eight pounds of force, but ours weren't shifting when they applied over sixty. As a result of this the parachute was grounded, and the course was stopped until the problem could be resolved, so for the next week we squeezed in as many jumps as we could on other parachute types before flying home.

By the 1st of December the MTVPS parachute was fixed, and we were back parachuting in El Centro to complete the course. Strangely, I was never asked to re-do the last jump, so I had to take their word for it that the handle now worked. Military tandem parachuting is a much slower process than standard freefalling, especially during a course. We had to pack our own parachutes, practice emergency drills, brief our passengers, conduct the descent, then get thoroughly debriefed by an instructor before starting over again with the next passenger. On average we'd complete three jumps per day, and that was plenty. By the 5th of December I was on my 14th descent of the trip, a night HALO from fifteen thousand feet onto Shade Tree DZ. My passenger was an RAF officer called Rich, a nice bloke that I'd never met until earlier that day but had been kind enough to volunteer for the jump. Military parachuting can be extremely uncomfortable because of the amount of equipment we carry, and it doesn't get much worse than tandem HALO with full equipment. Attached to the front and sides of Rich's body was a heavy bergan, two rifles, an oxygen tank, and an oxygen mask. Attached to the front of my body was Rich, and on my back was the heavy tandem parachute system and my oxygen bottle. Pete and another student had already jumped on a previous pass when our time came, and we were waiting behind another student and his passenger for our turn. In front of us the other tandem master student was an experienced PJI called Jim that I'd known for a few years, and his passenger was his best friend Marc, another PJI who'd done about a thousand jumps himself. After a short wait, the green light came on and Jim exited from the ramp, immediately disappearing into the darkness. Rich and I waddled awkwardly under the weight of the kit to the edge of the tail gate and after a few seconds I received a thumbs up from the dispatcher. Weighed down with so much equipment it's very difficult to move and impossible to jump, so I tipped us forward and let gravity do the rest, falling in a steep vertical dive, momentarily going upside down before settling in a belly-to-earth position.

Freefalling at night is fun, but quite eerie and lonely. There's not a lot to look at high above the desert, so you just concentrate on keeping stable and search for the landing area lights on the drop zone thousands of feet below. Sometimes you can identify other parachutists by the small red lights of their altimeters or the strobe on the back of their helmet, but your main focus is keeping track of your own altimeter as the needle slowly rotates anti-clockwise. Our altimeters resembled an oversized wristwatch, with numbers 12 at the top and 6 at the bottom, so there was a small amount of maths to do when jumping above 12,000 feet. We'd gone out at 15,000 feet so the needle pointed to the number 3, but sometimes we'd jump from 25,000 feet which meant the needle pointed at number 1, then rotated 360 degrees anti-clockwise twice during our descent. That's a long time in freefall, and when you can't see the ground because of darkness or clouds, it's impossible to get any visual perception of your height. We wore two altimeters, which was a clever idea, because if one broke you could just use the other. The problem with that was, you might not be able to determine which one was showing the correct reading, so you'd be none the wiser anyway. During my service audible altimeters were brought into use, so you'd also hear a beeping noise in your ear at pull height too.

Our jump was going perfectly, the fifty-five seconds of freefall was nice and steady, the parachute had paid out smoothly at five thousand feet, and the three bright lights that marked the DZ were clearly visible as we glided across the desert towards them. Judging height at night is difficult because you have no reference points to gauge it from, so when the internal lights of a vehicle on the DZ suddenly came on, it was a bonus. I handed my passenger the spare steering toggles and explained to him that we'd conduct a slow 180 degree turn into wind above the vehicle. I had no idea at the time, but the reason for those lights coming on was the medic had just opened the door to retrieve her medical pack from inside it, after witnessing Jim and Marc crash into the ground violently. They had made a terrible error in their approach and misjudged their altitude, resulting in them hitting the ground while still performing a turn, and therefore moving at a forward and downward speed much greater than anticipated. Some good friends of mine witnessed that event, and all knew immediately that the injuries would be very bad. Pete, my friend from PF also on the course said the sound alone, with all the equipment clattering together on impact was horrendous, and he'd immediately feared fatalities. My own landing was pretty good, and Rich and I skidded on our asses to a halt on the periphery of the inner circle that marked the landing area. I hadn't even released his harness buckles when one of the PJI's came over to check we were ok. Paul was a very experienced skydiver with thousands of jumps under his belt, so I was surprised by the sense of worry and urgency in his voice.

"Jim and Marc have had a really bad landing!" he told us. "Jim's conscious, but Marc's in a really bad way. I'm not sure he's going to make it!"

In all honesty I suspected he was probably being a bit overdramatic and was quite dismissive at first. "Calm down for fuck's sake." I said. "They'll be alright." The RAF are much more human than the army and tend to wear their hearts on their sleeves a bit more, but Paul's instinct was right, he'd seen enough parachuting accidents to know when it was serious. Jim was conscious, immobilised on the floor, with a broken back and obviously in severe pain, but his only concern was for his good friend who was also immobilised, but unconscious. Marc was stripped down to a pair of shorts where he'd been examined for injuries but lay motionless with no obvious signs of trauma visible. Before long there were fire and rescue trucks, police, and a medical emergency helicopter in attendance, and Jim and Marc were rushed to a local hospital for treatment. Sadly, despite the best efforts of many, Marc's injuries were too severe, and he died two days later. Jim's physical recovery was slow, but he was able to continue his service in the RAF. Due to the accident the parachute was grounded once again, and the course suspended so an investigation could take place.

My sixth, and final operational tour with the army was back to Afghanistan, on Operation HERRICK, in 2006. Although called HERRICK 4, it was actually the first brigade-level deployment to Afghanistan since operations had begun in 2002 and was launched to deal with a deteriorating situation in the country caused by Taliban fighters. Unlike most of the tours I'd been on, this one was planned in advance, with time for pre-deployment training and specific preparation before we left. Because it was the first brigade-sized deployment of the operation and our role was unclear, it was decided that the PF would only deploy half its strength, swapping over the men at around the three month point. As the platoon sergeant, along with the rest of the headquarters I planned on completing the whole six months, but my wife was pregnant with our first child, so I was hoping I'd be able to get back to the UK when the baby was born and spend a couple of weeks on paternity leave before going back out.

During pre-deployment planning it was decided that for this tour the PF order of battle (ORBAT) would be revised, in order to afford us some enhanced capabilities and flexibility. We took on a combat medical technician from 16 Close Support Squadron, three engineers from 9 Parachute Squadron, and a four-man light electronic warfare team from the Royal Signals, a total of eight extra men. Of course we were apprehensive at first, we didn't know who they were, what their personal skills or fitness were like, and most importantly, whether or not they'd fit in. The nature of reconnaissance soldiering means working under stressful conditions, in small teams, with little rest, and no privacy, so it's vital that people can get along. Seemingly insignificant personality imbalances can become very disruptive to a group when you are living in each other's pockets, and there's nowhere to go to escape for a few minutes. Argumentative, impulsive, selfish, or narcissistic traits could be devasting to the morale and harmony of a patrol, and fortunately those kind of people are normally weeded out during training or specialised courses. The blokes we had were all fantastic, and proved themselves countless times during the deployment, integrating seamlessly into what was called the Pathfinder Group, and performing to the highest standards throughout. I have no doubt in my mind that without them the PF casualty rate would have been far worse than it eventually was.

We got to Afghanistan in April, and spent a couple of days at Kandahar Airfield, going through the arrivals procedure of briefings and documentation, before being deployed on task to Helmand Province. The day we left Kandahar the entire PF group was lined up outside, preparing our vehicles for the move, when an American soldier came up to me and offered me some 7.62mm machine gun ammunition. His unit had just completed an eighteen-month deployment, and were heading back to the US imminently, and while packing his kit he'd found some excess ammunition he'd forgotten about. To avoid dropping himself in trouble by telling his commanders, he asked if I wanted it. It was armour-piercing tracer, a type of round I'd never even seen before, so I had no hesitation.

"I'll have it mate." I said. "If you guys have got any more, we'll have the lot."

Over the next ten minutes quite a few of his colleagues

wandered across bearing gifts they needed to get rid of, including more 7.62mm, some .50cal ammo, and a bunch of flash-bang grenades. Everyone was a winner.

From Kandahar we drove our Land Rovers onto C130's with two on each aircraft, then flew to a disused airfield near Lashkar Gah where we drove off, then headed north-east for the town of Gereshk about fifty kilometres away. On the western outskirts of Gereshk was a Forward Operating Base called FOB Price, a small camp still under construction, and at the time, home to some Afghan Army soldiers, US special forces, and UK special forces. The task we were taking on had previously been the responsibility of a UKSF unit who spent a few days handing it over to us before departing for the UK. They'd covered a lot of ground in the area of operations, discretely gathering intelligence on people, places, politics, and allegiances, all the while gaining priceless knowledge and experience of operating in the terrain, and the capabilities of the equipment in the harsh desert environment.

Once the hand-over was complete we started planning our first patrol. It was nothing too complicated or ambitious, just a few days on the ground, exploring the area and finding our feet. Everyone was keen to get cracking with the job and get a feel for the place. I took the lead on the planning, and we quickly worked out a route that took in some villages that were yet to be visited by anyone from the coalition. Against my judgement it was decided that we would adopt the same command structure that our predecessors had used, which meant I became the Patrol Commander, and an officer took on the new leading role of "Ground Commander". To me this made no sense at all, we'd never worked like that before, and it created confusion as to who was actually in charge at any given time. I raised it with the boss.

"If I'm the one doing the planning, giving the orders, leading the patrol, and making the decisions on the ground, how is someone else in command?" I asked him. "What exactly are they in command of?" We rarely saw eye to eye on anything, and I was counting the days till his incoming replacement took over as the new boss. I suppose in some ways our relationship worked, as far as we scrutinised each other's work in detail, so everything was always cross-referenced, and any flaws brought to the fore. At the end of the day though, I was just a sergeant, and when my argument was rejected, I had to take it on the chin and crack on. I'd made my point, but I always understood my place in the pecking order, and when to shut my mouth and do as I was told.

After many hours of map study and planning, our first independent patrol was cancelled at the last minute. Much of the battle group hadn't arrived in theatre yet, and it was deemed there were insufficient assets to support us if we got into any trouble. Frustratingly the same thing happened again after we prepared to deploy on an alternative mission, and randomly, as a distraction, I decided to write a little story in my notebook to keep myself entertained for a couple of hours. I don't like hanging around aimlessly, I hardly ever read books, and don't watch a great deal of T.V, so once I'd done a few hundred push-ups and sit-ups I'd quickly get bored. Not knowing how to start my story I decided to describe the scene in front of me and see where it went from there. I wrote: "*It was like a scene from a 1970's American prison movie*".....................

After a couple of hours I stopped and read through the few small pages I'd managed to write, and it was actually quite rewarding, I hadn't done anything like that since I was at school. I decided to carry on with the story the following day, and as I continued with it I quickly realised my notebook wasn't going to be big enough and took some A4 paper from the Ops Room to use instead. After a few more pages my friend Adie offered me his laptop computer to borrow, and I typed up what I'd written to that point then carried on, writing several thousand words over the next few weeks, and giving it the working title of "Meatheads".

My concerns over our new command structure soon proved to be justified when we came under fire for the first time a couple of weeks into the tour. Not only was it our first contact, but it was also the first contact of any British troops on Operation HERRICK. Driving through the night we were approaching a small town from the south when a burst of machine-gun fire cracked directly above our heads. I quickly spoke into the microphone mounted on my left shoulder. "All callsigns, this is One-Zero-Alpha, stand-to, stand-to!" The noise and trajectory of red tracer rounds gave us an indication of where they'd come from, and we halted in our tracks to see what happened next, instinctively swinging our own vehicle-mounted machine-guns towards the likely firing point. The bullets seemed to be quite high, so initially I wasn't sure if they were even intended for us. The Middle-East is a volatile place where lots of people own weapons, and it's not uncommon for them to fire into the air in protest or celebration. The next burst cleared that up though, when the bullets zipped by much closer, and we could hear them striking the stony ground around us. All at once our formidable arsenal of twenty machine-guns burst into life, including mine, sending a hail of 7.62mm and .50cal rounds back towards our attackers, who must have immediately regretted firing first. We'd practiced that scenario so many times, I knew exactly what to do straight away, as did every other patrol commander in the group. We spent every second of a patrol anticipating contact from the front, right, left, or rear, that was our job, continuously adjusting our plans depending on the terrain. A few seconds passed, with hundreds of rounds fired in both directions before I made the command decision we were all expecting from the Ground Commander. Speaking into the fist-mic I gave the order;

"All callsigns, this is One-Zero-Alpha, peel right, peel right!"

As the lead vehicle and closest to the enemy I was first to move, so my driver Andy quickly executed a 180° turn and headed back the way we'd come from, closely followed by the next vehicle, and so on. The drill was going smoothly, with tracer rounds flying in both directions as we extracted from the killing area, when it was announced on the radio that a vehicle had overturned. The side of a wadi had collapsed, and the wagon had rolled into it, landing on its roof. In the chaos of the noise and darkness it was difficult to work out exactly what had happened, but I knew one vehicle was down and two of the blokes from it were safely onboard another one. That left one bloke unaccounted for, my good mate Chuck. I didn't want to risk leaving anyone behind, so I halted the withdrawal and moved back along the line until I saw the upside-down Land Rover. I jumped down from my seat and ran towards the overturned vehicle, using it as a shield from the enemy's bullets, and I heard several impacting on its metalwork and many more cracking overhead. The wagon was definitely empty, so I moved to the WMIK that had driven next to it in support. "Have you got Chuck on this wagon?" I shouted over the noise of the guns firing.

"I'm here Steve." called a voice from the back of the vehicle that was instantly recognisable as Chuck, so I double checked that everyone was accounted for then got back into my own wagon. As we continued, the incoming fire receded and once it was apparent the enemy couldn't hear or see us anymore we stopped firing completely, not wanting to identify our location by muzzle-flash. Our SOP at the time was to have the GPS of every second vehicle permanently navigating to the emergency rendezvous (ERV) and the remainder navigating to the next waypoint. That way we could quickly get ourselves back to a safe location without the faff of waiting for someone to reconfigure their GPS. I told my 2i/c to take the lead and we all followed on behind. The ERV was a small hill about 1500m away from the enemy position and when we got there we immediately got into all-round-defence, positioning the vehicles so that the gunners could observe their surroundings and engage targets, while protecting the drivers as best as possible. In the darkness the Afghans couldn't see us, but they knew the ground well enough to guess where we were heading and continued to fire sporadic bursts in our direction. I debussed from my vehicle and made my way over to speak to Mick, my lead Forward Air Controller who was in another wagon, about a hundred metres from mine. We'd already called for air support, and I wanted to hear the conversation with the pilot when he arrived on scene. As I walked I heard some loud snapping sounds on the ground next to me, followed by the unmistakeable noise of automatic gunfire in the distance, and I realised there were bullets striking the stones around my feet. I was in dead ground to the enemy, but out in the open, with nowhere to take cover, so I just carried on walking. There wasn't much else I could do really. I think it was just good luck on their part that the fire was so accurate, but the rounds seemed to be falling down rather than zipping past, so I reckoned they were beyond their effective range anyway. To be honest, getting shot at is quite exciting. Our blokes began returning fire again and one of them noticed a group of eight men moving across the open ground towards our upturned wagon. Seemingly they were in an extended line, using fire and manoeuvre tactics, switching between firing at us and the vehicle. I passed the order to prepare the MILAN missiles and await my order to fire. We couldn't let them have the vehicle, there was still a machine gun on it, stuck under the roof, and if it was still working they could use it against us. The soldier watching them through the thermal imager gave a running commentary as the enemy closed in on the vehicle, and we could hear the bullets ricocheting off it as they increased their rate of fire in an attempt to kill anyone still inside. Gaz, the same bloke who'd taken out a tank in Iraq with a missile, now had another one loaded, and was also watching the scene unfold through the thermal sight of his MILAN.

"There's a bloke climbing on the wagon!" he said.

"Stand by." I replied.

The urgency in Gaz's voice was increasing. "There's two on the wagon now!"

"Stand by!" I repeated.

"Three! They're pulling stuff off it!"

"Fire!" I ordered.

"Firing now!" BANG! The missile launched, and we watched as Gaz guided it onto the target successfully, exploding in a bright flash as it struck the vehicle. To their credit the Afghans shook themselves off and went straight back to the wagon to try and strip it of kit, but Gaz fired a second missile, and they abandoned their efforts, running back to the safety of their trenches, and taking their casualties with them.

The air support was taking forever, and the Sun was threatening to breach the horizon, so I checked in with Mick for an update. It turned out there was a conversation taking place at a diplomatic level about whether to drop a bomb on the target or not. The local police chief had reported an attack on his men too, so the jets were put on hold until the situation was fully understood. As dawn broke our telescopic sights afforded us a better view of the enemy position and the blokes started reporting on what they could see, including a man in what looked like a police uniform. To be honest, at the time, I didn't really care who it was, I just wanted to blow them to kingdom come. They'd tried their best to kill us, and came pretty close, and someone putting on a blue shirt, trousers, and cap, made little difference to me. I wasn't convinced.

A few minutes later the boss got a call from an officer in the higher echelons telling him to stand down. Apparently it was the police we'd been fighting. He took down the police chiefs phone number and called him directly, so they could authenticate each other as friendly forces, and arrange safe passage for us back towards the town. We'd just started driving back to our overturned wagon, when two white Toyota Hilux's appeared in the distance, and started racing towards it at speed. Leaving a huge dust trail in their wake they bounced across the desert, with uniformed police stood in the back, holding on tight. Our blokes sped up too, not wanting the police to get their hands on our kit before we got there, and we arrived shortly after them, just in time to take back the stuff they were already trying to steal and load onto their Hilux's. They weren't being shy about robbing stuff, they'd removed the machine gun and some of the blokes' personal kit that had been trapped under the vehicle. They were proper rogues, and I didn't trust them at all. Within seconds they were asking for an ammunition resupply and some RPG's, but I told them bluntly they weren't getting anything from me. I still think they were corrupt to this day, and I think they knew exactly who they were shooting at. I took two vehicles and drove up the hill to their fortified position for a look around. There were obvious signs that our fire had been pretty accurate, with blood trails on the ground, and bunker positions riddled with bullet holes. A couple of the men wandering around sported blood soaked dressings, and they said two more had been taken to hospital, one with a gunshot wound to his face and another who's fingers had been shot off. I think I speak for everyone who was there when I say we felt no guilt or concern for those blokes whatsoever, especially after they told us they employed two fourteen-year-old boys, who they used solely for sex, and justified it by saying their wives lived many miles away, so they couldn't always get home.

As well as the first contact, PF were also involved in the first mine-strike of the tour during a patrol in the Sangin Valley. Leaving our base at FOB Price under the cover of darkness we headed north on the western side of the valley, to take a look at the areas that surrounded Sangin itself. At that early stage of the tour we adopted our predecessors policy of not using tracks in order to remain unpredictable, avoid ambushes, and utilise the natural cover afforded by the hills and folds of the terrain. Deserts are littered with dirt-tracks that criss-cross the open expanses between villages and towns in all directions. Created by the local populace, who navigate them at death-defying speeds, they are not shown on any maps, and can be single-track or a hundred-feet wide. Using night vision goggles we manoeuvred slowly through the wadis and re-entrants, maintaining a low profile, and keeping noise to a minimum, but the creaking of the suspension and chassis, as the overloaded vehicles strained under the immense weight was unavoidable. With a couple of hours' darkness remaining we reached our destination and deployed a handful of men forwards on foot to look into the valley below with powerful telescopes and thermal imagers. As the day began, from our vantage point we were able to identify many things in the valley that weren't represented on our maps such as new buildings, river crossing points, and markets. We could also record the pattern of life, making note of things like popular routes, busy periods, quiet periods, gathering places, and local demographics.

Our task coincided with an artillery bombardment by the Canadian army to the north, and the only noise we could hear was the sound of their rounds exploding, echoing down the valley. Apart from that it was quiet, but through our telescopes we observed the hustle and bustle in the distance, like we were watching a silent movie, as people went about their day to day business. Several hours later we withdrew, re-mounted our wagons, and continued on our patrol, heading for the next village on the map. As we moved west the sound of the Canadian artillery continued, and all of a sudden there was an explosion which seemed much closer and louder than the rest, loud enough to make me turn around in my seat and check behind us. To my horror a black cloud of dust and smoke was billowing upwards in the middle of our convoy, and I immediately suspected an ambush.

"Stand to! Stand to!" I called on the radio, expecting to take incoming fire from somewhere imminently.

Seconds passed, with no sign of a follow-up attack as we waited, scanning our surroundings urgently, looking for the enemy, and I looked back towards the blast site. As the smoke was slowly dispersed by the breeze, a severely damaged Land Rover started to appear, and with complete disregard for his own safety, our medic Nick, a great bloke from the Royal Army Medical Corps, could be seen sprinting to the stricken vehicle with his medical kit to attend the casualties. The rest of us maintained our fire positions behind our machine guns and observed our arcs, looking and listening for any sign of the enemy, and our signaller, Jim radioed headquarters to alert them of the incident, calling "Contact! Explosion! Wait out!" My initial thoughts were that it was an IED that had been buried under some dirt and detonated remotely by an ambush party, so I was braced for an onslaught of incoming fire. A few more seconds passed without further incident, and I started to think maybe it wasn't an ambush. My mind was racing, trying to work out what was happening. Maybe it was a stray Canadian artillery round, or a pressure-plate IED that had been placed ahead of us, or an old anti-tank mine left over from the Soviet war. Whatever it was, it had inflicted severe damage to the vehicle and life-changing injuries to two of the three men on-board. Medical evacuation was requested immediately, and Nick did a fantastic job on the casualties, administering life-saving first aid until a Chinook helicopter arrived with a full medical team, and they took over the treatment. The vehicle that was blown up was manned by the three soldiers from 9 Parachute Squadron, Royal Engineers who were attached to us for the tour, two of which were very seriously hurt, with multiple injuries, including a leg amputation and broken back. After a long period of recovery and rehabilitation both were medically discharged from the army. The medics and Chinook crews were awesome that day, quickly recovering the casualties and the vehicle back to Camp Bastion. The only man on that wagon not physically injured, was a great soldier called Dave, who along with Nick the medic, volunteered for service with the PF straight after the tour. Both passed the cadre and became highly respected members of the Pathfinders.

Shortly after our mine-strike incident, PF were asked to escort a small special forces reconnaissance team into the same area, so they could look at a proposed site for a covert observation post. Obviously the task was accepted, and we met with the two soldiers who needed our help so we could pass on our knowledge of the area, both of whom were really good blokes and very grateful for our help. Their mission was to locate and capture a high-value target, a key player in the Taliban, and I suggested they relay the importance of the mission to my blokes, so they'd understand why it was necessary to go back into an area that we'd already established was mined. Dave and Paul did a great job of outlining their mission without giving away too much information, and afterwards, despite our original misgivings we were all pleased to help. Their target was a despicable creature, responsible for countless atrocities, and his capture or death would undoubtedly save innocent lives. This time we flew in by helicopter, landing quite close to the proposed site in some dead ground to the west, then walking the rest of the way, making the use of any goat tracks that headed in the right direction as a proven route. After only a few hours on the ground Dave and Paul decided the area was unusable for their purposes. Even though we were high above Sangin the high-tech cameras and scopes they had at their disposal were of limited use because of all the high-walled compounds in the town that blocked their view. We'd all suspected that would be the case, but they were very professional and thorough in their planning, and if nothing else it ruled out that option for them. We patrolled back to another area of dead ground for pick-up and flew back to camp. That night Dave and Paul were invited to our compound for a barbeque, and to say thanks they bought a load of beer with them, which was gratefully received and shared by us all. A short while after that patrol Dave and Paul were on another mission in Sangin town when they came under attack by insurgents, who greatly outnumbered and outgunned their small team. Sadly, despite a heroic effort, both men were killed in the fierce firefight that ensued.

One task that came to us that I wasn't expecting, was a foot-patrol into Gereshk town centre, to meet with the Chief of Police at his HQ. To me that sounded like a classic rifle company task that 3 PARA would have been perfect for when they arrived in a couple of days' time, but instead it was given to us. Despite its proximity to our base no patrols had been into the town, and I think the general idea was to show our support to the police, and at the same time show the Taliban that we could go anywhere we wanted. My first question was who was providing the QRF. The quick reaction force would be the people on standby, ready to come to our assistance at short notice if it all kicked off, but it soon became obvious there wasn't one.

"There's a few Marines that could probably help out." was all the assurance I was offered.

People talk about "gut instinct" and mine was telling me that this was a bad idea that someone had drafted on the back of a cigarette packet. Your gut will always tell you not to do something that's blatantly stupid or dangerous, but on operations it's overruled by necessity, because you're doing dangerous things all the time. The US special forces guys on camp had been in country for a long time, so I went to speak to one of their team leaders for some advice.

"There's no fucking way I'd do that!" he told me bluntly. "How many guys you got?"

"Eighteen. Three teams of six." I replied. That was the most I could muster, taking into account someone needed to drop us off and pick us up as well.

He was visibly shocked by that answer, leaning back in his seat wide-eyed. "No..Fucking..Way!" he said. "Who's your QRF?"

"We haven't got one." I answered, looking forward to his response. They already thought we were nuts because we didn't have any armour for our vehicles, and his advice was not to do it at all, saying he'd only go in there if he had a company of infantry in support. They were a good bunch, and they were doing some cool stuff. But when they went somewhere it was usually to smash it to pieces with an overwhelming force. Quickly in and out, they didn't muck about.

I decided to conduct the patrol like we did in Northern Ireland, with my team of six in the middle, and a team either side of me on separate streets that paralleled mine. Some of the blokes had never done urban patrolling before, and several were non-infantry so there was a bit of preparation to be done, but everyone was more than capable, and keen to get on with it. We got dropped off on the outer limits of the town in the middle of the night, and using night-vision goggles, patrolled towards the centre. We moved quietly, but not quiet enough that a dog in a nearby compound didn't hear us almost immediately, and like any good guard dog it started barking, blatantly telling all the other dogs we were coming. I love dogs, but those one's were right pricks.

The world's luckiest man lives in Gereshk. I know this because I met him that night when he suddenly appeared on top of a wall behind me, probably investigating what all the dogs were barking at. The sound of his AK47 clattering off the wall as he climbed on top of it alerted me to his presence, and when I turned with my rifle in the aim I soon saw that every other bloke had heard him too. For a couple of seconds eighteen red dots weaved around in small circles on his torso as we all trained our weapons on him. Fortunately for him his weapon was hanging by his side on a sling and not pointing at us, or we'd have turned him into a human golf course, with eighteen holes in him. He didn't hang about when he saw those dots, rapidly dropping back down the other side of the wall and disappearing. We had no idea who he was, he could have been police, a guard, Taliban, or just a hyper-vigilant home owner, but he was very lucky not to get shot that night.

Before the Sun even came up people started to slowly appear in the streets. A few street traders began setting out their stalls, a delivery-man on a bike rode past, with a big pile of freshly baked bread balanced on the back, and others made their early morning walk to work. All of them stopped still in their tracks when they saw our sinister silhouettes moving malevolently through the shadows.

"Salaam alaykum" we said quietly, in a subtle display of non-aggression.

In the darkness our pathetic language skills immediately identified us as non-Afghans, and the locals just nodded in reply, waved hesitantly, or completely ignored us. They were understandably cautious, and as much as we were trying to present a non-threatening posture, a group of well-armed foreign men patrolling through the streets is inevitably going to cause some alarm to the population.

We arrived at the police station without incident and met with the local commander to be told the usual spiel that he was in control of the town, but needed more men, weapons, uniforms, vehicles, and money. It was the same story wherever we went, and the commanders would always claim they hadn't been paid for the last six to twelve months. Whether they had or not was impossible to know, but they never missed the opportunity to plead poverty, hoping we'd be able to do something about it. The problem was, there was so much blatant corruption, and so many conflicting statements about who was really in charge, we didn't know who to believe. In some towns the locals would tell us that the police were working for the Taliban, or that they were just a bunch of rogue vigilantes who beat and robbed people every night with impunity. The best we could do was record it and report it, because they were all very desperate, and equally convincing. The truth probably rested somewhere firmly in the middle.

Accompanied by a couple of police officers we left the station and continued our patrol around the town, this time deliberately overt, and making our presence known. Almost immediately after leaving the police compound a Toyota Hilux drove past my team with eight armed men sitting in the back. They wore civilian clothes, mostly black or blue dish-dashes, and turbans, and all had long beards. They also looked extremely displeased to see us, exchanging dirty looks with my blokes as they continued down the road. From what I knew about the Taliban, that was exactly how I'd have expected them to look, but I also knew that there were a lot of police who didn't own uniforms, and there was no way the Taliban would be so audacious as to brazenly drive past a police station and foot patrol in broad daylight. I called my interpreter over.

"Who were the men in that vehicle?" I asked him. Pointing to the Hilux driving into the distance. "Are they police?"

"No. They are Taliban." he replied matter-of-factly.

I shook my head. "No, no, they can't be Taliban." I said. "Ask the policeman who they were."

The interpreter ushered one of the police men over and spoke to him in Arabic, but the only word I recognised from the officers mouth was "Taliban". He turned back to me and translated.

"He says they are Taliban." he confirmed.

It was an extremely frustrating situation, because in all likelihood they were Taliban, but there was no way for us to know with any certainty. Lots of people wore the exact same clothing as them, lots of people had weapons, and lots of people looked at us like they wanted to kill us. Even if we'd stopped and searched them, they'd have just lied, and we'd have been powerless to prove them wrong or do anything. It was similar to Northern Ireland in that sense, the enemy were hiding in plain sight, and the only time we got to engage them on equal terms was when they made the first move and we reacted. Our hands were tied behind our backs, and they knew it.

On the 13th of May 2006, the PF Ops Room in Gereshk received a call from my wife to say she'd gone into labour. I'd been out on a patrol but was heading back to base and received the news as soon as I returned. Two of the other blokes were flying back to the UK that night and both offered to give me their places on the plane, but there was no way I was messing up someone else's leave just so I could get home a bit quicker. All three of us took a helicopter flight to Kandahar Airfield, and within a couple of hours my good friend Gilly had secured me a seat on a plane that was leaving the following morning. I don't know how he did it because the flight was full, but Gilly had an ability to get things done like no one else I ever met, he was the kind of bloke who could sell sand to an Arab, ice to an Eskimo, and bacon butties at a Bar Mitzvah.

In Kandahar I received a message that Carmen had given birth and that her and the baby were both in good health. Gilly got hold of a satellite phone from somewhere and I called her to learn I was the father of a baby boy. It was a short call, but it was good to hear everything was ok, and to be able to tell her I was on my way home.

In my early twenties I once told a girlfriend that my top three priorities were: Beer, the army, and then her. She was unsurprised. "Yes, that sounds about right." she replied.

I was a little bit disturbed she accepted that so easily, I was obviously underperforming in my role as a boyfriend.

"I'm only joking! Of course they're not my priorities. What

kind of man do you take me for?" I said, before setting things straight. "My priorities are the army first, then beer, then you." It was intended as a joke, but in reality we both knew there was an element of truth in it.

The first time I saw my son Luke was the 14th of May 2006, the day after he was born in Colchester hospital, and that day, for the first time in my life, my number one priority was suddenly apparent to me. Before then it had always been cloudy, with my job and relationships competing for the top spot. Now it was crystal clear, my family came first and whatever came second was a long way behind. It's hard to appreciate that rapid onset of responsibility, and I certainly wasn't expecting it, but it was real. Everything I did from that moment forward was for that tiny, one-day-old boy, to do my best to ensure he'd grow up safe, protected, and loved. That evening we returned to our two-bedroom, terraced house on the married quarters as proud parents, and I spent paternity leave learning how to feed, burp, bathe, comfort, entertain, and nappy change a baby.

While back in the UK it was announced that my ill-fated tandem master course was going to recommence in July, almost a year after we'd started it. It was decided that I would stay in the UK, fly out to the US, complete the course, then redeploy to Afghanistan on return. The PF blokes were coming and going from the tour periodically, so there was plenty of work to get on with in Colchester with many of them getting on military courses while they could. When July came I went back to California with the RAF, finally qualifying as a tandem master on the 26th of July 2006. While at the US Naval Air Facility in El Centro I was able to stay in communications with the PF ops room and received daily emails about their situation. It was hideous to learn that while I was in America the blokes were having daily battles with the Taliban, who were constantly attacking the compound they'd occupied in the town of Musa Qala. Under siege from hundreds of well-armed militants who attacked from all sides, the PF, led by the new O.C Major Nick Wight-Boycott, acquitted themselves excellently, repelling multiple assaults with limited resources and fire support from the RAF and Royal Artillery. Luckily when a Danish reconnaissance squadron eventually arrived and took over command of the compound the PF had suffered only one serious casualty, Andy the sergeant major, who'd been accidentally shot in the arm by an Afghan policeman. That siege was a testament to the command, leadership, skills, discipline, and tenacity of the PF soldiers who were there, and is another proud piece of British airborne forces and PF history. The significance of the siege was acknowledged by the awarding of the Military Cross to my good friend Mark Wilson, who risked his own life to rescue a Danish soldier under intense enemy fire. Mark, who was a private at the time, was the third recipient of the MC during my first seven years at Pathfinders, along with one MBE and several Mention in Despatches amongst the ranks, phenomenal for such a small unit.

I finished the tandem course and shortly afterwards redeployed to Helmand to see out the final months of the tour. While I'd been away the fighting had been intense, and it was starting to show on the soldiers faces, who looked tired. After four months of rations and irregular routine most had lost several pounds in weight, and looked lean in their baggy desert combat clothing, which was already becoming tatty and faded from the harsh conditions. Being at home while my mates were fighting the enemy had made me feel extremely guilty, like I'd abandoned them, so it felt good to get back. However, within hours of returning the harsh reality of conflict struck like a bolt of lightning when I learned that my good friend Bryan Budd had just been killed during a firefight with the Taliban. In recognition of his outstanding bravery Bry was posthumously awarded the Victoria Cross, Britain's highest military ward.

Since I'd left, some of the others had also gone back to the UK and their replacements had taken over, and it wasn't long before my entire team comprised of different men to those I'd started with in April. Once again I had a strong bunch of excellent soldiers in my patrol, and we were soon on another reconnaissance mission, this time to a suspected supply route for foreign fighters and munitions. That patrol presented us with the most challenging driving conditions I've ever experienced, pushing the vehicles and drivers to their limits. There were steep climbs and descents, sharp granite rocks that punctured the tyres, and worst of all, areas of deep, soft sand that the over-laden Land Rovers sank into up to their axles. We spent hours digging out the vehicles, using the shovels and sand-channels we carried. There was one day where we were doing it every five minutes, and even the best drivers got stuck. If the Taliban had attacked us that day, we'd have been in a world of pain. In my patrol report I recommended that nobody should ever attempt driving wheeled vehicles in that area again. Through sheer determination we got through it, and eventually onto firmer ground, but the wagons had taken a battering, and one of them needed a new clutch. A Chinook helicopter, with the spare part and a team of two vehicle mechanics was despatched, and we secured a landing site for their drop-off. They arrived with the new clutch, heavy lifting equipment, and tools, and got cracking with the task, grafting into the evening. Before they finished I received a call over the radio with new orders to move south to the town of Garmsir. The Afghan army were launching an attack on the Taliban there first thing in the morning, and we were tasked with gathering information on a bridge in the target area before the assault began. Based on the slow progress we were making across the terrain I was sceptical that we could get there on time but promised to do my best and briefed the blokes on the new plan for the night. Assisted by the PF lads, the REME mechanics did a fantastic job fixing the wagon in sub-optimal conditions, and once they finished I called for their extraction.

Two Chinooks arrived overhead soon afterwards, and one came in to land, kicking up sand with the downwash of its huge rotor blades. The dust settled, but to my surprise it hadn't landed, and I could hear it flying away into the distance. It was a different crew from the drop-off, but the exact same landing site, and the pilot had decided there was too much dust for him to land. It's hard to avoid dust in the desert, so I was very surprised to hear that, but he was gone, and when I asked what I was supposed to do with the mechanics I was told to take them with me and leave their equipment behind. We made space for them in two of the vehicles and set off for Garmsir, about sixty kilometres away.

Fortunately, the ground was much more forgiving on that stretch of desert, and we were able to make good speed towards the target, leaving the toils of the soft sand behind us. It was almost morning when we reached the outskirts of Garmsir, and as we cautiously approached I picked up a mass of heat sources through the thermal imager that I assumed to be the Afghan army. Using the radio I was able to confirm it was a combined force of three hundred Afghan soldiers and police officers, led by a nine-man operational mentoring and liaison team (OMLT) from the British army. Speaking directly to the Brits, to avoid getting shot at we informed them we were operating in close proximity on their flank. As we talked we identified ourselves to them by flashing infra-red light in their direction, and once they acknowledged it we continued on task. From our map study we'd identified a viable location to observe the bridge from and headed towards it. The map was old though, and like everywhere else we went the town had expanded in the years since it had been printed, meaning there were a lot more compounds between us and the river than anticipated. Time was against us, and the Sun wasn't far from breaking the horizon, so we continued as planned, as it was still the best option. I halted the patrol momentarily and told everyone to swap over their night-sights to daylight ones.

That's not something you want to be doing in the middle of a firefight, so it's better to be prepared. The task was conducted quickly and silently, and while I waited I received a message in my earpiece from my LEWT team saying they'd intercepted a radio transmission from a Taliban radio. The interpreter had translated it as, "They are coming. We are ready."

There was no way of telling if they were talking about us, but I had to acknowledge it as a possibility. I knew at least one person had seen us when a man had walked out of his gate, then darted back inside again, but it seemed much more likely that the message referred to the three hundred men and vehicles amassed a few hundred metres away. It only took about a minute to get everything switched over and stowed away, before we were on the move again, slowly navigating our way to the north-eastern quarter of Garmsir. Moving west towards the Helmand river in the lead vehicle I directed my driver Dan towards a large clearing that was about three-hundred metres wide and flanked on both sides by high-walled compounds. It was a vulnerable point for sure, but that's the nature of operating in any populated or urban environment, the threat quickly escalates and envelops you from all sides. The clearing was uneven and difficult to drive through, because it was littered with deep holes, high mounds of earth, and shallow trenches, like some kind of partially-excavated, neolithic, archaeology site. My vehicle and at least one more behind me were inside the bottleneck when it all kicked off.

"Boom!" An RPG exploded in the earth just ahead of me to my right side, followed by a hail of automatic fire from the left flank. Dan halted the vehicle, and I immediately traversed my machine gun to the left, returning fire with some of the armour-piercing ammo the Americans had donated. Behind me, Craig was doing exactly the same from the rear turret, firing at the muzzle-flash from the enemies weapons, and our tracer rounds gave a good indication to the rest of the patrol where the enemy was. Within seconds those firing points were being hammered by the PF firepower behind us, enabling us to move out of the killing area. Dan did a great job turning us around in a tight space and we sped back the way we'd come under the covering fire of the others, closely followed by the vehicle behind us and the remainder. We were lucky that morning, I think the Taliban could have caused us a lot of damage if they'd held their fire for a couple of minutes and waited until a few more vehicles were in the ambush site. They were just too damn eager to kill us and messed it up. We came out of that firefight unscathed, and also survived a subsequent rocket and mortar attack, but that was more because of their terrible accuracy than our good skills. The blokes were laughing out loud and giving the Taliban a proper slagging for their slack drills when the bombs started landing about half a mile away. Soldiers are relentless when it comes to mocking the opposition, regardless of the situation.

Shortly after our engagement, air support arrived on scene in the form of AH64 Apache helicopters, and A10 Thunderbolt attack aircraft, two of the most formidable close-air-support assets ever made. The sight and sound of those beasts firing their guns and missiles at the enemy was absolutely awesome from our standpoint but must have been terrifying for the Taliban on the receiving end. The sound of the A10's canon firing was particularly impressive, a sound I will never forget, like an eerie heavenly roar from above. High above us at altitude there were also fast-jets circling the airspace, armed with precision bombs. Having identified the location a Taliban mortar firing-point, one of the PF Forward Air Controllers guided one of those bombs directly onto it, destroying that threat completely. I went over to speak to the British OMLT and the officer in charge told me they were about to launch a major offensive on the town. I knew very little about the role of the OMLT's and assumed they would be acting in a purely supervisory or advisory capacity.

"At least you won't be going in with them." I said. The noise coming from the town was exactly what you'd imagine from a full-on battlefield. Afghan soldiers from the town were already fighting the insurgents with rifles, machine guns, and grenades, and the three-tiered air-support was pounding their positions relentlessly.

"Oh, we're going with them alright." he replied. "I'm leading the assault. They won't go if we don't go first." They were a brave bunch of blokes on that team, and I didn't envy them on that task at all. There were a lot of good men in the Afghan army and police, and plenty who fought courageously alongside the coalition, but amongst them there were also many who weren't so trustworthy or loyal, saboteurs and extremists who'd put a bullet in your back at the first opportunity. I didn't like the idea of having the Taliban to my front and people like that to my rear. I wished them good luck, and shortly afterwards the gunfire intensified to a whole new level when they entered the town to drive out the enemy. I monitored their advance on the radio, listening to the OMLT commander report his progress and casualties as they pressed forward. At one point he was halted by Taliban snipers who shot at his men from the tower of a mosque. They did that deliberately, knowing full-well that the coalition would be reluctant to damage a place of worship and risk the political backlash. Those kind of tactics worked for them all the time, using culture as cover. They'd often cache weapons and explosives in places that were considered out-of-bounds or forbidden for foreign soldiers to enter, like mosques, and female-only areas, and would feign outrage if ever we dared go inside. To their credit, it was a weakness that they identified and exploited. Our top-brass were desperate not to offend the impartial people of the region, and the one thing that united all of them, regardless of political allegiance, was religion. Any act that could be interpreted as anti-Islamic could be used as propaganda to rally everybody against us.

Our tour ended in October 2006, and I don't mind

admitting I was glad to see the back of it. Friends and colleagues had been killed, wounded, and bereaved during that deployment, and to me it always felt like we were fighting a losing battle. Nobody seemed to want us there, we couldn't trust half of the Afghan army or police, and we were bound by a moralistic ruleset that our opponents had no regard for.

Craig, Dan, and me on patrol in Helmand Province 2006

On subsequent tours the British Army was introduced to a new NATO strategy, intended to reduce civilian casualties and collateral damage. However, for many soldiers "Courageous Restraint" became yet another frustrating obstacle in the decision making process, disrupting essential support like artillery and air-strikes. Being brave enough not to shoot back at an enemy that's trying to kill you, because someone else might get hurt, is a philosophy that's never going to wash with the soldiers who are actually involved in the fighting. It's like watching a girl beat the crap out of a boy because she knows he won't hit her back. My mum taught me from day one that I should never hit a girl, and it stuck, even after being punched, hit over the head with a heel, and glassed by women. In hindsight it's bad advice, everyone has the right to self-defence, and once the line has been crossed it's jungle-rules, survival of the fittest.

The last thing you want in a firefight is soldiers on your team who are hesitant to return fire in case they get into trouble for it. Soldiers should never be put in that situation, their priority has to be the safety of their mates and themselves, and they need to know that if that safety is jeopardised, they must take decisive action. Operating in a small group, with limited support, whether you're a special-forces team, six-man PF patrol, eight-man infantry section, or a convoy protection team, there's no time to ask for permission when it all kicks off. Every second counts, and the enemy need suppressing as quickly and violently as possible, to either deter them from continuing their attack, or destroy them completely. All soldiers should be confident that their commanders are going to support the decisions they make in the heat of battle. Those decisions are not made lightly, and are informed by detailed intelligence, situational awareness, and previous operational experience. They are also a product of intensive training in command, leadership, marksmanship, the law of armed conflict, and the rules of engagement.

In my opinion, if you don't trust your commanders to make command decisions, don't put them in command in the first place, or at least revise your leadership criteria. The sanctimonious twerps who sit comfortably, high in their ivory towers, far away from the battlefield, passing judgement on how their soldiers are carrying out their duty should walk a mile in their shoes before commenting. And that mile should be through the booby-trapped alleys, swamps, ditches, and sewers that their soldiers are navigating through on a daily basis while carrying heavy loads and being shot at.

In 2007 I learned that I was getting promoted to the rank of colour sergeant, after three years as the Pathfinders' platoon sergeant. My boss at the time, Major Nick Wight-Boycott was a great bloke from the SCOTS Regiment who

I'd served with in Afghanistan in 2006. We had an excellent working relationship and a mutual respect for each other, and he offered me some advice.

"You should look at a posting outside of the PF." he said. "There's a lot more to the army than the Parachute Regiment and the Pathfinders. I think it would be good for you to broaden your horizons for a couple of years."

Back then I had no interest whatsoever in broadening my horizons beyond my own cap badge. Although I'd chilled out a lot, I was still blinkered by the airborne ethos and mentality and working outside of that was not on my agenda at all. He suggested I apply for a job at the Royal Military Academy, where army officer recruits are trained.

"Have you ever thought about going to Sandhurst as an instructor?" he suggested. "You'd do well there, and it would be good for your career."

I'd definitely never considered that before because it sounded like Hell on Earth to me. I imagined it to be like baby-sitting a bunch of posh, croquet playing, cravat wearing, public schoolboys, with degrees in sociology, anthropology, or modern art, and it held little appeal. Historically I'd not got on very well with most of the officers I'd met, sometimes due to their personality and sometimes due to mine, but in the PF I'd made some good friends with the captains and majors that I'd served with. Nick's intentions were good, and he was right. I didn't know it at the time, but I was naïve to the opportunities on offer outside of airborne forces. Fortunately, a good friend of mine called Ash was actually attending Sandhurst as an officer cadet at the time, so I gave him a call to see what it was all about. Ash was a young lance corporal from 1 PARA who was very fit, capable, and level-headed, and we'd served together in PF for a few years, so he knew me pretty well, and I valued his opinion.

"You would hate it here Steve!" was his immediate response,

laughing at the suggestion. He explained how everything there was very formal, with strict dress codes, etiquettes, and traditions, all things I detested, and he strongly advised against me applying to go there. I didn't need telling twice.

My son was approaching his first birthday and we'd always said that when we had kids we'd have them no more than two years apart. My brother is two years older than me, and we hung around together as kids, but Carmen grew up with three much older brothers who had all left home by the time she was about ten. We both wanted our kids to be of similar age, so they could be friends and companions for each other. The problem we faced now was that PF were deploying to Afghanistan again in 2008.

"I'm not going through that on my own again." Carmen told me, referring to her pregnancy with Luke while I was deployed. It was a fair comment and left me with two choices. I needed to either move away from the hectic lifestyle of PF for a while to build my family or accept that our kids would have a four year age gap between them, and I'd be deploying again within a year.

Another possibility I was told about was an instructor job at the Survival, Evasion, Resistance, and Extraction (SERE) school in Gosport, Hampshire. This was one of only two establishments in the military that taught survival and conducted escape and evasion courses, and that got my attention.

I found out that a couple of army blokes were already working at the SERE school and reached out to one of them, a Scottish colour sergeant called Smudge from the SCOTS Regiment. Over the phone he told me that the school was located in a Royal Navy base in Gosport called HMS Sultan, the training team were a mixture of army and navy personnel, and they spent a lot of time teaching sea and land survival, as well as escape, evasion, and resistance to interrogation. It sounded really interesting and after a lot of deliberation I decided to apply for the job, which I got, and started in August 2007.

Working alongside the Royal Navy took a bit of getting used to, but they had to get used to working with army personnel as well, and fortunately we had a great team led by a brilliant chief instructor called Chief Petty Officer Colin Towell. Most of my time was spent on courses, or teaching in the New Forest, the Solent, and the classroom, and I had a lot to learn. Colin was one of those people that taught you something amazing every time you worked with him and made extremely difficult things look easy. More often than not it wasn't even intentional, just something he'd say or do while sat around the fire having a brew.

The stability and predictable working hours of my posting to Gosport finally gave me the opportunity to get back into martial arts. I'd hardly done anything other than bag work for years, and I missed it. A friend in PF called Mac was from Gosport, and he told me about a good mixed martial arts gym he'd trained at there, called South Coast Submissions. The club owner and coach was a professional MMA fighter called Brian Adams and I called him to see if I could come to his classes, to which he said yes. The club was located in a small industrial estate just a couple of miles from my house, so I cycled there and made my way up the narrow concrete stairway to the windowless gym. Although my striking was still ok, my first class was a massive eye-opener, because we did wrestling and jiu jitsu too, where I got mauled by just about everybody. I had no idea what to do against someone that knew how to grapple, and the notion that I could simply keep the fight on the feet quickly disappeared after repeatedly being taken down, put on my back, and getting my arms, legs, and neck contorted into all sorts of unnatural positions. I got the bug immediately and started training at SCS three times a week.

In March 2008 my daughter Jasmin was born in Gosport Maternity Hospital, and this time I was in attendance, although like most blokes during childbirth I was absolutely useless. We were now a family of four and returned home with her wearing the little pink woolly hat the nurses had given her. After only one year in Gosport the MoD decided to close the SERE school in HMS Sultan, and merge it with the one in RAF St. Mawgan, Cornwall. I was gutted, because I was on a two-year posting, and that meant I'd be moving house every year, three years in a row. I'd gone from Colchester to Gosport in 2007, I was going from Gosport to Cornwall in 2008, and I'd be going back to Colchester from Cornwall in 2009. I made that point to my boss at HMS Sultan during a chat, and he responded by offering me an extension at the SERE school, which I accepted, and in the summer of 2008 I moved to Cornwall to continue my job as a SERE instructor. For the first time ever, instructors from the navy, army, and air force were all working together to deliver SERE training from one centralised training establishment under the watchful eye of a new chief instructor Flight Lieutenant John Hudson, another amazing teacher.

For the next three years I immersed myself in SERE, studying survival in my own time and completing many overseas exercises in desert, Arctic, and jungle environments. It was a great job, and there were always new things to learn so I liked it, plus the stability afforded me time to continue learning MMA and Brazilian Jiu Jitsu. I found a new club in Newquay called Koncept Martial Arts where I trained under another fantastic coach called Mark Rowlett.

It was during this period that I started to question my state of mind. I think being away from the hard, fast, and aggressive nature of airborne forces and working alongside "normal people" made me realise that I wasn't normal myself. I was inexplicably unhappy, unexcitable, and uncompassionate, and I'd been that way for quite some time. My thought processes were extremely violent, I saw threats everywhere, and was totally unable to relax or enjoy anything. In the PF

I'd never have admitted these things to a doctor for fear of being medically downgraded or putting my job at risk, but as a SERE instructor it would have little effect. I went to the medical centre, asked the doctor for help, and was given an appointment at the Department of Clinical Mental Health (DCMH) in Plymouth. I went to the appointment, but left the DCMH feeling worse than ever after a dreadful experience with a young clinical nurse who made me fill out a questionnaire, asked a few questions, told me I didn't have PTSD, then sent me on my way feeling like I'd wasted everyone's time. Years later I'd return to that same building as a patient with a diagnosis of PTSD and an apology for the way I was treated the first time.

I finished working at the SERE school in 2011 as the team leader for survival, escape, and evasion, before moving to South Wales to join 1 PARA on promotion to Sergeant-Major.

CHAPTER THIRTEEN
THE SERGEANT
MAJOR

My first day at 1 PARA was rather odd. I reported to Battalion Headquarters to be told that the decision on where I was going hadn't been made yet. I was either going to become the Operations Warrant Officer, or the Capability Development Warrant Officer, neither of which sounded particularly enticing to me. My main focus before settling into my new job was to convince everyone that I was only there for a year.

"I'm only here for a year, then I'm going back to Pathfinders." I'd say to every officer I met. It was nothing against 1 PARA, I was extremely proud to be there, and it was full of some the best soldiers in the British army with unparalleled operational experience. The problem was my window of opportunity to get the job as the PF sergeant major was finite. The bloke in the job at that point was leaving in a years' time, and that might be my only chance to do it. On day two it was agreed that I'd be working in the Capability Development Cell.

In my entire career I was only interviewed by a Regimental Careers Management Officer once, and that was when I was at 1 PARA as a sergeant major. The RCMO was a decent bloke, who'd gone through the ranks, been the RSM, and then commissioned as an officer. His job was to ensure the soldiers in his battalion reached their full potential, by completing the right courses and taking on the best roles for their development and career progression.

"How long have you got left in the army?" he asked me.

"Four years Sir." I told him. I'd already served eighteen years by then.

"Is that including Veng?" he queried. Versatile Engagement or V-Eng was the optional two year extension I was eligible for but hadn't committed to.

"No Sir, that's without Veng." I replied.

"So that's six years if you stay on for Veng." he said. Soldiers aren't necessarily renowned for their mathematical prowess, but between us we could at least agree on that.

"That's correct." I nodded.

His next comment was surprising, but at least he was honest. "Well let's face it, you're not going to be an RSM." he stated bluntly.

I didn't know how to respond to that. For most career soldiers, becoming a Regimental Sergeant Major is their ultimate ambition, the pinnacle of their career. In fairness, to me it wasn't, the prospect held no interest for me whatsoever, but he didn't know that, and I was quite shocked that he'd actually say it out loud.

"Oh, okay." I said.

He explained that I'd spent too long away from the battalions by going to Pathfinders and the survival school, and the RSM roles would be awarded to the men who'd served their careers in 1, 2, or 3 PARA and followed a more traditional career path. In reality I knew that already, and I agreed with it too, they'd do a much better job than me, and they deserved it. I'd have been like a fish out of water as an RSM in a battalion. I had no idea about the formalities of the Sergeants' Mess and had spent the majority of my career working in small teams, on first-name terms with everyone I worked with. I loathed formal occasions, parades, and mess etiquette, and the mere thought of carrying a pace-stick everywhere because it was tradition, really irritated me, plus I'd definitely lose it within a week unless it was velcroed to my hand.

As a career management interview I suppose it achieved the aim, as far as managing my expectations, but it wasn't the inspirational, or motivational spiel I was expecting. I'd worked hard for eighteen years, and had excellent reports throughout, but here I was being told I'd reached my ceiling. For some that might have been enough to convince them to stop grafting, to rest on their laurels and take their foot off the gas, but it just reassured me that returning to the Pathfinders was my best course of action. In PF I was a round peg in a round hole.

The next year was filled with research, liaison, trials, and project management as I settled into the complex world of capability development. I learned a lot in that job about processes, procedures, and inter-organisational communication, met some fantastic soldiers, and had some good successes with infrastructure and equipment, but the main lesson I took away from it, was that it wasn't for me. The amount of time I spent jumping through hoops, negotiating red-tape, and justifying the need to spend money on essential kit was extremely frustrating. One year of dealing with self-important dinosaurs in the civil service, who didn't know one end of a rifle from the other was more than enough for me.

I continued training MMA and BJJ, heading up my own little club in camp with a few of the blokes, and training at a fantastic club in Cardiff called the Chris Rees Academy whenever I could. I also took classes with two brilliant coaches from Chris's academy, who were purple belts at the time, attending classes with Rob Taylor in Bridgend, and private lessons with Ash Williams in Cardiff. Both of those men are highly accomplished black-belts in BJJ now.

During my time at 1 PARA I overheard a conversation

between two paratroopers that made me realise how, as soldiers, we were all very expendable and replaceable. I'd known it for a long time really, but that day was the first time I fully understood it. For one of the men it was his last day in the army, and he explained to his friend that he was only in camp to sign some forms and hand in his army I.D card. From that day forward he was a civilian. They had a brief conversation in the corridor and left in opposite directions. I never saw either of them, but heard everything, and it was the standard non-emotional exchange of best wishes, and pledges to stay in-touch that I'd heard many times before. The talking ceased, and a few footsteps echoed down the corridor before a door creaked open, then slammed shut again, leaving the building in silence once more, like they'd never even been there. That few seconds massively resonated with me. For all I knew that man was the best soldier in the entire battalion, with unparalleled skills and experience, but the second that door closed behind him he was gone, and whatever roles and responsibilities he held before that moment were already being fulfilled by someone else. The wheel just kept on turning, and rightly so.

2011 was the year my step-dad Dave died. My mum phoned me to say the doctors had given him 48 hours to live, so I drove to Northampton to support her and say goodbye to him. He was a peculiar man, but he was good to me, and from the day I left home to join the army our relationship had grown into a strong one of mutual respect. Dave was in a private room, and heavily sedated, with rare moments of consciousness as he was intravenously administered morphine on an auto-injector. On the few occasions he did wake up, he would either be screaming in pain or totally confused as to what was happening before quickly falling back to sleep. He was dying of bowel cancer and the nurses did their best to clean up the foul smelling mess being expelled from his body, regularly changing the soiled sheets and nappy-like pants he was wearing.

At the hospital I saw my step-brother Michael for the first time in twenty or so years. He and Dave were best friends, and he struggled with seeing his dad in such a helpless state. Not wanting to witness his dads decline and suffering, Michael decided to say his goodbyes while Dave was sleeping restfully and went home, with a promise from me that I'd let him know of any developments. Essentially we were just waiting for him to die, and I spent several days watching over him as that horrible disease ravaged his body and sucked the fight from his soul. I monitored his heart rate and respirations when we were alone together, noticing a steady decline in both, as he battled well beyond the predicted 48 hours, and by day five he was taking only four breaths per minute when the doctor came in to check him over.

I stood up to take a break and leave him to it. "I don't think he's got long left has he Doc?" I said. "His breathing rate has dropped massively overnight."

The doctor looked at me and nodded. "I think you're right." he replied solemnly. "It will be today."

I left the room and went to join my mum and brother, who were in the hospital canteen having a cup of tea.

I hope nobody ever has to watch me die slowly. If I end up in Dave's position I'd much rather my family do what Michael did and leave while they still remember me with some dignity. I felt guilty, because in the end I just wanted him to die, for it to be over for all of us. He'd had no food or water for the best part of a week and been mostly unconscious, so he was obviously in a terrible condition, and I'd barely slept in an effort to be there for him if he did wake up. On one of the few occasions he did awaken he noticed me sat in the corner of the room.

"What are you doing here?" he said, surprised to see me.

He was delirious on morphine, and completely unaware that

I'd spent the best part of the last 72 hours by his side, but selfishly I was a bit put out by his question. "I've been here the whole bloody time mate!" I replied defensively. He looked around the room and fell back to sleep, and that was the last conversation we ever had.

I'd barely finished my brew when the doctor I'd just been speaking to in Dave's room approached our table, looking very sombre. Dave had died right after I left, and the MacMillan nurses were already cleaning him up, so he looked presentable for us to pay one last visit. I phoned Michael to give him the bad news and he said he'd pass it on to his older sister Kim, who lived in South Africa. Before leaving the hospital I went back to say goodbye with my brother but found it very awkward with us both there. Dave looked peaceful, and the nurses had brushed his hair and cleaned him up, but I couldn't think of anything poignant or meaningful to say. I patted him on the shoulder, said something like "I'll see you in the next life" and left. My brother hung around for a while after I'd gone which I found surprising, because he and Dave had never been close. I reckon he probably apologised for the times he'd been a pain in the ass and thanked Dave for all the good things he did for us, but like me he couldn't say those things in front of someone else.

Returning to Pathfinders in 2012 after only a year at 1 PARA was very satisfying. It was the only sergeant-major job in the army that appealed to me, where I felt like I truly belonged, and could fulfil my potential. There were a few blokes still there from my days as platoon sergeant, but most were people I had no former relationship with. I'd always kept my ear to the ground, so I'd heard all about the strong characters, the rebels, the rogues, the super-keen, and the stand-out soldiers. Unfortunately I'd also heard a few negative stories that circulated, claiming that the PF was losing its way and the blokes were cutting corners and getting too big for their boots. I must admit, I almost started to believe it and hoped I wouldn't have to go in there guns blazing to sort it out, but the rumours were false, and it didn't take long to settle back in. The blokes were still the same, ducking and diving the shitty jobs and trying their best to get on the exciting stuff like overseas exercises and parachuting trips. They took the piss out of each other incessantly and nothing was off-limits, fat bastard, skinny bastard, ginger bastard, old bastard, bald bastard, some things never change. No doubt I was the old, bald, grumpy bastard. There were some fantastic soldiers there, some of which were junior patrol members when I left and were now mature patrol commanders and sergeants. On my first brigade exercise as the sergeant-major I watched on proudly as one of my corporals briefed the brigade headquarters on an enemy position he'd reconnoitred over the previous few days. With the aid of some excellent hand-drawn sketches, Craig provided intricate details of the site, including the location of tripwires, landmines, sentries, and even described the state of the ground inside the enemy harbour area. When he recommended avoiding one approach route because of a dense mass of brambles that would slow down an assaulting force, one officer voiced his scepticism.

"How can you be so sure of that?" he asked suspiciously.

Craig's answer was brilliant, and clearly surprised everyone, including me.

"Because I was in there last night Sir." he said confidently.

It was impressive. Using night-vision goggles, him and one of his team had stealthily walked through the position undetected, identifying and recording every detail for the forthcoming attack. It was the best target briefing I ever saw, far better than anything I'd ever produced as a patrol commander, and I told him so afterwards.

In 2012 London hosted the Olympic Games, but it quickly became apparent that the company responsible for the security of the venues and stadiums was drastically ill-prepared and couldn't fulfil the role. Predictably the army was called upon to do the job, and 16 Air Assault Brigade was told to stand-by. Initially the brigade was split into about fourteen tiers, where tier one would be the first to go and tier fourteen, probably consisting of the NAAFI manager, and the brigadier himself, going last. I think PF were tier twelve, so the optimists amongst us were fairly confident we wouldn't be getting involved. Not me though, I knew that crappy task had our names all over it, and before long we were sent to Tobacco Dock near Tower Bridge in London, to act as a Quick Reaction Force. While there we were partnered up with D Squadron of the Household Cavalry Regiment, who's boss held the rank of Squadron Leader. I served with three men in PF who were from the Household Cavalry, and they were all excellent soldiers and brilliant blokes, so I had some understanding of their unique rank structure. Because of its long history the HCR is very different from the rest of the army. Their appointed ranks include Trooper, Corporal of the Horse, and Corporal Major, and their badges of rank are arranged differently to the rest of the army too, making everyone appear very important, but in my experience they have always been down-to-earth, decent blokes. Tobacco Dock was an old disused warehouse built in the early 1800's, but during the Olympics it was a busy makeshift barracks for hundreds of soldiers. Rows of camp-cots and roll-mats filled every room and corridor, army chefs set up a fully operational field kitchen, and sentries were posted at the entrances. Our first task as QRF was to secure Lords Cricket Ground for an archery event, and with little warning or direction we were hastily loaded onto coaches and driven to the venue. To our surprise when we arrived there was already a large group of other soldiers on duty, conducting searches and operating the scanning equipment. Strangely, we were made to queue-up and go through the security checks alongside everyone else, emptying our pockets, placing daysacs onto scanner conveyor belts, and walking through metal-detectors under the supervision of the soldiers doing the job we thought we were supposed to be doing. In a separate queue and out of sight to me one of my blokes was stopped and questioned when something in his daysac caught the attention of the x-ray machine operator. After a brief discussion with some civilian security staff he was handed back his bag and told to wait outside the stadium. I cleared security with no problems and made my way to where everyone was gathering. I noticed two of my blokes acting suspiciously, fidgeting anxiously and repeatedly looking towards the entrance so I stood next to them to eavesdrop, pretending to be distracted by something else.

I didn't hear much of what was being said but there were two words that leapt out at me and really got my attention, "Gaz" and "grenade". I interrupted the conversation.

"Has Gaz got a grenade?" I asked, hoping I'd misread the situation.

The blokes looked at each other awkwardly, not wanting to snitch on their mate.

"Tell me now. Has Gaz got a fucking hand grenade with him?" I said sternly.

"I think so yes." Hodgy replied reluctantly. "He's been sent back outside on the street."

Through the metalwork of a fence, I could see Gaz standing outside the stadium on the pavement and made my way back through security to where he was.

"Have you got a hand grenade in that daysac?" I asked him straight away.

Gaz looked gutted, we'd been good friends for many years, and I could see he was kicking himself.

"Sorry mate. It must have been in there since I came back from Sennybridge. It was stuck inside a tear in the lining." He explained.

I wasn't angry, nor was I disappointed in him. It was a genuine mistake that could have happened to anyone. He was an excellent soldier who I'd watched develop from a quiet private to a confident, well respected sergeant.

"Don't worry, I'll sort it." I told him. Inside the stadium was a police officer who looked very important with his rank displayed on his epaulettes, so I approached him for some help. "Excuse me Sir, I've got a bit of an issue that I think you might be able to help with" I said. The officer wasn't flustered at all when I told him of the live, high-explosive hand grenade about fifty feet away. It turned out he was an ex-Royal Marine.

"Is it an L2?" he asked, referring to the designation of the weapon. That type of grenade had been out of service for about ten years by then but would have been what he'd used during his service in the Marines.

"No, we don't use them anymore. It's an L109 Sir, but it's perfectly safe. I just want to get it off the street." I was being extra polite to keep him on side.

"Where do you need to get him to?" the officer said, obviously wanting to help.

I answered with the only military barracks I knew of in London. "If I can get him to Regents Park Barracks, I can sort it out from there." I replied. At the time I had no real idea where I was in the city, but that was only a mile and a half away from the cricket ground.

The copper was happy with that, and within a couple of minutes Gaz was picked up by a squad car and taken to the camp, where I arranged for someone to come down from Colchester to collect the grenade and take it back to the garrison.

The rest of the Olympics went without incident for us and apart from the inevitable hanging around, we actually managed to make the most of being in the capital. I went to the

Tower of London, did some Jiu Jitsu, and went to a nearby gym every day.

I did a few different jobs as a sergeant-major, but those two years at PF were by far the most challenging. Because it's a stand-alone unit everything is done organically, but there's no real staff to support it. In the battalions you have dedicated personnel to deal with specific areas of concern. There's a career manager, a welfare officer, an ammunition NCO, a training officer, a courses clerk, and plenty of other people covering specialist roles. In PF, although on a much smaller scale, those roles still need to be fulfilled, but are covered by the platoon sergeant and sergeant-major, and to make it complicated we had to do it for soldiers from multiple regiments and corps across the army as well as blokes from the RAF too. For two years I was on-call 24/7 and on high-readiness to deploy at short notice. I worked long days covering multiple roles and did my best to keep the PF moving forward without overworking the blokes. I've been led by some great people in my time, as well as some not-so-great, and I've tried to educate myself along the way on how to treat others. My philosophy is to work hard, be good at your job, then reap the rewards if there's any time left over. Nothing is free. Everything you want has a cost, and that cost can come in many forms, including physical, psychological, financial, and your time. Fortunately there were always plenty of excellent soldiers in PF to ensure standards were kept to the highest levels, so we were able to work hard and play hard.

In 2014 I was offered the opportunity to stay on at PF as the sergeant major for my final year, but I declined. I was honoured, but I knew it would be a bad idea, the workload there was phenomenal.

"To be honest, I can't think of anywhere worse to resettle from." I replied. If I stayed on I'd never have been able to concentrate on resettlement. The job was so busy, there simply wasn't enough time to do both. I'd have grafted right to the last day, then left the army with zero preparation. I turned down the offer and waited to see what other job I'd be getting for my final twelve months. A plan was made for me to be posted back to the survival school for my last year and thinking that was all agreed I began the process of buying a house in Cornwall and securing places in a school for my kids.

A few weeks later I received a message that I'd been lined up for a job in Canada for six months. This was extremely disappointing, and I'd only just informed my wife when the phone rang again to tell me there had been a mistake and the job wasn't in Canada, it was in Afghanistan, and it was for nine months not six. I called headquarters for some clarification and was told the job was definitely in Afghanistan, working in an Afghan army special forces base.

"I take it I'm not going to the survival school now then?" I said.

The answer was shockingly apathetic. "You've already had your little holiday in Cornwall Sergeant Major. You can forget going back there now!"

"You do realise that I'll be in my last year of service don't you?" I asked them. "Is there nothing else available?" I had the option of staying on for an extra two years if I wanted to and planned to take it if I was at the survival school. Outside of that though, I was ready to leave. Spending so much time away from the battalions had left me in an awkward position.

I was informed of two other possibilities; a permanent instructor job with the reserves in Leeds, or a training development job with Army HQ in Warminster. I was snapping. In the space of a few hours I'd gone from thinking I had a job in Cornwall, to Canada, then Afghanistan, and now I had to choose between Leeds and Warminster.

"Well I'm buying a house in Cornwall, so I'll ask for Warminster please." I said reluctantly. That would be a commute of 150 miles which was a fair distance, but nothing compared to the 350 miles to Leeds. Once the job was confirmed I visited Warminster with my family to look at the married quarters and town and consider the option of us all moving there together. It was an easy decision. We'd almost completed the purchase of our house in Cornwall and the kids had moved around enough already. At age seven Luke was in his seventh house and fourth school, another short residency was the last thing we needed. The final nail in the coffin was when my daughter said, "These houses are horrible Daddy, who lives here?"

I knew exactly what she meant. "Not us Jasmin." I answered. She was already in her fifth house by the time she was five years old too.

We decided right there and then to continue as planned with the move to Cornwall and I'd live in the Sergeants' Mess in Warminster from Monday to Friday, coming home by train and bus at weekends. I left PF in 2014 and began working at the Land Warfare Centre in Warminster.

The job itself was working for a training development team within Army HQ and my role was in training validation. However, because of a huge backlog in another department, I was asked to help clear that before beginning any of my own tasks. It soon became apparent why the work was backed-up when I saw how much effort was being put in by some of the civil servants responsible for it. Their office was next to mine, with paperwork stacked high on their desks gaining in height daily. The staff in there gossiped incessantly, either to each other, or to their friends and family on the phone, with one of them laughing hysterically every few seconds to everything she was told. Initially I thought it was nice to be around someone so happy, but the novelty rapidly wore off and the shrill cackle started causing me to fidget and twitch in my seat. The lack of a sense of urgency in that office was what annoyed me the most, closely followed by the complete lack of military intuition. Their complacency directly affected operational capability and morale, but they were either oblivious or indifferent. Once I got involved in clearing up their mess I worked until 0200hrs every night until it was done, only stopping to eat or do fitness. It was boring computer work, and I never got any thanks for it, but it made me feel like I was doing something of use for the blokes on the ground.

For some of the men in the Warminster Sergeants Mess, evenings were exclusively reserved for drinking cheap beer in the bar, regaling each other with stories from their illustrious pasts, and convincing themselves that things were tougher in their day. Despite their obvious aversion to the gym or any form of physical training they liked to talk about how fit they used to be, and how the younger generation would never have been able to cope with what they'd been through. I stayed well away from those people and instead found a few blokes to train MMA with a few nights a week, like I'd done at 1 PARA. Living in the mess was depressing enough without adding alcohol and hangovers to the mix, I think that would have finished me off.

It was during my time in Warminster that I decided to seek help once again for my mental health. I was in no way qualified to self-diagnose, but I felt confident in my prognosis of an imminent psychological breakdown. In truth, nothing had really changed since I first asked for help, except my symptoms had worsened, left to burgeon in the absence of medical intervention. I was extremely angry, disillusioned about the army, completely unhappy with my personal circumstances, and highly stressed by crowds or busy places. My legs were bouncing while sitting, my jaw was constantly flexing as I bit down on my teeth, I was rocking in my seat, rubbing my head, and even developed a twitch in my face when agitated. I was an accident waiting to happen. It was actually another warrant officer in the team who gave me the push to speak to a doctor. Adam was very open to me about his personal mental health issues and recognised my signs, symptoms, and behaviours as similar to his own. Under the care of the DCMH in Tidworth he was taking a prescribed medication and attending counselling sessions every week, which he said helped him massively. A big, strong, square-jawed infantryman, who was always immaculately dressed and seemingly full of confidence, he was the last person you'd expect to have such emotional demons at first glance, but he was broken. A particularly horrendous tour of Afghanistan had decimated the soldiers under his command, with many killed, and even more very seriously injured. On his office wall hung a large, framed photo of his rifle company that was taken near the beginning of their deployment, and one day he talked me through the personalities within it, drawing a finger across the glass frame as he did so. It was the usual scene of soldiers standing or kneeling with their rifles, some sporting beards and looking dirty from operating in harsh conditions.

"He lost a leg above the knee. He was killed by an IED. He lost an arm. He lost both legs below the knee. He was killed by a sniper. He's in a wheelchair now. Him I carried onto the helicopter after he was blown up." he told me, never skipping more than a few men before describing the next casualty. It was horrific and listening to him talk explained why he was so psychologically injured. I'd suggest that every man in that photo suffered some form of trauma, with many of them probably never receiving any medical attention. It was on Adam's advice that I went to ask for help for the second time. I told him about an incident that had happened at home over the weekend where I'd smashed up my vacuum cleaner in front of my children in an angry outburst, visibly frightening them.

"They'll never forget that you know." he told me. "That will stay with them forever."

I knew he might be right. They were only young, but from my own experiences as a kid I knew that the impact of being frightened could be long lasting. I already felt extremely guilty about it, but someone else highlighting the possible effects of my behaviour made it even worse.

In military medical centres you don't always get to see the same doctor as you might expect in a civilian G.P surgery. In big garrisons there could be several doctors on duty, often a mix of civilian locum G.P's and military Medical Officers. I was nervous the day I went to the Med Centre in Warminster, unsure how I was going to ask the doctor for help. I was in uniform, displaying my rank and regiment, and quite self-conscious about showing weakness in front of another person. The doctor I saw that day was an R.A.F Squadron Leader that I'd never met before and after the usual brief formalities he asked me how he could help. I explained to him that I was in my last year of service, severely depressed, and in a permanent state of anxiety and anger for no apparent reason.

"I think I need some help." I said. I hadn't prepared or rehearsed what I was going to say, and I didn't mean to sound dramatic, but I was speaking the absolute truth as I saw it at that moment in time. "I'm so angry all the time, I think I'm going to end up killing someone. Probably someone who doesn't even deserve to be killed." At the time I could totally empathise with people in the news who'd murdered someone or gone on a rampage, because I felt like they'd probably been where I was emotionally just before they'd done it, then something had tipped them over the edge. I had no sympathy for them and didn't see it as any kind of justification for their horrendous crimes, but I genuinely felt like that kind of psychological meltdown could quite easily happen to me if I were exposed to the wrong circumstances or triggers. I'd kept it together up until that point, but actually verbalising my inner thoughts and fears really struck a nerve, and I started crying as I pleaded with the doctor. "Please help me. I think I'm going fucking mental. I think I'm going to leave the army a basket case" I sobbed. It was embarrassing, but it needed to be said, and to be honest it probably made quite an impression on the doctor, because I clearly had issues. He prescribed me some anti-depressant medication to be started that day and referred me to the Department of Clinical Mental Health as a priority, before reassuring me that everything was in-hand and sending me on my way. I collected the prescription of Sertraline tablets on my way out, went straight to my room in the sergeants' mess and took them with some water immediately, hopeful they'd make a difference.

Within a week I had my first appointment with a clinical nurse from the DCMH, a staff sergeant called Emma from the Royal Army Medical Corps, who came across as very knowledgeable and likeable. Talking to her was humbling and enlightening because she asked questions that nobody had ever put to me before about my thoughts and emotions, and while trying to verbalise and explain them to her, I gained an understanding of them myself. It was during these early consultations that I slowly began to realise I'd been struggling with low-mood, depression, anxiety, and hypervigilance for a long time. She wasn't throwing labels at me or jumping to conclusions, instead it felt more like an education, which was great because that felt like progress. I always struggled answering questions about things or places I enjoyed during our sessions, and that got me thinking hard about my own happiness, or lack of it. I'd become a very unexcitable, and apathetic man, who neither felt nor showed emotion, describing myself as numb, cold, and robotic. I took joy from nothing, and the only thing that could make me worried was the thought of my kids being in danger. However when she first mentioned the possibility of PTSD I was very dismissive. "There's plenty of people who've been through a lot worse than me." I said.

I wasn't being modest or humble, I truly believed it, and still do. There are thousands of servicemen and women who experienced far worse events and situations than I ever did.

People say that when you stop being afraid of doing dangerous activities it's time to stop doing them, but after a while I never really felt fear from any thing I did in the army. The problem was I never felt any joy either. Whether it was deploying on operations, abseiling from a helicopter, or jumping out of a plane at 25,000ft, I felt nothing, it was just part of my job. Everything I did in both my personal and work life was a task, and once one task was completed I immediately started thinking about the next, never stopping to enjoy the previous success. For a long time I thought I'd stopped enjoying things because of the responsibility that came with being a platoon sergeant, because it was about then that I stopped enjoying life. However, that was also around the same time that we went to Afghanistan. It was 2014 when I was formally diagnosed with PTSD and realised that I'd been suffering with depression and anxiety for at least eight years, and probably longer, with every year worse than the one before. After speaking to several nurses, psychologists, and psychiatrists who were all of the same opinion, I humbly accepted their evaluation, and began working towards wellness with weekly visits to the DCMH in Tidworth, a forty-five minute drive from Warminster. The psychologist assigned to me there was a good guy, and despite him being German, he did a good job of speaking to me in plain English to help me understand what was going on in my brain. He made me realise that PTSD wasn't something extraordinary, that it wasn't a mark of self-pity or weakness, and also that it was probably prevalent among my friends, colleagues, and peers too.

Warminster was a terrible place for someone like me to work. The handful of soldiers in the team were all good blokes but I had nothing in common with the vast majority of the other people there. Some of the civil servants were unbelievably arrogant, strutting around with their noses in the air and truly believing that their "equivalent rank" status meant something to us mere soldiers. They used some kind of alpha-numeric ranking system that only they understood or cared about, which apparently equated to our rank structure, usually as a captain or a major. Nobody in the army recognised that though, especially not grumpy old sergeant majors like me, it was ridiculous. If they wanted to be an officer they should have joined the army, not the civil service. On a daily basis my friend Mitch, who I shared an office with would notice me getting angry and intervene.

"Go and get some fresh air Steve." he'd say. "Get outside for a while and clear your head."

He was a good bloke, another sergeant-major, who was at the end of his service in the SCOTS Regiment. I must have looked like a proper nutcase to him sometimes, sat rocking in my chair, rubbing my head, and talking to myself. Because of my deafness he used to tell me when my phone was ringing all the time too. I'd often think it was his phone, or one in another office, or not hear it at all, and Mitch would have to alert me.

"Your phone is ringing!" he'd shout, while pointing to the landline on a shelf right next to me. He probably thought I was quite special.

My second and last-ever face-to-face meeting with a career management officer occurred during my final year in the army, when I received a surprise visit from the captain who'd arranged my posting to Warminster. Strutting like a peacock he swaggered into my office.

"Fucking hell, have you got enough folders in here?" he said sarcastically, referring to the vast amount of military pamphlets and reference books we had in there.

"Hello Sir." I replied, deliberately avoiding the boredom of a conversation about documentation.

"How's the job? Not what you wanted but could have been worse right?" he asked. It was blatantly apparent that he didn't care, his facial expression and body language made that loud and clear. The questions were mere formalities before he got to the real point of his unannounced visit.

I wasn't going to lie, I hated it there, but I wasn't going to be rude either. "It is what it is Sir." I answered diplomatically.

His flippant reply confirmed my doubts about his authenticity. "Well I never told you it was going to be fucking good did I Sergeant Major?" he blurted out arrogantly.

I was disappointed more than I was angry. I'd grafted for twenty-one years in every post I'd been in, and this was likely to be the last time I saw a career manager. If I was ever going to get a pat on the back or thank you from one of them, this was it. Instead I got an indirect telling off.

"Why have I got a full colonel in the Parachute Regiment asking me why you haven't done WO1 CLM yet? Why am I getting it in the neck?" he asked. Evidently he'd just been talking to a colonel that worked in the same building, who'd been my platoon commander as a captain many years before. The course he referred to was a command, leadership, and management course that was a condition of being promoted to WO1 / Regimental Sergeant Major. He didn't give me a chance to answer, so I let him carry on. "If you want to reach WO1, then you have to do the right courses. It's not difficult, if you apply for the course you'll get on it. But I shouldn't have to be explaining this to a colonel like it's up to me!"

To be honest, the more he spoke, the more smug I felt, and the more assured I was that my so-called managers had no real interest in my career. "Well, obviously I've signed off Sir haven't I? So there'd be no point in me doing CLM." I said it like he already knew it, because we both knew he should have done, and that must have made him feel quite awkward.

Unsurprisingly, he looked surprised. "What? You've signed off have you? When was that?

"About two months ago, I'm pretty sure you authorised it Sir." I replied. I'd had a notification from his office acknowledging my decision.

"Then why the fuck don't I know about it then?" he snapped,

feigning disappointment.

It was an awkward conversation that I just wanted to end. "I have no idea Sir." I answered, and he promptly left.

"Who the hell was that?" Mitch asked me, shaking his head, and looking dumbfounded.

"That bloke there mate?" I said, nodding towards where he'd just been standing. "Believe it or not, that was my career management officer."

Mitch had quickly established an opinion on him. "Wow, he's an arrogant bastard!" he said.

I just shrugged my shoulders. It was hard to argue otherwise.

I completed my last year as a regular soldier in Warminster, leaving in July 2015 after over twenty-two years' service, and just like the soldier I'd overheard in the 1 PARA corridor the door closed firmly behind me to mark the end of my career. There were plenty of other sergeant majors to take my place, the army didn't need me. The wheel kept on turning.

Just before I finished at Warminster I heard about a job opportunity that was being advertised at the SERE school in Newquay, where I'd worked before. The job was FTRS, or full-time reserve service, and advertised as a Lead Instructor role in evasion and extraction. The start date was just a few weeks after my termination date, so I applied for it, and got it, remaining a Parachute Regiment sergeant-major and moving seamlessly into the new job after a bit of leave. I'd always promised Carmen and the kids that we'd go to Disney World when I'd done my 22 years, so we booked a two week trip to Florida and had the best holiday ever, before returning to RAF St Mawgan on a two-year contract. Working at the SERE school was great, because outside of martial arts my only other real hobby was survival, so once I re-joined my old BJJ club in Newquay I got to keep doing both. After about a year a new role was created at the school and I was appointed the

Training Warrant Officer, overseeing all aspects of the training we delivered, and after a couple of extensions I stayed in that job until 2020. Every job has it's frustrations, and SERE was no different, but overall it was a great place to work, with some excellent instructors and great friends from across the Army, Navy, and RAF. I was lucky to conduct and deliver training all over the world as a SERE instructor, including the worlds driest desert, the worlds hottest place, the high-arctic, the high-desert, salt-lakes, frozen seas, and rain-forests. Teaching and studying survival will always be a passion of mine, because like Jiu Jitsu there is always so much more to learn.

In September 2019 I decided to spend some time updating my CV in preparation for my fast approaching retirement from the army. I'd originally written it in 2015 and had a few things to add, so I spent several hours re-writing it and printed off a copy. The following day at work my friend Nathan was telling me about a job vacancy at a sports centre in Newquay where his friend worked as the manager.

"Why don't you apply for the job?" Nath suggested.

The closing date for applications was coincidentally the following day so there was no time to procrastinate.

"Fuck it, I will." I said. I didn't expect to get it anyway, they wanted someone to start immediately, and I wasn't out of the army for another four months. If nothing else it would be a valuable experience to go through the application process.

A few minutes later Nath had spoken to his friend at the sports centre and arranged for me to go down there and meet him, so off we went. Simon was a nice bloke, very passionate about the centre, and keen to increase the staff numbers. We spoke for a while, and he suggested I apply and send my CV via email.

"I've actually got a copy of my CV with me now." I told him. "I wrote it yesterday by chance."

While he'd been talking about the job roles and responsibilities

I couldn't help but think my CV was already a great fit. I handed him the document, conscious that it might look like I'd prepared it specifically for the job.

"It might look like I've written that for this job, but I honestly haven't." I said. "I wrote that as a generic CV yesterday, and only heard about this job a couple of hours ago."

Nath and I returned to camp, and later that night I formally applied for the job online. Within a couple of days I received an email stating that I'd made the shortlist of applicants and was invited to attend an interview. The interview went well, and on the promise that I'd complete a civilian personal trainer course at my own expense I got the job.

The personal trainer course was well taught but far less informative or useful than the army PTI course I did in 1998. From the outset it was clear that half of the students had absolutely no interest in physical fitness whatsoever and were only there for the kudos of the qualification. Individuals were late every day, took multiple days off, and spent more time on their phones than listening to the instructor. If it were a military course they'd have been thrown out on day one. The other half were good though and included a former Royal Marine and an ex-Guardsman, who were both very keen. On the final day it was frustrating to learn that everyone had passed when some had made no effort at all, and others had grafted throughout. I raised it with the instructor, who despite his own obvious passion for the industry had obviously stopped caring. He'd done his bit and had another course starting in a few days' time where he'd do it all again. It was a money-making exercise, and if he didn't do the job someone else would gladly take his place.

CHAPTER FOURTEEN
THE CIVILIAN

I started working at the sports centre part-time, using my remaining leave and resettlement days as work experience instead of taking time off. I'd committed to it when I did the personal trainer course and wanted to give it a fair go, so I worked there for free, spending the rest of my time at the SERE school. I took bootcamp, circuit training, and military-style battle fitness and spent a lot of time preparing my classes so the clients both enjoyed them and found them challenging. However, I quickly learned that civilians don't do fitness the way we did in the army. Although there were some very fit people who loved a good beasting, for many it was more of a social event where they met up with friends and chatted while exercising leisurely. Most of them wanted to do the same old exercises they'd been doing for years and were comfortable with, and none of them wanted to listen to me explaining or demonstrating anything. It took all of my self-control to not start shouting at them and dishing out push-ups, but they were paying customers not soldiers, and they could do whatever they wanted. Controlling civilians was much harder than soldiers, because in the army everyone understands the same terminology, but I had to find alternatives to the commands I was used to:

Military language	Civilian language
"On me!"	"Can everyone come over here please?"
"Listen in!"	"Can I have your attention please?"
"Cover off!"	"Stand next to your equipment."
"In position, ready!"	"Prepare to begin the exercise."
"You're late. Give me fifty push-ups!"	"Join in when you're ready."
"You fuckers are not working!"	"Well done guys, keep up the hard work."
"Do not fucking stop until I tell you to!"	"Stop if you feel any discomfort."
"If you don't start working, I'll keep you here all fucking day!"	"We'll finish exactly on time so you can get on with whatever you need to do."
"I'm going to beast you until your fucking eyes bleed!"	"Today we'll be doing some anaerobic training."
"At the speed of a thousand Gazelles!"	"When you're good and ready."
"Are you fucking stupid?"	"Sorry if I didn't explain myself clearly enough for you."
"Get away you wretched creatures!"	"Thanks for coming. Goodbye."

My contract with the army finished in February 2020 and I left quietly after almost twenty-seven years' service, immediately starting full time employment at the sports centre as a senior coach. Along with the fitness classes, Simon and I also began running a community mental-health support project called the Pathfinder Programme. Open to walk-ins and NHS referrals, we taught morning and evening survival lessons to local people who were struggling with their mental health. Conscious we weren't trained in psychotherapy, we didn't ask personal questions or push agendas on our guests, instead our sessions were based on mindful activities such as fire lighting, cordage making, knot tying, and foraging etc. It was a whole new experience for me, but very rewarding to watch many of them grow in confidence and develop new skills. We had men and women who suffered with depression, anxiety, PTSD, schizophrenia, addictions, learning difficulties, agoraphobia, and personality disorders. Some had experienced domestic abuse, childhood trauma, bullying, and imprisonment, and some had attempted suicide or been sectioned. It didn't matter to us why they were there, we never asked, and we never judged, but several of them would talk openly about their problems once they settled in, with some disturbing stories from their troubled pasts. Without doubt I met people through that programme that I would never have met otherwise, and In all honesty I'd probably have actively avoided some of them based solely on their appearance before getting to know them. It made me realise that as human beings we really do have more in common than what divides us. As group we probably held some strongly opposing political, societal, and ethical views, but a shared interest in the great outdoors, and learning about the environment gave us enough common ground to sit down together and enjoy each other's company. Of course the fact we were all complete lunatics helped too.

When the Covid 19 pandemic forced the closure of the sports centre and everyone went in to lockdown, the pathfinder programme was permitted to continue under a medical waiver. Apart from that I had a lot of time on my hands, so I decided to use it to finish the book I'd started in 2006. Over the years I'd added to "Meatheads" sporadically during quiet periods, but it was still only half complete. I knuckled down, writing for several hours a day until it was done, then thought about getting it published. After two months I'd received six or seven contract offers from publishers, but I didn't really understand the jargon in their emails or what they were actually offering, and after talking to some friends who'd already had books published I considered doing it myself through Amazon. While waiting for a response on "Meatheads" I started to write another book called "You'd Be Nuts Too!" which I completed quickly and decided to go ahead with self-publishing. I'm far too impatient to wait around and didn't see the point in having two complete books sat idly on my laptop. I released them in quick succession, both hitting number one in their respective categories, then started on book number three "Don't Ask". In the space of a year I wrote and released three books, and not long after that I started on this one.

In the first "Rambo, First Blood" movie, there's a scene near the end, where an angry John Rambo is surrounded by police and facing capture or death. In a bid to deter him from further violence his old special forces commander, Colonel Trautman intervenes with a radio call.

"It's over Johnny!" he tells him.

"Nothing's over!" Rambo yells. "You just don't turn it off!" He then goes into a furious rant where he tells Trautman how civilian life has nothing for him after serving alongside his military brothers. "Back there I was in charge of million-dollar equipment, now I can't even hold down a job cleaning fucking cars!" he shouts. Rambo was a leader of men in the Vietnam War, responsible for life or death situations, but in civvy street he'd become a lonely wanderer, a nomad, aimlessly walking from town to town without any real purpose.

It's a great scene that has resonated more and more with me as I've grown older, the significance of the words and emotions reflecting those of my own.

As a private soldier in 3 PARA I was in charge

of a million dollars' worth of equipment when I ran the communications detachment for the commanding officer. Even at that stage of my career I was accountable for Land Rovers, BV206 over-snow vehicles, radio systems, cryptographic material, and weapons. Twenty years later, as a civilian, working in a sports centre I was in charge of a v-mop, eight toilet brushes, and a vending machine, it was hideous. Many soldiers, including myself, genuinely predict that civvy street will be a doddle, and the prospect of having no responsibility seems quite alluring while they're still serving in their twilight years, but in reality, it's not that simple. I made a point of cleaning the toilets daily when I worked at the sports centre. Partly, I did it to show my colleagues that I wasn't afraid of getting my hands dirty, partly to deliberately start as I meant to go on, and partly because they needed cleaning after a day's use anyway. The problem was, most of the others didn't share my standards of cleanliness and rarely did it themselves. One day I was vigorously brushing the skid marks left by a thousand schoolkids and gym users in the male changing rooms when I heard the door open, and someone enter. Stooped over in the cubicle I turned my head to see who it was and imagined how I'd react if it was one of my old soldiers from the Pathfinders walking in. I thought about how I'd feel if one of the men that I'd been the sergeant major for was to see me stood there, toilet-brush in hand. I've never felt above any task, no matter how menial, and have always kept my feet firmly on the ground, but in that moment I realised how disappointing it would be for that soldier to see me in that situation. It wasn't that I was better than that, it was that I had a lot more to offer than that. I felt like a right fucking loser, like I'd let my soldiers, myself, and my regiment down.

Over the years I've heard loads of soldiers say that a job stacking shelves in B&Q or Tesco's would be perfect when they've finished their service. "No responsibility", "No bullshit", "No accounting", "No inspections" they'll say. If it's not that, it's the idea of being a postman that gets the juices flowing. "Early start, early finish", "Gets you outside", "Don't have to talk to anyone", "Keeps you fit" is what everyone sees as the positives. In my limited experience, the joy of these perks would be short-lived for most people, especially anyone who'd worked at the higher levels of capability or responsibility.

On completion of twenty-four years' service in the army, a good friend of mine recently told me he'd applied for a job as a house-keeper on a large property owned by a wealthy family.

"What do you mean, like an estate manager?" I asked. House-keeper sounded like a cleaning job to me.

"No mate, house-keeper." he confirmed, before explaining the likely cleaning and tidying tasks he'd be responsible for around the home. My initial thought was that he was massively under-selling himself, and that he should be aiming much higher, but I knew that he was struggling with his mental health, so I held back, and instead wished him luck. A few days later I called him again, and he was pleased to tell me that he'd been offered the job. At the same time as being pleased for him I was gutted, because I knew from personal experience that the job would never be fulfilling for a man of his calibre. He was a Parachute Regiment sergeant major with vast operational and command experience in some of the most challenging environments imaginable. Picking up other people's dirty washing and making their beds was not the best use of his skills or abilities. I'm not suggesting that cleaning jobs aren't important or honourable, I'm just highlighting the fact that many veterans don't appreciate the potential value they hold for prospective civilian employers and will sometimes settle for any job they can get when the end of their military career suddenly becomes a reality.

In the army I was qualified and competent in many things. I was a physical training instructor, military ski instructor, weapons instructor, combatives instructor, survival instructor, escape & evasion instructor, forward air controller, and tandem master, with many years' experience managing people, training, infrastructure, and complex projects. However, when I left the army all of this seemed immediately irrelevant when I started scrolling through the job opportunities on websites and social media. When leaving the military you are sent on courses to help you transition into civilian life, and on those courses they do their best to convince you that you are full of great qualities and transferable skills that employers are yearning for, but on paper your submitted CV could easily be your downfall. You can try to put it in generic terms, but there's no escaping the fact that you have been in the army, and you are inexperienced in the nuances of civilian work-life. In civvy street I was back to being a Joe Crow, with no experience in many day-to-day problems that a man of my age should understand intimately. I didn't even know how to arrange a dental or doctor's appointment, and the whole bill-paying process is still a mystery that remains entirely under my wife's control.

As a sergeant major, people of all ranks would often come to me for advice, and more often than not I found that I could help them out in one way or another. By the time you reach that rank you're invariably one of the older people in a unit, so it's a fair assumption that you'll have some experience in the kind of situations people are struggling with. It could be welfare, discipline, medical, psychological, financial, social, or professional, but I almost always knew what to do or say, and if I didn't, I knew where to find out. After a few years in the army there wasn't much left that could shock me, and after two decades there was even less that I hadn't seen or heard about before; ABH, GBH, PTSD, ADHD, breakdowns, break-ups, affray, arson, assault, adultery, AWOL, A-holes, amputation, asphyxiation, decapitation, paralysation, murder and rape allegation, self-harm, firearms, vandalism, Naziism, kidnap, theft, mutiny, drunk-and-disorderly, suicide, fratricide, lewd conduct, BDSM, cross-border, cross-dressing, homosexuality, bisexuality, transsexuality, bestiality, snuff, scat, steroid abuse, alcohol misuse, domestic abuse, incest, civil unrest, accidental death, prostitution, retribution, you name it.

When I left the army and lost my identity as a soldier I think I needed to find a new belonging to replace it. I'd been a paratrooper for more than half my life and almost all of my adulthood. Whenever someone asked me what I did for a living I used to proudly tell them I was in the Parachute Regiment, and when filling out on-line documentation, if paratrooper wasn't an option, I'd scroll down until I found a suitable alternative like "Armed Forces", "Army", or "MoD". As a civilian I felt like a bit of an outcast, a loner. I was no longer part of a tribe and didn't know where I belonged. For a while I told people I was Cornish and justified it by stating that I'd served my country for a long time, could choose wherever I wanted as home, and had chosen Cornwall. It didn't matter where I chose really, you could argue I wasn't truly from anywhere. Now I don't care, it doesn't matter, just like you don't have to pledge your allegiance to a particular football or rugby team, you don't have to be from a specific town either. I know I'll never be a part of something as substantial as the paras, the airborne brotherhood, or the PF again, and that makes me a little bit sad sometimes, because nothing will ever replicate the feeling of pride, camaraderie, and esprit de corps I felt as part of that family. I worked hard to earn my place there and did my best to uphold and represent the standards and ethos that it stood for, never resting on my laurels, or accepting anything less. As a civilian I'll always be proud to call myself a former paratrooper and pathfinder, but I'm under no illusions, those days are over for me and before long there will be nobody left in the army who even remembers me, I'll be just another name beneath a picture on the wall, and rightly so. I was nobody special, but hopefully I made a positive difference to someone or something during my time there. No one is, or ever should be irreplaceable in the army, because the wheel has to keep on turning and moving forwards. If you work hard, act respectfully, stay humble, and stand up for what you believe in, you'll be remembered by the people that matter to you for the right reasons, and you'll be able to sleep at night knowing you did your best. That's about as good as it gets.

An old friend of mine in 3 PARA used to vociferously claim to be Scottish, despite the fact that he wasn't born there, and had never even lived there. To be honest, I don't think he'd even visited the place, but he was adamant that he was a true Scotsman, proudly wearing his Hibernian Football Club shirt, and flying a Scottish flag above his bed. It really wound me up that he had, what seemed to me, a totally illegitimate loyalty to a place he clearly didn't belong, and I'd actually get quite angry about it. The problem was, he wasn't really from anywhere. His father was Scottish, his mother was Irish, and he was born in Germany while his dad was serving there with the British army. As a military family they moved around a few times, and Danny had eventually joined the army himself from his home in Cyprus. One day after challenging him on his nationality, he said to me "Alright then Steve, where am I from then?"

I had no answer. It was way too complicated. "Not Scotland!" was all I had. I just didn't get it.

About twenty years later, I realised I was in the same situation Danny had been in all those years before. Enjoying a few pints with a friend in a Wadebridge pub, we were approached by a local who started a conversation. Predictably the question soon came.

"Where are you two from then?" he asked.

"I'm from Bath." Will replied. He'd bought a house in Wadebridge, and lived a short distance from me, but still called Bath home.

The man nodded, then looked at me.

"I'm from Wadebridge." I told him. As far as I was concerned I was from Wadebridge. I lived there, paid my council tax there, my kids went to school there, and my wife worked there.

The local wasn't convinced though, my accent was telling him otherwise. "Yeah, but where are you *really* from?" he quizzed.

I was bored of this conversation, it seemed like I was having it every other week, but I'd realised I held a trump card. "I've been in the army for the last twenty five years mate, so I've moved around a lot. But now I live here, so I'm from here." I told him. That seemed to hold a bit of weight and appease him somewhat.

"Ah okay. What part of the army are you in?" he asked, suddenly a bit more respectful.

"I'm in the Parachute Regiment." I replied.

There are some military units that everyone has heard of and require no further explanation. The Paras, Marines, Gurkhas, and only a few others tend to be in that category. We got on fine after that.

I was actually born in Salisbury but only because it was the nearest hospital. By some peoples reckoning that means I'm from Salisbury but I've never lived there, and I can't name a single street there. My first seven years were in Andover, then Haslemere, and then Aylesbury where I spent the longest amount of time and did most of my schooling. Once I joined the army I lived in Lichfield, Catterick, Aldershot, Dover, Ipswich, Colchester, Gosport, Newquay, South Wales, Warminster, and Wadebridge. Nobody wants to hear all that to work out where I'm from, and to be honest their guess would be as good as mine anyway.

In the military when someone asks you where you're from they normally mean which unit, not town, which is much simpler and less ambiguous. Special forces guys just say the name of their town, "Poole" or "Hereford". Royal Marines will respond with a number in the forties "Forty" "Four Two" or "Four Five". Scottish infantry are 1 SCOTS through to 7 SCOTS. Some units are a bit more of a mouthful, like the PWRR, JCTAT or the now disbanded RGBW and KORBR .

Increasingly these days people tend to identify themselves by their race, religion, gender, or sexuality, like that is what defines them, but these traits and characteristics were of little significance to us during my service. I can't speak for other units but assume they operate the same, where nobody really cares about that kind of stuff. As long as you are fit, capable, and loyal, you'll get the respect you deserve regardless, and expecting preferential, or special treatment because of your personal choices will only alienate you. Pronouns, politics, and preferences are trumped by rank, role, and responsibility, and so they should be.

In the army there was a protocol or procedure for just about everything. When marching we always stepped-off with the left foot first, when patrolling we adopted different formations for different terrain. There were six section-battle-drills, four platoon-battle-drills, four types of fire-control-order, seven reasons why things were seen, and four priorities of survival. When answering the telephone there was only one way to do it properly, and I must have said "Pathfinders, Sergeant Major Brown Sir" thousands of times. When speaking on a radio there were specific words to begin a message, acknowledge a message, and end a message. Words like "Roger", "over", "wait", and "out" ensured messages could be passed uninterrupted and efficiently. Sick-parade was at 0800hrs every morning at the Medical Centre, and breakfast, lunch, and dinner were served in the cookhouse at the same time every day. There were also specific people to deal with specific issues. The CQMS dealt with equipment, the clerk dealt with admin, the PTI organised the fitness, the MT dealt with vehicles, and the medical centre dealt with injuries. Life was simple.

The military has a well-established hierarchy that's understood by everyone too, and each individual knows exactly where they sit within it. Among the services of the Navy, Army, and Air Force these structures differ slightly, with their own unique ranks and traditions, but the rules remain roughly the same.

-Civilians are not like you, and they will never fully understand you. You are not one of them.

-Recruits are almost civilians. Treat them with the disrespect they deserve.

-New soldiers, sailors, and airmen are almost as dumb as recruits. Assume they are stupid but demand the highest standards anyway.

-Old soldiers, sailors, and airmen with no interest or desire for promotion have nothing to lose so handle them carefully.

-Junior Non-Commissioned Officers are at the peak of their physical fitness, ability, and motivation. They need either encouragement and guidance, or to be kept on a leash.

-Senior Non-Commissioned Officers are volatile, stubborn, and cynical beyond their years. Their job is to prevent young officers from messing up, and to prevent young soldiers doing the things they used to enjoy doing before they had responsibilities.

-Warrant Officers are grumpy old bastards that know everyone and everything that's going on. They have done all the stupid things you've done, but they got away with it.

-Lieutenants, or junior officers are stupid. They have a finite amount of time available to be ridiculed and abused, so make the most of it. Make them think that your idea was actually their idea, and they'll do exactly what you want.

-Captains have paid their dues and learnt the ropes. They have the confidence to call you out if you don't salute them. If they are going to turn into a prick, it will be during this period that their true colours will come through.

-Majors are no longer acceptable targets for abuse. Respect them, or at least pretend to, because they can make your life a misery.

-Lieutenant Colonels are the big cheese of their empire, and interactions with them could be career changing. Act sensibly, salute them, and call them Sir or Ma'am.

-Officers above the rank of Lt Col are seldom seen outside of headquarters establishments. You don't even need to learn their ranks, so long as you understand they are called Sir, or Ma'am and they are in a different class to you. They won't tell you if they don't like you, they'll just hint it to someone else and let them ruin you instead.

-Outside of work there is a time and place for rank, but it cannot be used and abused like a get-out-of-jail-free card. If one man treats another disrespectfully or with contempt, especially after alcohol has been consumed, he should be prepared for that man to defend himself.

In civvy street these rules seem far less established and in a society where respect is becoming an old-fashioned trait, politeness is too time consuming, and compassion is seen as a weakness, I was like a fish out of water as a civilian. Several friends were surprised that I got a job where I was sometimes front-of-house, spending time at a reception desk, welcoming customers. They were right to be sceptical because I hated it. Dozens of people walked past every day, doing their best to avoid eye contact. Some were attempting to gain free access to the gym, some just wanted to use the toilets, and some were simply rude, but I quickly learned that to them I was insignificant, just some annoying man with inconvenient questions like "Can I help you?" and "Are you a member?"

One man seemed exasperated when I asked him his name

once. He wanted me to give him the keys to one of the out-buildings.

"Don't you know who I am?" he snapped.

"Nope." I said. "I have no idea. I've never met you before."

With his head held high he proudly let me know the significance of his authority, that he held the high office of Treasurer of one of the resident sports clubs. "I've been on the committee since before this place even opened!" he told me.

I think I was supposed to be impressed by that. "Nice to meet you mate." I said. "I'm Steve, what's your name please?"

As a former paratrooper it might seem ironic or hypocritical for me to say this, but I detest people who think they're better than everyone else or look down on others, and abuse of power through rank, status, or reverence disgusts me. It took me a while to reach the mindset I now have, but rest assured, I've been humbled, impressed, and inspired by other people so many times, that I long ago stopped judging individuals by the superficialities of appearance or accolades. I've been fortunate enough to be part of some fantastic units, training teams, martial arts clubs, and support groups, but as an individual I've never been the best at anything at all. There's always been plenty of soldiers, students, athletes, coaches, and instructors who were better, more knowledgeable, or more skilled than me. I've always known and accepted this, and I think that has both helped and impeded me in my own personal development. I'm not a particularly competitive person, because I'm well aware that I can be beaten by someone in any contest, so winning is not always that important to me. As long as I don't let myself or my team down through lack of trying, I really don't care. For me, competitiveness will often take the enjoyment out of something, because there will inevitably be a winner and a loser in any competition, and nobody likes losing. I don't want to feel bad from losing, and I don't want to feel bad about making someone else feel bad if I beat them either. People who turn everything into a contest really irritate me. For them it makes things more fun and incentivises them, but for me it has the opposite effect, I'm just stressed about who will be left feeling demoralised. Some of my best friends and family are hyper competitive and it motivates them to put 100% effort into what they're doing which is great, but I'll avoid doing it with them if I can. Anything against kids I'll happily let them win, especially if they're learning something new, because I want them to enjoy it and carry it on afterwards. If I can engineer it, I'll do my best to make it difficult for them to win, but I think we both get more out of it when it's a close match, but they are the ultimate victor. I know some people are opposed to that style of teaching, and I understand why, but there's nothing worse than watching a fully grown adult ruthlessly destroy a kid Ten-Nil at a game of Connect 4, draughts, or shooting hoops, then justify it by saying something like "They need to learn they can't always win". These are the same people who wonder why the kid never wants to play the games again, and are surprised when they find an abandoned, deflated ball at the bottom of the garden a few weeks later, or an unused chess-set gathering dust on top of a wardrobe. I do understand how important healthy competition is though. It drives people to excel in their chosen field and rewards hard work, discipline, and determination. Striving to be the best will draw out the full potential of any individual or team, and the best people in anything are always the competitive ones.

In the military, when you're taking anti-depressants, you have regular reviews with your doctor to see how you're getting on. I had a really good Medical Officer called Liz for my last five years of service, who seemed to have a genuine interest in my well-being. When a doctor talks to you as a person, rather than a patient, I think it makes a massive difference on how you communicate, enabling you to be more honest, and speak freely. I've always kept it professional with doctors, addressing them as "Doc" to acknowledge the hierarchy in the room, but also kept it informal and friendly. One day I was talking to Liz after she'd just given me a repeat prescription when I said something that I've thought about many times since. We'd had a good chat about how I was feeling at the time, and I was stood in the doorway of her office, about to leave, when, as a parting shot I solemnly said, "Depression is depressing." I'd never said or thought that before, and on the surface it probably sounds a bit stupid, stating the obvious, but it was actually a moment of realisation. Depression *is* depressing! It's a vicious cycle, that's really difficult to get out of. For me, there is often no explanation for it. My life is pretty good, compared to some it's a relative paradise, but that doesn't stop me from suffering bouts of deep depression that sometimes last for many months.

Years ago my mum expressed concern as I walked her to her car after a visit to my house. "I don't know why you seem so unhappy." she said. "You've got a nice home, a wife who loves you, and children who adore you. You should be happy." I had no answer, she was right, and it was as much of a mystery to me as it was to her. I just shrugged my shoulders and feigned a grin.

"I'm alright mum." I replied. "Don't worry about me."

It's not self-pity, in fact it's probably closer to self-loathing that keeps you down when you're in a depressed state. I've questioned my own existence many times and felt guilty that life has been wasted on me, when it could have been gifted to someone else, who'd have been more grateful and done more with it. The truth is, as much as I'd like to have me as a friend, I don't actually like myself very much at all, but I don't know why.

Sometimes when I'm driving my car fast along a

motorway or main road, I think about closing my eyes and letting the inevitable happen. The thought makes me feel peaceful, relaxed, for just a few short seconds. I imagine that death from a high speed collision would be instantaneous, like turning out the lights, or dying in your sleep. I wouldn't alter my speed or steering, just close my eyes. I wouldn't even close them tightly, just let them rest gently as if going to sleep. After a few seconds I think about what I might have collided with in that last short distance if I'd actually done it. Maybe I'd have carried on dead straight and hit nothing for a long time. Maybe I'd have smashed into the car heading towards me at speed on the other side of the road, or maybe I'd have slammed into the solid, concrete base of the bridge I'd just driven under. The selfish part of me briefly enjoys the macabre thought of ending it, and the relief it would bring, but within another few seconds I start to consider the possible consequences. My suicide would ruin my family, especially my kids. It would change them and their lives forever. A suicide note or video would never be enough to answer their questions about why I'd done it. They might blame themselves, or even each other, or they might understandably blame me, and hate me for the rest of their lives, forever angry about what I'd done.

And what about the others involved in my crash? People in any other vehicles involved would be just as likely to die as I would. It could be an innocent family with children in the car and they could become orphans, grieving parents, amputees, or mutilated casualties, for what? Because I was feeling sorry for myself? Unacceptable. Even the emergency services would be psychologically scarred for life, attending a scene like that. Why should a paramedic have to try and save the life of someone who's been so reckless. If I wasn't killed instantly, they'd have to deal with the aftermath, taking on that huge burden of critical care.

Another factor to consider is the excellent safety features in modern vehicles. Seatbelts and airbags could save your life but leave you with permanent disabilities, you could end up paralysed and unable to finish what you started, sentenced to a life in a wheelchair or on life-support.

A while ago, I walked into the kitchen and my wife was in there tidying up. Emptying our dishwasher, she stood up with a large silver knife in her hand. I looked at that long, shiny blade and almost smirked, as I fantasised about her thrusting it into my body. We'd had a bit of an argument, but there was no actual threat or likelihood of her doing that, it's not in her nature at all. A few days later I was making myself a brew in that same kitchen when I noticed two sweetener pellets on top of the small plastic dispenser they belonged to. It was strange to see them there, I suppose somebody had accidentally clicked the button too many times in a rush. I pondered that they could be some kind of poison, placed there deliberately, but inconspicuously by my wife, in the hope that I'd use them, and unwittingly seal my own fate. Again I knew it was highly unlikely, but the thought of it was quite exciting, and I picked the tiny caplets up and dropped them into my mug. Having undergone a significant amount of psychotherapy, I recognise that is not necessarily a normal thought process. I'd guess that those ideas wouldn't enter most people's mind at all. You could argue that there was no real threat, and that I knew they were safe, and I would probably agree. But thinking like that all the time, even considering it as a possibility, in the safety of your own home, that's not healthy.

Some people with an addiction to alcohol or drugs will continue to class themselves as alcoholics or addicts, even after many years of disciplined abstinence from the stuff. This is because they recognise and understand that they are not "cured", and they never will be. Instead, they are merely managing their condition with the help of medication, therapy, or coping mechanisms to effectively suppress their unwelcome urges and cravings. They know that they will always be addicts, and that they sit permanently on the edge of a precipice that falling from would cause devastating consequences. This is the same way I view mental illness, with those affected never really cured, but hopefully able to reach a point where they have enough self-awareness and control to exist in relative peace, even if it's only for short periods at a time. Hypervigilance and the accompanying anxiety that it brings can be all-consuming, with every person, vehicle, sound, movement, and gesture becoming a potential trigger. The reactions to these perceived threats can be varied, sometimes you'll feel fear, other times it will be anger, frustration, excitement, nervousness, confusion, self-doubt, paranoia, or a combination of them. Any one of these psychological reactions will have a physiological effect too, releasing stress hormones like cortisol and adrenaline into the body, and raising your heart-rate and blood-pressure due to your natural "fight or flight" response. In my experience it is extremely difficult, if not impossible to switch these thoughts and emotions off, because they are ingrained deep into the psyche. However, I do believe that it's possible to manage them, at least to some degree.

My old psychologist used to set me challenges between sessions sometimes, giving me at least a week to attempt them. One week the challenge was to sit somewhere in a café or restaurant that made me feel vulnerable or uncomfortable. Like many soldiers, my default setting is to sit with my back to the wall, with good arcs of observation across the room, especially the exits and entrances. I'd previously told her that sitting like this makes me feel better prepared for an attack. I could see people come and go, identify any threats early by observing the other customers' behaviour, and use the wall to protect my back.

"How many times have you actually been attacked in a café?" she asked.

I knew where she was heading with that line of questioning. "None." I replied. "But you could argue that that kind of proves

I'm doing the right thing. Maybe I would have been attacked if I was unprepared." As soon as the words left my mouth, I knew I was fighting a losing battle.

She continued. "And how likely do you think it is that someone will randomly decide to attack you in a café in Cornwall?"

I took a deep breath through my nose as my mind raced through a dozen scenarios. Not only had it never happened to me before, but none of my friends or family had ever had it happen to them either. Outside of gangster movies I couldn't actually recall a single such incident. "Not very likely I suppose." I conceded.

That afternoon, straight after the session I went into a Starbucks coffee shop in Plymouth and sat right in the middle of the seating area with my back to the door. It was uncomfortable, and I didn't like it very much, but I did it, and although I finished my drink in record time, I completed the challenge successfully.

One of the many things that trigger my hypervigilance is someone driving too close behind me on the road, especially at night when I can't see their face in my mirrors because of the glare from their headlights. To me, tailgating is an act of aggression, a bully tactic of intimidation that makes me angry, stressed, and anxious. I know the majority of people probably aren't deliberately causing me stress when they do this, they are most likely just ignorant, or bad drivers, but until they overtake, or we go in separate directions my automatic assumption will be that they mean me harm. My heart rate increases, my grip on the steering wheel tightens, and I frown deeply as my mind starts racing through different scenarios, all with explosive outcomes. If I'm already in a bad mood the thoughts can be quite exciting, and I sometimes hope they materialise, grinning maniacally at the prospect of impending violence. Thankfully it's never come to that.

Getting on trains is something I dread, but only when

I have a seat reserved. As I approach the carriage I always assume that someone will be sat in my seat, and I think about how I'll deal with it. Multiple scenarios go through my head based on who it is and how they react. If it's an elderly or pregnant person I'd just try and find another seat or stand up. If it's a young person, I'd probably tell them the seat was reserved for me and hope they apologised and moved. If it was a man I'd definitely have to ask them to find another seat and be prepared for confrontation. Other variables race through my mind and make it much more complicated than that though; What if they are drunk, on drugs, asleep, aggressive, anxious, with a group, with a kid, mentally ill, armed, or don't speak English? It's actually only ever happened to me a couple of times and both times it was men who moved on and sat somewhere else. I remember one of them told me that somebody was sat in his seat, so he'd taken mine, like that was a fair enough excuse.

"And how does that become my problem?" I asked him, staring into his eyes and shaking my head as I motioned with my thumb for him to get out.

Airplane journeys elicit the same emotions from me, but for a different reason. It's unlikely someone will be sat in the wrong seat on a plane, and even if they are it will be a genuine mistake where they'll just be a little bit embarrassed and promptly move. What stresses me out about air travel is overhead luggage space. I always travel with a small backpack, well within the dictated size dimensions, but when I look around at what other people are carrying while we're waiting to board, their blatant disregard for the rules gets me quite vexed. So many people carry small suitcases on with them nowadays, normally accompanied by another bag that they'll perch on top of it, taking more baggage into the cabin than I've got in the hold. Once on the plane it's dog eat dog, with people desperately filling cabinets that aren't even near their own seats, and I always convince myself that by the time I get to my seat some selfish prick will have already filled the small space above it with their oversized "man-bag" or stupid little suitcase on wheels. I walk down the aisle trying to think about something else, avoiding eye contact with all the people I'm quietly fantasising about throwing out as soon as the seatbelt light goes off, swiftly followed by their shiny designer bags. If I did do that the cabin crew community would probably claim me as their patron saint.

Laziness and rudeness are probably the two things that anger me more than anything else on this planet. I've been punched in the head, bricked, glassed, rocketed, bombed, and shot at without getting angry about it, but ignorance and idleness, they drive me absolutely nuts. If I possessed a magic wand that could instantly remove people from existence, I'd probably decimate the world's population within weeks. People that don't indicate, people who don't say thanks when you hold a door open or give way to them, people that queue jump, people who tailgate, and people who drop litter on the floor would all feel my wrath. People who are obnoxious to police officers, security guards, referees, shopkeepers, waiters, or any kind of service provider would all also be in mortal danger. It's only a quick flash, but those kind of folk enrage me, and in that second I'd enthusiastically banish them to the depths of hell with a quick flick of the wrist.

Being around people who are not listening to each other, which to me is a combination of rudeness and laziness is something I absolutely cannot tolerate. More often than not it seems to me like people are just waiting for their turn to speak, rather than listening to anyone else. In the military, when using radios, we had things called "voice procedure" and "net discipline". These principles of communication ensured that information was passed on in a timely and orderly manner, using the acronyms "ABC" and "KISS":

Accuracy – Facts, not guesses or opinions

Brevity – To the point. No waffle. Short sentences

Clarity – Plain English. Phonetic alphabet

Keep

It

Simple

Stupid

Deep down, despite my sometimes horrible thought processes, I'm pretty sure I'm a decent human being. For the most part I play by the rules, and when I don't, I accept there will be consequences if I'm caught. If I exceed a speed limit or illegally park and get a ticket, I won't complain, I know the rules. Play stupid games, get stupid prizes. I'm a big believer in treating others as you'd expect to be treated yourself, and by my reckoning I'm fairly considerate, polite, and honourable. Because of this, something that used to really bother me until a few years ago was the thought that someone didn't like me. A disapproving look, a second hand comment, or a reluctance to speak to me could quite easily ruin my day, and either make me feel anger towards them, or start questioning my own actions and behaviour that may have upset them. To some this might sound a bit self-righteous or reek of insecurity, and I can understand that, maybe I am a little of both.

I once had a neighbour who lived directly opposite my house but always did his best to ignore me whenever we were in close proximity. One day whilst weeding my front garden I made an extra effort to get his attention as he got out of his car and crossed the road to introduce myself.

"Hello mate, my name's Steve." I said, extending my arm to shake his hand. "I live opposite you, but we've never actually met."

My neighbour seemed a bit surprised and nervous but accepted my handshake. I'm well aware that to some people I look like a miserable bastard or an angry hooligan, but it's not intentional and I try my best not to. I'm also conscious that I speak quietly, but that's mainly because I sound very abrupt if I speak loudly, which makes people think I'm having a go at them. I learned that his name was Peter and after a short conversation I shook his hand once more, said it was nice to meet him, and went back to what I was doing. The next night I saw him again, this time with his wife.

"Alright Peter?" I called. When he didn't respond I gave him the benefit of the doubt and tried again. Maybe he was a bit deaf like me. "Alright Peter?" I said, this time a bit louder. His wife looked at me and smiled, but he continued to ignore me, so I started walking towards him. "Peter....Peter.....Peter!"

His wife spoke up nervously as I got close. "Is there something wrong?" she asked as he turned around to face me.

"No, I'm just trying to say hello to Peter, but he's not answering me." I said, looking him straight in the eye. "You do remember me don't you?" I asked him abruptly. Pointing to myself, then the ground. "We had a conversation yesterday, right here."

"Oh yeah, of course mate, is everything ok?" he replied. He knew he'd been ignorant, and he knew I was calling him out on it. His wife knew too.

"He's not being rude or anything, we just didn't recognise you that's all." she bluffed.

"Well I'm Steve, and I live in that house right there." I clarified, pointing at my house. "When you didn't answer me I thought you might be thinking I was some kind of random weirdo, walking around shouting your name in the street, so I just wanted to make sure you knew it was only me." I explained. I doubt it made them feel any better though, if anything all I'd done is convince them that I was not only some kind of random weirdo, but I was also quite an angry and aggressive one too. What I really wanted to happen of course, was for Peter to act aggressively towards me, so I could justify punching him in the face, but in hindsight that was probably more down to my own insecurities than his ignorance.

I always try to make eye contact and say hello to everyone I interact with, to me it's just basic manners. People who don't respond when I greet them in the street or shops frustrate me too, and sometimes when I'm in a bad mood I can't let it go unaddressed. Many a time I've called people ignorant pricks or told them to go fuck themselves when they've blatantly ignored me or failed to acknowledge a polite gesture such as holding a door open for them. People at the shopping tills aren't safe sometimes either:

"Hello mate, you alright?" I'll ask. The ones that don't even look up and immediately start scanning my stuff are the worst. "I take it you're not alright then?" I'll continue, standing still and staring at them until they look at me. "Are you okay?" They'll answer eventually, they always do. I realise they might have had a shitty day, or they may be shy, or bored, but when I'm in a bad mood ignorance really gets my goat.

COVID facemasks made communication difficult, especially for people with hearing loss who rely on lip-reading, and I massively struggled to understand people, especially the staff in shops, who were often behind a cloth mask and a protective plastic screen. I absolutely detested wearing those masks, but there was a plus side. I found it much easier to walk around talking to myself and was far less self-conscious about looking like a nut case. Most of the time I can keep it under wraps, but when I'm super-stressed I can't contain it, chatting quietly to myself or bitching about everyone and everything I see or hear. Face masks made it possible to talk the whole time you were out, because nobody could see your lips moving. People often say that talking to yourself is the first sign of madness, but I hope they're wrong, because I not only talk to myself quite a lot, I have 3-way conversations. It's not deliberate, it just comes out, but sometimes it even makes me laugh. The following are a few text messages I sent to my good friend Will, a close confident of mine who I often tell about the stupid things I do or say:

> Just did an exercise in the gym and said the following:
>
> > "That's a good one that. We like that one don't we?
> > "Yeah we like that one mate."
> > "You like that one do you?"
> > "Yeah, we do, you got a fucking problem with that?"
>
> There's 3 of me. Got to work out which one is the angry one.

> Conversation I had with myself earlier. There's definitely 3 of me:
>
> > "You talk to yourself a lot don't you?"
> > "Yeah, I've noticed that. You do talk to yourself a lot."
> > "I suppose so mate, yeah. Do you talk to yourself too?"
> > "Not as much as you mate!"

> "I walked past some blokes in Aldi today, and one said to the other "Ooh look, Marmite!" Under my mask I said, "Fuck you, you fucking prick." Like he was calling me Marmite.

> "Right, what are we doing?"
>
> "I don't know what we're doing!"
>
> "Who's we?"
>
> "Us you fucking prick!"

Over five years of therapy there weren't many times that I didn't agree with my psychologist Dr Barrett, but I remember at least one session where it felt like she couldn't relate to my experiences. It was during one of my early consultations with her when I said something like;

"Once you've accepted death, you stop worrying about it, you stop caring."

Her response was along the lines of; "But you never had to accept death, because you didn't die."

I think it's probably very difficult to understand that mindset, unless you have spent a substantial amount of time in high risk environments, where you genuinely believe that your life is under a real threat. It's not defeatism or pessimism, nor is it capitulation, it's simply living each day with the understanding that it might realistically be your last. In places like Afghanistan and Iraq this is how thousands of soldiers had to live their lives, because people were being killed every day, more often than not by pure bad luck, rather than any tactical error or oversight on their part. Anyone could become the chosen target of an enemy sniper or suicide bomber, just as anyone could drive over an IED or step on a mine. Nobody was exempt from these threats, regardless of their personal skills and abilities. These dangers aren't dwelled upon by soldiers, they are just a fact of life on operations, and in some ways they are what makes being on tour exciting for many.

One of the more morbid things you are encouraged to do when deployed on operations is write a letter to your loved ones that they will only receive in the event of your death. Like many soldiers I've written a couple of these in my time, but obviously none of them were ever delivered. It's a challenging thing to do, to write a letter like that when you are sat at a table in perfectly good health. You know it's unlikely to be required, but in the event that it is, you want it to be poignant and meaningful, without being melodramatic or overly sad. The last one I wrote was for my wife in 2006 and it was very unremarkable. I'd just returned to Helmand to complete the PF tour after spending time at home on paternity leave and the situation on the ground was deteriorating rapidly. I was grateful that I'd been able to see my new-born son, that was hugely important to me. The idea of being killed and never meeting my own child had weighed heavy on my conscience while my wife was pregnant, so when I returned to Afghanistan I felt blessed that I'd been afforded that opportunity. He wouldn't remember it, but there were photographs of us together, and I'd been able to hold him in my arms, kiss him on the head, and tell him I loved him. It didn't absolve me of the guilt I felt for not being there for my family, but it did let me focus on my job, knowing I'd done what I could. I kept that letter, and sometime after returning from the tour I found it and showed it to my wife, after explaining its purpose. She was clearly underwhelmed. It lacked emotion and depth, and fell short of her expectations, evidently I'd done a poor job. If ever I write one again, I'll try harder.

My Golden Retriever Barney was almost sixteen years old when he died in 2021. He was the first pet I owned as an adult, and most of my friends and family knew him because he often accompanied me on my travels. Barney wasn't an overly affectionate dog, he liked company, but didn't like being smothered, and he loved being outside, especially by water. Over the years we ran and walked thousands of miles together, and he followed me on many hard slogs across the moors, coastal paths, and forests where we lived in Essex, Hampshire,

South Wales, and Cornwall. The day Barney was put to sleep at the veterinary surgery, we were all by his side, me, my wife, and two children, and together we comforted him as he drifted off peacefully for one last time. It was sad saying goodbye to such a loyal friend, but it must have been so much harder for my kids. Barney had been in their lives since the day they were born, they didn't know life without him. He'd got in their way every morning before school and welcomed them home every afternoon afterwards. For Carmen he'd been a great companion too, keeping her entertained and protected while I was regularly away with work. Everyone was crying as we said our goodbyes, except me, and I was conscious they'd all noticed that too. I tried my best to offer some sympathetic support, but did a poor job of it, patting them on the back and saying it would all be ok as I ushered them outside. It seemed the natural thing to do, to remain stoic and pragmatic. There was nothing more I could do really, and the vet needed to get on with her job too. A few days later my daughter asked my wife why I hadn't cried when Barney died, and it made me wonder if she saw it as an act of indifference or cold-heartedness. It wasn't, I was just acting in the way I thought was appropriate, being strong for my family in their time of sadness. Getting visibly upset would only have made the situation worse, or so I thought anyway. In retrospect, if I'd been alone in that room with Barney I think I'd have given him a massive cuddle and cried like a baby, he was my best mate. I'll never know if the way I acted suppressed the emotions of everyone else around me or made it awkward for them, but my intentions were good. Against my better judgement I watched a film called "A Dogs Purpose" with Carmen about a year after Barney died. On the front cover is a picture of a beautiful Golden Retriever, so I knew it might be a bit of a test. If it had been a test, I would have failed miserably, because at one point I literally had to leave the room. There's a scene where a Golden Retriever gets put to sleep while his family comfort him, and it was just like what happened to us. I'd sooner watch Marley &

Me, Bambi, Lassie, and Watership Down back to back whilst chopping onions, than watch that again. I was in tatters.

Despite my internal angers, frustrations, and perceived external appearance I hate confrontation, and will normally go well out of my way to avoid it. I don't know why, but I think one of the reasons is my macabre mindset where I assume every form of conflict will result in extreme violence. Assuming the other person will take offence, become outraged, or be psychologically unstable, I have to ask myself how important an issue is to me, and how far I'm prepared to go to make my point, and unless the answer is "to the death!" I'd rather just avoid it completely.

It was only recently that someone brought it to my attention that not everyone thinks the way I do when it comes to physical violence. I was teaching some self-defence to a civilian friend and talking about the opportune targets that presented themselves during a certain scenario.

"From this position I can bite the neck, I can gouge the eyes with my thumbs, I can try to tear the ear off, and I can smash the groin with hammer-fists." I said, all the while going through the actions, but without making physical contact with his vulnerable body parts.

For him this was not a natural thought process at all and at the end of the lesson while we were chatting he explained that to me. "The thing is, I don't see what you see when I'm in those positions Steve." he told me honestly. "What I'm thinking about is how I can get away as safely and quickly as possible. But you're instinct is to keep looking for ways to do more damage. I wouldn't have thought any of that stuff if you hadn't pointed it out to me, my brain doesn't work like that at all."

In the military we were taught to find and exploit weaknesses, and an attack was broken down into three phases; the approach, the assault, and the fight-through. Once the attack was launched, it was seen through to the end, and it didn't end until the enemy was destroyed.

To be fair I've only ever met one other person who shares my mentality for self-defence or self-preservation, and the day I did meet him, I asked him to be my coach. My first Jiu Jitsu lesson with Mark Tucker was so enlightening and inspiring that I had to have more. A former Royal Marine, close protection officer, and professional fighter, he'd experienced combat in many forms and understood it intimately. He also understood how my brain worked, and his method of instruction suited me perfectly, giving clear context and utility to everything he taught, whether it was for sport or a street fight. He was definitely someone I'd want to have on my side in a bar fight and would hate to see on the opposing team.

Making friends outside of the army has been quite difficult. I don't like crowds, parties, or large social gatherings, and my first, instinctive thought when I meet someone new is to assess the immediate threat they pose to me, and how I'm going to deal with the attack they might launch. When my children were young I met quite a few of the other local parents during the walk to-and-from school and did my best to learn their names while we walked home in the same direction or waited for the kids to come out of the gate when school finished. The vast majority of my friendships outside of the army have been formed through martial arts, especially Brazilian jiu jitsu where I've made many good friends.

The word "martial" literally means military, and the arts were mostly created during periods of feud and conflict. Like the army there is a rank structure, usually in the form of coloured belts, and also like the army there are protocols and formalities to observe. Jiu jitsu in particular has been fantastic for my mental health, because no matter what's going on in your life, when you are sparring, you're thinking about jiu jitsu and nothing else. Stresses about debts, relationships, work, or any other problems quickly disappear when you're concentrating on defending a choke or choking someone else. For me, from my first Karate lesson aged six, to the numerous classes I attend today, martial arts have been about survival, about defending myself, and the people I care about. I think not being able to protect my mum from a violent man when I was a young boy had a profound effect on me that shaped my personality greatly. I think I felt guilty about that for a very long time, well into adulthood, even though it was way beyond my control. But I don't anymore, instead I feel sorry for that helpless little kid, because children can't win fights against grown men. That boy did nothing wrong, he shouldn't be ashamed.

Today I teach survival, situational awareness, self-defence and jiu jitsu to men, women, and children because I don't think anyone should ever feel helpless. Obviously there are extreme variables in physicality and mental state that could be almost impossible to overcome, but knowledge and training can be the difference between becoming a victim, or a victor, and victory could mean survival, escape, or even avoiding a situation altogether. Moving forward I plan to continue writing, because as frustrating and time-consuming as it can be, it gives me a defined mission, and without a mission I have no purpose. Martial arts, especially Jiu Jitsu will always be another key activity for me too, and I hope to develop my knowledge, skills, friendships, and club for as long as I am breathing. Ultimately, everything I do is for my family, and if it wasn't for my children I honestly think my demons would have gotten the better of me a long time ago. I learned a lot in the army, and I've learned a lot since, I've done good and bad, had extreme highs and extreme lows, seen good and evil, and met legends and scumbags. All I know is it's good to have friendships, trust, and respect with people, and to be able to look yourself in the mirror without contempt. Stay away from people you dislike, and close to people you admire.

Keep low, move fast. Out.....

Lessons Identified

Don't be afraid to ask questions. If you don't understand, others don't either.

To ask is a moments shame. Not to ask and remain ignorant is a lifelong shame.

Don't ask a question if you're not prepared for the answer.

Everyone knows something you don't.

You know something everyone else doesn't.

Nothing is free.

Treat people how you'd like them to treat you.

Politeness is not a sign of weakness, it's a sign of strength.

Say please and thank you.

Look people in the eye when you meet them and when you say goodbye.

Always nominate a specific individual as responsible for any task.

Always set a deadline for any task.

A volunteer is worth ten pressed men.

Everyone likes a pat on the back.

Always give credit where it's due.

Superior rank does not make you a superior human being.

There are excellent soldiers in every unit of the military.

There are incompetent soldiers in every unit of the military.

Medals are a record of where you've been, not what you've done.

Teaching and coaching are two different skills. Being good at one doesn't mean you're good at the other.

If all your students are crap, you are probably not a very good teacher.

Try not to worry about things beyond your control.

If you are a good person and someone doesn't like you, they're probably not a good person.

If you don't know who the idiot in the room is, it's probably you.

Don't take a knife to a gun fight.

Mnemonics and other ways to remember things that are deeply embedded in my brain:

First Aid:

AVPU

Alert

Voice responsive

Pain responsive

Unresponsive

The 4 B's

Breathing, Bleeding, Breaks and Burns

EAR

Exhaled Air Resuscitation

ECC

External Cardiac Compression

TWELVE FLAPS

Tracheal deviation

Wounds and bleeding

Emphysema

Larynx

Veins distended

Expose chest

Feel

Look

Auscultate

Percuss

Search sides and back

CPR

Cardiopulmonary Resuscitation

DRCABCDE

Danger

Response

Catastrophic bleeding

Airway

Breathing

Circulation

Disabilities

Exposure

Map Reading:

DDCRAPS

Direction

Distance

Conventional signs

Relief

Alignment

Proximity

Shape

Grid to Mag = Add. Mag to Grid = Get rid.

Weapons:
HELMDD
Hard extraction
Expended ammunition
Live round partially fed, due to damaged link
Misfired round
Damaged link
Damaged round

Tactics:
AMBUSH
Advanced preparation
Maximum firepower
Battle discipline
Unseen, unheard
Security, simplicity, speed
Home run

PACESSDO
Protection
Ammunition
Casualties
Equipment
Searchers
Sit-rep

Dig in

Orders

PAWPERSO

Protection

Ammunition

Weapons

Personal camouflage

Equipment

Radios

Specialist equipment

Orders

SAD

Speed

Aggression

Discipline

Orders:

CLAP

Clear

Loud

As an order

(with) **P**auses

FBI Detective

Full

Brief

Individual

Delayed

GRIT

Group

Range

Indication

Type of fire

Para **S**oldiers **M**ake **E**xcellent **S**ection **C**ommanders

Prelims

Situation

Mission

Execution

Service support

Command and signals

Communications:

ABC

Accuracy

Brevity

Clarity

RSVP

Rhythm

Speed

Volume

Pitch

SAD

Security

Accuracy

Discipline

More Military Terminology:

1 up – One unit (Section / Platoon / Company etc.) at the front of an advance

2i/c – Second in command / the wife

2LT – Second Lieutenant

2 up - Two units (Section / Platoon / Company etc.) at the front of an advance

5.56 – Calibre of ammunition round

7.62 - Calibre of ammunition round

9 mil - Calibre of ammunition round

9x9 – Small tent

12x12 – Big ten

12x24 – Two big tents tied together

'37 Pattern - British Army personal equipment system used from 1937 to 1959

50/50 – Half of the people do a task at a time

51mm – Mortar ammunition calibre

'58 Pattern – British Army personal equipment system used from 1959 to 1996

60mm - Mortar ammunition calibre

66 – US anti-tank rocket system

81mm – Mortar ammunition calibre

82mm – Soviet / Russian mortar calibre

84 – Anti-tank rocket system

90 – Short wheel-based Landrover

94 – Anti-tank rocket system

95 Kit – British military clothing system issued between 1996 to 2011

105 – Calibre of artillery ammunition

112 – Type of radio

110 – Long wheel-based Landrover

120 – Mortar ammunition calibre

303 – Historic bolt-action rifle used by the British Army 1895-1957

319 – Type of radio

320 – Type of radio

338 – Type of sniper rifle

349 – Type of radio

350 – Type of radio

351 – Type of radio

352 – Type of radio

1033 – Receipt and issue document

1157 - Receipt and issue document

A - Alpha

AB - Airborne

AB jacket – Airborne jacket (Green bomber jacket)

ABF – Airborne forces

ABI – Airborne initiative

Ablutions – Wash room

ABTF – Airborne task force

Adjt – Adjutant. An officer who deals with discipline issues in a battalion

Admin – Administration

AFV – Armoured fighting vehicle

AH64 / Apache – Attack helicopter

Airborne – Specific to airborne troops

Airborne stew – Meal brought out to soldiers on exercise. Meat and potatoes with dumplings

All-in – Meal where everyone puts their rations into one communal pot

Ally – Cool, different, flashy

Ammo – Ammunition

Antler – Type of electronic counter measures equipment used in Northern Ireland

Area cleaning – Daily, outside cleaning task carried out by the privates of each company

Arty – Artillery

AT4 – Anti-tank rocket

A/TK – Anti-tank

B - Bravo

Baboon – Method of punishment involving the backside being struck with various weapons

The Badge – The Regimental Sergeant Major

Bag meal – Packed lunch

Basha – Shelter

Basics – Basic soldiering skills

Beasting – Vigorous fitness session or verbal dressing down

Bed block – Method of laying out bedding for inspection

Bedspace – Area of a room that belongs to an individual

Bedford – Type of troop carrying vehicle

BFA – Blank firing attachment / Battlefield ambulance

Biff – Person who is injured or incapable of performing a task

Biff chit – Document from a doctor excusing types of physical activity (sick note).

Bine / Biner – Cigarette / Smoker

Binos – Binoculars

Blue rocket – Cleaner in MoD camp who wears a blue uniform

Body - Person

BOS – Battalion Orderly Sergeant

Bouncing bomb – Issued sleeping bag

Bowman – Communications system used by the British Army

Bn - Battalion

Brew – Hot drink. Usually tea

BT80 – High-altitude parachute system

Buckshee – Easy / Spare / Free

Buddy buddy – System of soldiers helping each other out

Bull – Clean something to inspection standard

Bullshit – Acts done for no practical reason. Usually relating to parades or inspections

Bumper – Device for polishing floors

Burners - Sideburns

C - Charlie

C130 – Transport aircraft used for parachuting

Cam and Con – Camouflage and concealment

Capt – Captain

CBA – Combat Body Armour

CBRN – Chemical, Biological, Radiological, and Nuclear

Charlie Charlie One – Pretext to a message that is for everyone's attention

Chinook – Twin-rotor helicopter

Civvies – Civilians / civilian clothes

Clansman – Obsolete communications system used by the British Army

Claymore – Ant-personnel mine

Col – Colonel

The Colonel / Colonel Gadaffi – The NAAFI

Colour Man – Colour Sergeant

Comms – Communications

Comms cord – length of paracord between two positions that's tugged on to signal to each other

CO – Commanding officer

Cookhouse – Dining area / canteen

COS – Company Orderly Sergeant. A duty normally carried out by a Corporal

COS – Chief of Staff

Cougar – Type of radio

Coy - Company

Cpl – Corporal

CPR – Cardio-Pulmonary Resuscitation

Craphat – Non Parachute Regiment soldier

Crow – New bloke

CSgt – Colour Sergeant

CSM – Company Sergeant Major

CSPEP – Carrying Straps Personal Equipment Parachutist

C*ntcap – Baseball cap type headdress

CWS (Common Weapon Sight) – Telescopic night-sight

D - Delta

DAF – Troop carrying truck

Daily detail – Daily orders issued to a Company

DB's – Desert boots

Diffy – Deficient / Missing

Diggers – Cutlery

Dems – Demolitions / explosives

Denims – Single colour, green trousers

Depot – Parachute Regiment recruit training establishment

Desert rose – Urinal, consisting of a tube sticking out of the ground

Dhobi - Washing

Dhobi dust – Washing powder

Dicking – Crappy job

Diggers - Cutlery

Dixies – Kitchen duties

Double - Run

Dry kit – Spare set of dry clothes

DS – Directing staff / instructors

DSO – Demolitions (Explosives) Safety Officer

Duff – Untruth / Simulation

DZ – Drop zone

DZ flash – badge worn on an airborne soldier's right arm to identify their unit

E - Echo

EAR – Exhaled Air Resuscitation

ECC – External Cardiac Compression

ECM – Electronic Counter Measures

Egg banjo – Fried egg sandwich

Endex- End of exercise

ERV – Emergency rendezvous. Place you will meet-up in an emergency

F - Foxtrot

Fat Albert – C130 Hercules transport plane

FFR – Fitted for radio (communications vehicle)

Fives – Infamous Parachute Regiment drinking establishment in Aldershot

Fireteam – Half of a section (4 men)

Fire picquet – Firefighting duty personnel

FOJ – Friend of Joe (Crow)

Four-tonner – Troop carrying truck

FRV – Final rendezvous

Full screw – Corporal

G - Golf

G10 – Issued equipment

Gen – Genuine / True

Gibbers / Gibbersville – Cold / Cold place

GS – General service

Guard duty – The duty of guarding a camp or establishment

Gun – Machine gun or artillery piece. (Not a rifle or personal weapon)

Gimpy / GPMG / The General – 7.62mm General Purpose Machine Gun

Gimp – Weirdo / freak

GMG – Grenade Machine Gun

H - Hotel

H83 – Type of ammunition container

HAHO – High Altitude High Opening parachute insertion method

HAI – Helicopter Abseil Instructor

HALO – High Altitude Low Opening parachute insertion method

Hand grenade – Person who's a nightmare after a few beers / Hand-thrown explosive device

HAPES – High Altitude Parachutist Equipment Straps

Haraldo – Non Parachute Regiment soldier

Haverbag / Horrorbag – Packed meal from the cookhouse

Headshed – People in charge / Headquarters personnel

Herc – C130 Hercules aircraft

HHI – Helicopter Handling Instructor

HHTI ("Hootie") – Hand-Held Thermal Imager

HMG – Heavy Machine Gun

Housewife – Sewing kit / needle and thread

HQ - Headquarters

I - India

I/C – In command

IED – Improvised explosive device

Interrupter – Nickname for an interpreter

Int – Intelligence

IO – Int Officer

IRAD – Infra-red aiming device

IWS (Individual Weapon Sight) – Early generation night-sight

J - Juliet

Jack – Lazy / Selfish / Quit / Give up

Jackal – 4x4 vehicle

Jack wagon – Vehicle for people who either jack or fail to keep up during fitness

Javelin – Man-portable, shoulder launched missile system

JNCO – Junior non-commissioned officer (Corporal)

Joe / Joe Crow – New bloke or recruit

K - Kilo

Kangaroo court – Mock courtroom where soldiers are charged with an offence and others are nominated as prosecution, defence, judge, and jury

KFS – Knife, fork, spoon

KIA – Killed in action

L - Lima

L2 – Old type of hand grenade

L109 – Modern type of hand grenade

Lance Jack – Lance Corporal

LCpl – Lance Corporal

LEC – Locally employed civilian

LF28 – Type of laser target designator

LFTT – Live-Fire Tactical Training

Lick / lickout – Event, job, task that's demoralising, boring, or extremely difficult

Link – Linked / belted ammunition

Linkman – Soldier who connects one group of men to another for the passing of messages

LLP – Low Level Parachute

LMG – Light Machine Gun

Locker layout – Designated, inspection-ready layout for the contents of a locker

Locker Monster – Mysterious fiend who steals from and destroys locker layout

Long-Haired General – The wife

LPBG – Lead parachute battalion group

LSW – Light Support Weapon

Lt – Lieutenant. Pronounced Lef-ten-ant

M - Mike

Magazine – Ammunition container that fits to a weapon

Maj – Major

MANPAD – Man portable air defence

Man's flick – Coin toss to select someone for a crappy task

Matelot – Member of the Royal Navy

Medic – Appointed first-aider. Not a doctor

MIA - Missing in action

MD – Medical discharge

MiD – Mention in despatches

MILAN – Old anti-tank missile system

Milling – P Company event similar to boxing

Miniflare – Pyrotechnic pistol flare

Minimi – 5.56mm light machine gun

MMG – Medium Machine Gun

Mincing – Moving slowly / Not trying

M.O – Medical Officer

Mong – Stupid person

Monkey – Military police officer

MPI – Mean point of impact

MRE – Meal ready-to-eat. American ration packs

MRI – Map reading instructor

MSI – Military ski instructor

N - November

NAAFI – Navy Army Air Force Institute. The small, overpriced, "non-profit" shop on camp

Navex – Navigation exercise

NBC – Nuclear, Biological, and Chemical

NCO - Non-commissioned officer (Lance Corporal, Corporal, Sergeant, Colour Sergeant)

Net – Radio communications channel

No duff – True statement / non-exercise statement

Non-ferocious – Non Parachute Regiment soldier

Norweigan – Type of food and drink container and also a type of cold-weather sweatshirt

NVA's – Night viewing aids

NVD's – Night viewing devices

NVG's – Night viewing goggles

O - Oscar

OC – Officer commanding

Offr – Officer

One-pip wonder – Second Lieutenant

Op – Operation / tour

OP – Observation post

OpsWO – Operations Warrant Officer

Outrageous – Any behaviour or decision that a soldier

disagrees with or doesn't understand

Orifices – Affectionate collective nickname for officers

P - Papa

Pad – Married soldier

Pads estate – Married quarters

Pads wives – Soldiers wives

Pan bashing – Cleaning pots and pans

Parang – Type of machete

P Company – Test week of Depot Para

Pest – Person with a passion for a topic or subject

PF / PFPL – Pathfinders / Pathfinder Platoon

The Phantom – Mysterious, unidentified soldier who shaves the eyebrows off drunk soldiers while they sleep

PID – Positive identification

Pinz – Pinzgauer 4x4 vehicle

Pit - Bed

PJI – Parachute jump instructor

Pl - Platoon

Planks – Army issue skis

Player – Terrorist in Northern Ireland

Poncho – Shelter sheet / small tarpaulin

POL – Petrol, oil, and lubricants

POL point – MoD petrol / diesel pump location

Provo – Provost Staff. Team of disciplinarians within a battalion

PRR – Personal role radio

PSI – Permanent staff instructor

PsyOps – Psychological operations/warfare

Pte - Private

PTI – Physical Training Instructor

Pub paratrooper – Soldier who tells everyone how awesome he is down the pub, but is actually a bit of a mong

Punji pit – Booby-trap where sharpened sticks are placed inside a hole dug into the ground

Q - Quebec

QRF – Quick Reaction Force

R - Romeo

Rag order – In a bad state of disrepair / Untidy / Dishevelled / Exhausted

Rats / rat pack - Rations

Red-eye – Punishment where the victim gets pinned to the floor and humiliated by at least one other

Reg – Parachute Regiment

Remf – Rear echelon mother fucker. A soldier who is not on the front-line

Re-org – Re-organise

RMP – Royal Military Police

Road slappers – Army issue trainers

Room jobs – Daily cleaning tasks appointed to junior soldiers such as "Sinks and Mirrors"

ROP's – Restriction of privileges

Round – Bullet / mortar bomb / artillery shell

Rover – Land Rover

RQMS – Regimental Quartermaster Sergeant

RSM – Regimental Sergeant Major

RV - rendezvous

S - Sierra

SA80 – Standard issue British Army rifle

Sarn't – Sergeant

SAS – Special Air Service

SBS – Special Boat Service

Scoff – Food / Meal

Screamer – Non Parachute Regiment soldier

Screech – Squash / Cordial

Screw - Corporal

Sect – Section (8 men)

SF – Special forces / Sustained fire

SFSG – Special Forces Support Group

Sgt - Sergeant

Skiff – Smear a nasty substance onto something

Shell-scrape – Shallow trench used as a defensive fighting position

Shermuley – Hand-held rocket-fired parachute flare

Silver cross – Nickname for the Parachute Regiment cap badge

Slop jockey – Affectionate nickname for an army chef

SLR (Self Loading Rifle) – Standard issue British Army rifle 1954 to 1994

SMG – Sub machine-gun

Smock – Word used by airborne soldiers instead of jacket

Snatch – Armoured Land Rover

SNCO – Senior non-commissioned officer (Sergeant / Colour Sergeant)

S.O's – Standing orders

SOP's – Standard operating procedures

Spearhead – High-readiness battle group, stood-by to deploy on operations at short notice

Spoof – Game played to determine who gets the crappy job, forfeit, or pays the bill etc

STAB – Stupid T.A Bastard. Soldier from the reserves

Stag – Guard duty

Stand-down – Relax, end of work, end of stand-to

Stand-easy – Command given on parade permitting soldiers to adopt a relaxed posture

Stand-to – Be on high alert, prepare for an attack

Steeplechase – Cross-country run interspersed with obstacles and water courses

SUSAT (Sight Unit Small Arms Trilux) – Standard issue telescopic sight for SA80

T - Tango

T.A – Territorial Army

Tab – Tactical Advance to Battle. Speed marching over distance with a loaded bergan

Tac - Tactical

TCV – Troop Carrying Vehicle

TI – Thermal Imager

TOET – Test Of Elementary Training

Trainasium – Aerial obstacle course at heights of up to sixty feet

Tramline – Double-crease ironed into clothing

TrgWO – Training Warrant Officer

Trouser twists – Elastic bands to tuck your trouser legs into and keep them smart

Twists – Twisted parachute rigging lines

Two-pip wonder - Lieutenant

U - Uniform

U/S – Unserviceable / Broken

V - Victor

Vallon – Mine detector used by the British Army in Afghanistan

Vallon man – Front man of a patrol who searches for mines with the Vallon

VBIED – Vehicle borne improvised explosive device

Violet Joker - Type of electronic counter measures equipment used in Northern Ireland

VOR – Vehicle off road (not roadworthy)

W - Whiskey

Wagon - Vehicle

Warm kit – Extra layer of warm clothing

White sifter - Type of electronic counter measures equipment used in Northern Ireland

Windproofs – Windproof smock or trousers

Wings – Military parachutist wings badge

WMIK – Weapon Mounted Installation Kit. Vehicle firing platform

WOMBAT – 120mm Anti-tank recoilless rifle

WO1 – Warrant Officer Class 1 (RSM)

WO2 – Warrant Officer Class 2 (RQMS, CSM, OpsWO, TrgWO)

X – X-Ray

Y -Yankee

Z - Zulu

STEVE BROWN

Zeppie / Zepster – New bloke

BOOKS BY THIS AUTHOR

Meatheads

You'd Be Nuts Too!

Don't Ask - You Won't Believe Me Anyway